The Transiting Planets

Frances Sakoian
and
Louis Acker

ISBN-10: 0-86690-597-9
ISBN-13: 978-0-86690-597-8

Cover Design: Jack Cipolla

Published by:
American Federation of Astrologers, Inc.
6535 S. Rural Road
Tempe, AZ 85283

www.astrologers.com

Printed in the United States of America

Contents

Introduction

Although transits of Mars, Venus, Mercury, the Moon and the Sun do not normally sustain significant influence for more than one to four days, exceptions to this rule do occur when the planet in question is either retrograde or stationary in its zodiacal position. (Note: Such stationary or retrograde periods *never* occur in the Sun's or the Moon's respective motions.)

These transits function as timing factors for the long-range influences of the slower-moving planets, i.e., Jupiter through Pluto. Thus, such passages of the faster-moving planets and their associated transiting aspects to the natal planets do not as a rule produce events of major or lasting importance in a native's life unless by virtue of their transit influences these planets reinforce the transit of a slower-moving planet.

Let us take the event of marriage as an example. It is said that transit Venus trine natal Uranus could offer the native a marriage opportunity; yet this transit occurs twice each year in every horoscope. It is thus obvious that other marital indications must be present for this particular transit to culminate an event of such major importance in the life of an individual.

Utilizing this same example, should transiting Jupiter, Saturn or another of the slower-moving planets trine natal Venus from the seventh house, or should the ruler of the seventh house be making a major transit to Venus in the natal horoscope, then marriage can be considered a reasonable likelihood.

The strongest effect of this fast-moving transit of Venus to Uranus' natal position would be felt at the same time that transiting Uranus is trine the position of natal Venus, or some similar condition involving these planets. Such a combination would double the impetus of the vibratory quality inherent to the planets involved, making use of the Venus transit as a triggering mechanism for the events that ensue.

Without the background influences of major transits from slower-moving planets, such transits of Venus to natal Uranus would in all probability merely indicate a momentary enjoyment of social activities, friendship and music or an unusual opportunity to accumulate wealth.

A general principle applying to all transits is this: *No* transit can exert a powerful life-changing influence upon the native unless it reinforces an aspect promising such a potential event in the natal horoscope.

It should be noted that the Sun *never* retrogrades and that the effects of its transiting aspects are of approximately three to four days duration. In this way, they are much like transits of the Moon. In contrast to the Sun transits, which indicate dynamic positive self-expression, those of the Moon evoke a passive response in the native.

1

Transits of the Sun

Transits of the Sun are indicative of the directions in and means by which the native will exert willpower and creative abilities during this period. Whatever house the Sun is transiting at the time will receive the focus of this creative energy. There will be a greater self-awareness along with a self-directed expression on the part of the native.

Determination of the constructive or destructive nature of these influences will depend upon the overall maturity of the native as revealed in the natal horoscope. Natal aspects to the sign and house placements of the planet receiving the Sun transit will also exert some effect upon the outcome of such contacts.

Favorable transits of the Sun can be used to seek favor from those in power and authority, or to assume a role of personal authority in a given situation.

Should the Sun make adverse contacts to the natal planets, there is the danger of overexertion and egotistical self-expression.

Transit Sun Through the Houses

Transit Sun Through the First House

The Sun's transit through the first house increases the native's vitality. The native expresses himself or herself with increased optimism and a sense of personal power and authority, and will thus appear to others as a more lively, dynamic and magnetic individual.

Favorable contacts to the natal planets during the Sun's transit through this house will encourage the native to proceed confidently in the pursuit of life goals and purposes.

Adverse transits, on the other hand, are likely to give rise to displays of personal egotism and a desire for prominence and admiration. This may often manifest in a competitive attitude that ignores the rights and feelings of others. Problems and difficulties are apt to ensue.

Transit Sun Through the Second House

This transit usually emphasizes important financial dealings in the native's life, often directing dynamic self-expression toward the acquisition of money, material security and status.

Children and their education are likely to be a source of financial concern to the native during this period. There may also be a tendency to spend money in the pursuit of romantic and pleasurable activities. The native may even be involved in the purchase of art objects or gold, the metal ruled by the Sun.

Favorable transiting aspects of the Sun to natal planets during its passage through this house will promote the native's self-confidence and creativity in business affairs and matters of personal material value.

Adverse contacts set off either in the natal chart or by other transiting bodies can, on the other hand, lead to extravagant expenditures of time and money on pleasures and unwise speculations. Gambling and risky ventures should thus be avoided under such affliction.

Transit Sun Through the Third House

This transit usually indicates a period of creative, positive and forceful determination in the native's presentation and application of ideas. Creative writing, public speaking and communication dealing with artistic, social and educational matters will experience a demonstrable ease and effectiveness of expression at this time. Short journeys undertaken to pursue social, romantic or pleasurable activities will be especially meaningful to the native.

Likewise, the native will find it easier and more rewarding to participate in various activities with children and is apt to lend assistance to some venture or project designed to improve the nature and quality of their education.

A favorably-aspected Sun here will promote the native's ability to communicate with those in power and authority, encouraging the introduction and discussion of important tropics and information with these individuals.

Should the Sun make adverse contacts to the natal planets during its transit through this house, there is the danger of egotistical attitudes in personal ideas and notions.

Transit Sun Through the Fourth House

This transit denotes a period of increased creative, artistic, romantic and social activity in the home. Projects intended to beautify and improve the domestic environment can be favorably planned and inaugurated at this time. Romantic, sexual and social relationships are apt to be centered around the home.

A forthrightness in family relationships and in the expression of personal beliefs and views about domestic affairs will enhance the native's ability to command attention and respect in the home. Thus, a native experiencing this transit as a parent will find that he or she can express a positive, creative attitude toward matters of consequence as family leader and authority figure.

The devotion of time to children and family activities will be enjoyed during this period.

Real estate transactions and property purchases can be satisfactorily and often profitably expedited at this time if the Sun is not afflicted.

Afflictions to the Sun in its transit through this house are apt to give rise to problems in the native's handling of everyday affairs and family matters. Feelings of awkwardness or uneasiness experienced by the native in the home or domestic environment may lead the native to reassert his or her position as pilot of the family destiny. Ego confrontations between the native and other family members, even children, are often the result, and only tend to accentuate their differences. Home improvement projects, real estate matters and property acquisitions are not likely to fulfill the native's expectations under such adverse transits. Likewise, family relationships may also suffer temporary setbacks.

Transit Sun Through the Fifth House

This transit marks a particularly strong period for creative self-expression and usually brings a period of sexual stimulation and increased social involvement. The Sun's accidental dignity in the house of its natural rulership, corresponding to Leo in the natural zodiac, will incline the native to be more positive and dramatic in self-expression, more dynamic in social behavior and generally more attractive to members of the opposite sex. Thus, the native is apt to participate in romantic, artistic, social, educational or speculative activities. The native can display a dramatic flair in the performing arts or other artistic endeavors, or while attending social gatherings.

Children are apt to be a great source of pleasure and entertainment to the native during this period. Time devoted to their care and development will be meaningful under this transit.

Should the Sun be afflicted in its transit through this house, the native is likely to experience some blockage or obstacle to the immediate fulfillment of creative potential. A lack of artistic sense, impropriety in social behavior and improper management in financial activities are apt to pose obstacles and difficulties to the native. Romantic and sexual involvements, too, may suffer from wrong motives or an ineptness in the native's handling of such relationships.

Transit Sun Through the Sixth House

This transit indicates a period of increased self-expression in work, personal dress, hygiene and diet. Manifestations of leadership potential are likely to be evidenced in constructive attempts to organize the occupational environment to provide greater efficiency and effectiveness. Favors can thus be more readily sought from employers or superiors during this transit. Employers and those in positions of power and authority experiencing this transit will find it easier to deal with employees and subordinates. Those working with children or in the creative arts will be particularly assisted toward the practical accomplishment of tasks under this transit.

The native may make use of a heightened artistic flair in personal dress and adornment, style or trendsetting in order to attract the opposite sex or those who can confer favors. Vitality and willpower are enhanced by this transit, enabling the native to overcome illness or negative conditions and thereby express a more optimistic outlook in work and health.

Should the Sun be afflicted while transiting this house, the native is likely to experience difficulties with others in the working environment due to his or her own obstinate, overbearing or egotistical attitude, or those of others.

Transit Sun Through the Seventh House

This transit will usually correspond to the introduction of dynamic individuals into the native's sphere of activity.

During this period, the native will be disposed toward much social activity and the pursuit of pleasure in close personal relationships. If the Sun is well-aspected, he is likely to attract a romantic partner, and if this transit coincides with other important seventh house influences, it could usher a marriage or new partnership into the native's life. Close relationships with children can find positive constructive expression at this time.

Much activity is apt to revolve about the marriage relationship or other partnerships during this transit, stimulating the creative self-expression of *both* individuals involved. It would be wise for each to respect the other's free will and self-determinism in order to achieve the most favorable results.

Should the Sun be afflicted during its transit through the seventh house, ego confrontations are likely to arise. Difficulties and problems, under such affliction, are apt to be encountered in marital, business, legal, promotional or professional relationships.

Transit Sun Through the Eighth House

This transit often denotes a period during which the native can be involved in financial affairs dealing with corporate investments or joint money. Matters of insurance, taxes, inheritance or collective resources, can be favorably negotiated or handled at this time. Occult investigations can also be given positive impetus.

This transit may also act as a sexual stimulus, inclining the native to establish intimate relationships. Such involvements will be especially pronounced if planets in the fifth house, its ruler, Venus, or Mars receive transiting aspects from the Sun during this period.

In its broadest interpretation, this transit will inspire the native to take the initiative in regenerating personal life conditions, disposing of outworn modes of expression to make way for the new.

Should the Sun make adverse contacts while transiting this house, the native is apt to become callous and egotistical in business and financial dealings, giving rise to serious problems in relationships with others. Under such afflictions the native should always exercise caution in matters of speculation, or risk the ever-present danger of a disastrous loss.

Transit Sun Through the Ninth House

This transit often indicates renewed interest in religion or academics. Involvement in the study of foreign languages, cultures or histories will provide insight and understanding in the native's perception of world affairs and cultural trends. During this period, the native may assume a leadership role in espousing personal beliefs and attitudes. The training of children in religious and educational precepts could become important at this time. This is also a good period for pleasure trips or visits to foreign countries, and romantic attractions at this time are likely to involve those of foreign birth or extraction.

Afflictions to the Sun in its transit through this house may give rise to a fanatical, egotistical or dogmatic adherence to one's own point of view toward educational and philosophical values and a desire to impress those views upon others. Such attempts to force conformity, and consequent disregard of others' opinions, will often arouse resentment in and cause conflict with others or those in positions of power and authority. Problems may arise while traveling in foreign countries or in dealings with foreigners, when the Sun is afflicted.

Transit Sun Through the Tenth House

This transit acts as a general stimulus to the drive for status and position in life. It thus denotes a period of active involvement in career, professional or political affairs as the native seeks to assume a role of leadership in a professional circle or sphere of activity. Important individuals with positions of power and authority are likely to enter the native's life at this time, often through social activities connected with professional matters or through prominent business associates. The native's drive can be expressed as ambition for his or her children, engaging in efforts that will help launch them on successful careers.

Afflictions to the Sun in its transit through the tenth house can cause the native to adopt an egotistical and overbearing manner in the effort to achieve position, power and status. Power struggles could have a damaging effect upon the native's reputation.

Transit Sun Through the Eleventh House

During the period of this transit the native will be inclined to assume a leadership role among friends or in group and organizational activities. New associations and attachments are favored, and the native will tend to attract authoritative individuals into his or her circle of friends. Thus, the native may either be approached by or find it easier to approach those in positions of power and authority on a more casual and friendlier basis.

The native may become an active participant in scientific, humanitarian or occult groups and organizations. Likewise, group creative efforts in the fields of education, art, music and entertainment, social activities or matters dealing with children could be a subject of the native's concern. Romantic opportunities are apt to arise through friends or groups.

Should the Sun be afflicted while transiting this house, the native may seek to dominate friends and group associates, thus arousing their opposition and resentment.

Transit Sun Through the Twelfth House

This transit favors the native's inner spiritual, meditative self-development. Thus, to others, the native will seem to be more quiet, withdrawn and reserved than usual. Adoption of a subjective, introspective attitude at this time will enable the native to elicit and constructively utilize many of the resources of his deeper levels of consciousness. Often, the native will assume a leadership role in connection with a hospital or institution during this transit.

A well-aspected Sun in its transit through this house will confer the native with increased courage and determination to confront and overcome psychological problems, thus removing and releasing him or her from subconscious inhibitions and neuroses that afflict the mind.

Adverse contacts while the Sun is in the twelfth house, on the other hand, may give rise to the native's dramatization of subconscious issues, disposing him or her to seek attention and recognition through covert or abnormal behavior exemplifying these psychological neuroses.

Transit Sun Conjunctions

Transiting conjunctions of the Sun are indicative of the native's dynamic expression of the will in matters ruled by the planet receiving the contact through affairs ruled by its sign and house position. Further interpretation of such contacts will depend upon natal aspects to the Sun and to the planet receiving the conjunction, as well as transits from other planetary bodies, to determine their true import.

A favorably-aspected Sun conjunction both in the natal horoscope and by transit may incline the native toward a great deal of constructive accomplishment during this period. On the other hand, should afflictions be in evidence, the native may try to force his or her will in an inharmonious or destructive manner.

Transit Sun Conjunction Sun

This transit occurs once each year, marking the day of the native's birth. Social activities associated with a traditional birthday celebration are highly illustrative of the sign Leo and the fifth house, both naturally ruled by the Sun. An increase in or strengthening of the native's vitality corresponding to the period of this contact will encourage positive expression of dynamic creativity. The native will thus find this a favorable time to seek the favor of those in positions of power and authority, or to assume a role of personal leadership in influential matters. The exact time of this conjunction is frequently used to construct a cyclic prediction chart called a solar return, which is usually erected to determine areas of significant activity in the coming year. Supportive rationale for this procedure lies in the recognition that planetary energies are programmed into and directed through the basic solar energy representative of the source of personal power and creativity, and that each time this transit conjunction occurs, the true direction of the native's creative potential can be determined. Hence the solar return acts as a cyclic impulse, setting the pattern for activity in the ensuing year.

Transit Sun Conjunction Moon

This transit usually corresponds to a period of family and domestic activity and concern. Dynamic individuals may enter the native's life, often having dramatic influence upon one's family or domestic situation. Social activities, creative artistic endeavors and festive family gatherings can be successfully conducted in the home. Children and their needs also can be more readily and auspiciously handled at this time. In a woman's chart, this contact may coincide with an important event or occurrence of considerable emotional impact, usually precipitated by an important man in her life. Should this conjunction be afflicted either natally or by other transiting bodies, emotional upsets could be the result of a dominating attitude on the part of the native. Such disharmony in the home environment may often lead to an unfortunate clash of wills.

Transit Sun Conjunction Mercury

This transit is indicative of a period of dynamic mental activity. Studies, correspondence and necessary communication can be properly and often quite successfully handled at this time. Invitations may be extended by the native for social functions, and opportunities may arise for short pleasure trips with brothers, sisters or neighbors. This transit will usually encourage the native's confident expression of personal ideas and opinions. The native may even be inspired with ideas for creative artistic endeavors, tackling serious communication with a romantic partner about their relationship or taking a short excursion related to some personal romantic involvement. Important decisions will often be forthcoming at this time that directly affect future developments in these spheres of activity. Afflictions to this conjunction by either natal planets or other transiting bodies may incline the native to adopt dogmatic attitudes when expounding upon his or her points of view. Such "intellectual egotism" often gives rise to arguments and debates with other individuals.

Transit Sun Conjunction Venus

This transit often coincides with the introduction of dynamic romantic, social and artistic activities into the native's life. A happy, optimistic frame of mind conferred by this transit will attract friendships or favors from others. The native's cheerful disposition will make participation in these and other matters that much easier, more harmonious and more enjoyable. Business affairs or purchases of art objects and luxury items can be profitably handled at this time. Social affairs conducted by the native are apt to be well-attended, drawing together many congenial individuals. Strong romantic and sexual stimulation is frequently evidenced during this transit, usually with the native assuming a lead role. Should this conjunction be afflicted, the native may indulge in excessive social activity or spend extravagantly on luxury items.

Transit Sun Conjunction Mars

This transit is indicative of a period of increased energy and dynamic personal action, encouraging the native to undertake tasks requiring initiative and the expenditure of physical energy. Willpower and self-confidence are stimulated at this time, favoring the pursuit of business, professional, financial and creative goals. Interests in sports, working with children, social events and pursuits of pleasure, as well as other physical activities, are likely to arise, providing the native with many outlets for the positive energy flow now available. This transit is also a strong stimulus to the sex drive, tending to make one aggressive in romantic relationships. The native is thus apt to take the initiative in seeking out new romantic contacts or in deepening and energizing existing involvements. Afflictions to this conjunction, whether from natal or other transiting bodies, will incline the native toward egocentric attitudes, aggressiveness that is heedless of the rights and feelings of others, and hasty, ill-considered actions. Such tendencies must be closely guarded to avoid unpleasant consequences.

Transit Sun Conjunction Jupiter

During the period of this transit the native will usually display a happy, optimistic and self-confident attitude toward his or her life goals and objectives. This is often evidenced by a desire to expand personal consciousness and, consequently, further his or her aims through religious, educational or philosophical study and enlightenment, or travel or contact with foreign cultures. To fulfill these aspirations, the native may seek admittance to a university or school of higher learning, embark upon a long journey or cultivate correspondence and dealings with people from distant places. Assistance toward accomplishing these ends may often be found by seeking favor from those in positions of power and authority especially if these individuals are prominent in religious, educational or cultural institutions. Should this conjunction be afflicted by either natal or other transiting bodies, the native's dealings are likely to suffer from a lack of practicality, excessive optimism or grandiose displays of egotism in relating with others.

Transit Sun Conjunction Saturn

This conjunction corresponds to a period of intensified sense of responsibility. It denotes a period of important professional dealings, often affecting status and reputation. Creativity can be positively directed toward organizing and structuring one's work and professional obligations through acceptance of responsibility. If the native has done his or her work, a forward career step could occur, bringing honor and recognition. However, if the native's work load seems burdensome or oppressive, he or she may be subject to resultant depression and unhappiness. Afflictions to this conjunction by either natal or other transiting planets may incline the native to adopt an ultraconservative or pessimistic outlook on life. Dogmatic, authoritarian, egotistical attitudes are often evidenced under such afflictions. Problems with superiors, the government or those in positions of power and authority are likely to arise.

Transit Sun Conjunction Uranus

This transit denotes a period of impulsiveness in the native's desire to experience and express personal freedom and self-determination. The native refuses to be forced or molded into a life style that is not of personal interest or value. Thus, the native will be inclined to seek out and often lead others into new experiences. Humanitarian, scientific and reformist causes are apt to appeal to the native at this time. Such endeavors can in some way benefit from the native's personal leadership and original creativity. The intuitive faculties are strengthened and enhanced, and the native will display a greater degree of personal magnetism, sparkle and creativity. This will draw exciting new friends and, often, sudden and unusual romantic contacts. The sex drive will be stimulated, much like transit Sun conjunction natal Mars, resulting in the native's experience of sudden changes in existing romantic relationships or active furtherance of new romantic opportunities. New outlooks and lifestyles may be introduced by the native, often gaining acceptance from others. Unique approaches toward the rearing of children and their education often result from this transit. Adverse contacts to this conjunction from either natal or other transiting bodies are likely to dispose the native toward an egotistical attitude demanding absolute personal freedom. The native may thus refuse to adhere to necessary routines and disciplines, disrupting not only his or her own but also the lives of others, thereby incurring their resentment.

Transit Sun Conjunction Neptune

During this transit, the native's creative, imaginative and psychic abilities will be stimulated. Lacking affliction, it marks a favorable period for meditation and spiritual self-development, frequently coinciding with spiritual or religious experiences of an inspiring or uplifting nature. In many cases, impressions arising from deeper levels of the native's consciousness will strongly affect his or her personal attitudes and self-image at this time. Thus, the native will wish to see and understand his or her own subconscious motivations and inhibitions by confronting them and either using them to best advantage or overcoming them. Such self-realization, may often become a motivating factor for interest in the spiritual and psychological unfoldment of children. A vibrant personal magnetism or mystique is frequently expressed during this transit, enhancing the native's attractiveness and appeal to members of the opposite sex. If well-aspected, this conjunction marks an excellent time for creative artistic expression in music and the arts, especially the performing arts. Under affliction, on the other hand, the native should beware of placing emphasis on any neurotic or psychotic tendencies, usually the result of past experiences buried in his or her subconscious. The native may be prone to use alcohol, drugs, sexual overindulgence and other unwise pleasurable pursuits to temporarily escape these psychological fears; these pursuits, however, will only tend to aggravate the recurrence of this problem. Undesirable psychic influences, secret love affairs or ill-advised romantic associations can be a drain on the native's physical vitality if the conjunction is afflicted.

Transit Sun Conjunction Pluto

During the period of this transit, a dynamic stimulation of the native's willpower is usually evidenced, increasing personal self-confidence and determination to succeed. This helps the native to carry through on projects of creative self-expression. Psychic abilities and spiritual perceptions are enhanced by application of the will. Thus, if properly utilized, worthwhile accomplishments toward goals of physical and spiritual self-improvement can be effected. During this yearly transit, the native is likely to eliminate that which is outworn, unnecessary or superfluous. Even that which is not discarded will be subject to change, whether it be found in new uses or in minor improvements of some kind. During this transit the native may assume a role of leadership in such affairs as joint finances and corporate enterprise. Likewise, the native may seek to improve romantic relationships, affinity to children and creative self-expression in the fields of art, music, financial investments or social activities. Afflictions to this conjunction from either natal or other transiting bodies may incline the native to coerce, dominate or otherwise attempt to reform or reshape others to fit a particular concept or model. Such efforts, and their often accompanied self-righteous attitudes are, unfortunately, apt to arouse the opposition and resentment of others.

Transit Sun Sextiles

These transits usually coincide with periods of mental stimulation during which the native's friendships and ideas are emphasized. Impressions made by reading, communication and contact with friends and group associates can have an invigorating beneficial effect upon all types of creative self-expression, especially in the fields of teaching, artistic endeavors, sports, games, financial speculation, interpersonal communication and romantic and social activity.

All of these opportunities will arise through the affairs ruled by the planet receiving the sextile in a manner as determined by the aspects to the sign and house position of that planet.

Transit Sun Sextile Sun

During the period of this transit the native will usually display greater vitality and self-confidence in his or her actions and activities. The native is thus apt to take a more active leadership role among friends and group associates. The native's ideas, expressed with a positive degree of poise and self-confidence, will be demonstrative of his or her creative potential. Thus, the native is likely to find favor in communicating with those of power and authority who can help the native realize his or her goals. Social and romantic communication and activity can reflect the positive attributes of this transit, as can the native's participation in programs of child development and education.

Transit Sun Sextile Moon

The period of this transit usually corresponds to an increase in the native's vitality. Much can be gained by the exchange of ideas and communication with members of the opposite sex. Financial affairs in particular can be furthered by the native's positive direction of intellectual energies and expertise, especially in businesses dealing with food, farming, real estate and domestic products and services. Family and domestic affairs are likely to interest the native. Entertaining in the home and family get-togethers often coincide with this transit. Here, too, time can be rewardingly devoted toward insuring the emotional well-being and physical health of children. This is a favorable time to enhance the home environment. Thus, during this transit the native is presented with many opportunities to improve and make home and family life more meaningful.

Transit Sun Sextile Mercury

This transit is a helpful mental stimulus for all creative endeavors. It brings easy communication with brothers, sisters, neighbors, coworkers, group associates, romantic partners, children and those in positions of power and authority. This transit is helpful for inspiration and ideas for creative artists, especially those working in the literary field. It also stimulates ideas for the improvement of work efficiency and the betterment of health and hygiene, and this is a good time to approach a superior concerning work matters. The native could improve his or her dress, with a tendency toward what is more colorful or artistic. This transit also favors writing, communication, study and dealing with schools, as well as short trips, pleasure and romance. Romance could come through friends, neighbors, brothers, sisters, artistic activities, groups or organizations.

Transit Sun Sextile Venus

This transit is conducive to social, romantic, artistic and business endeavors, and helps the native display personal charm, attractiveness and consideration to the opposite sex. It is a favorable time for communication regarding the organization of social activities, and the native could have opportunities to make money through art, entertainment or luxury items. This can bring communication with the opposite sex which could present romantic opportunities. It is a favorable time for involvement with music, art and the theater, and the native will be more inclined to be sympathetic and kind, and also is likely to be affectionate and kind toward children, showing emotional rapport with them.

Transit Sun Sextile Mars

This transit indicates a period of energetic constructive action. Because of the intellectual nature of this sextile, the individual is more likely to think through his or her, which would not be the case with other Mars contacts. There is apt to be involvement with social activities of a physical nature such as sports, dancing and hiking. The native is apt to pursue professional, business, romantic and creative goals with self-confidence and determination, and to assume an active and aggressive role of leadership in professional and business affairs. There is a greater sense of competition with a drive to outshine others, and the native may become a leader in organizations and aggressively pursue romantic contacts. This transit is favorable for dealing with children, especially in physical activities such as sports and in youth organizations.

Transit Sun Sextile Jupiter

This transit stimulates the individual's energy, enthusiasm, thought and communication toward religious, philosophical, educational, cultural and group activity. There is a greater display of optimism, hope, enthusiasm and concern for the overall betterment of the social order, and opportunities can arise for higher education, spiritual knowledge and training. Long-distance travel for education, exposure to foreign cultures or spiritual philosophies, or for purposes of moving residence are possible under this transit. It is a good period for devoting time to the cultural, social and religious training of children. This transit can bring romantic opportunities through contact with those connected with religious, educational or cultural groups or institutions. The native can make gains through carefully thought out speculative ventures during this period, providing the rest of the horoscope concurs.

Transit Sun Sextile Saturn

This transit is favorable for the planning and organization of professional and business affairs. It is a good time for dealing with those in positions of established authority and power, especially if they are connected with conservative institutions. Creative projects and ideas can be organized and put in practical use at this time. This period helps stabilize a romantic relationship. It is also a good time to help children build structure into their lives by acquiring the discipline and character that will help them grow and mature. This transit tends to make the individual more conscientious about work and other serious responsibilities, so the native can accomplish much that has a long-term value. The native could take on responsibility for organizing group and organizational affairs. In general, this transit helps the native's managerial skills and gives personal authority. Romantic opportunities could arise through professional or business contacts. Artists experiencing this transit will have an enhanced sense of form and structure.

Transit Sun Sextile Uranus

This transit brings exciting new ideas, friends, groups and organizational affiliations. The individual's willpower and desire for personal freedom are stimulated, and thus the native is likely to seek new experiences and social contacts. Powerful new friends could help in the realization of goals. This is a favorable transit for occult activities and finding intuitively inspired solutions to existing problems, and the individual will display greater originality and unique insights in all creative endeavors. There will be opportunities for romance through friends and groups. Humanitarian interests will be intensified and bring new opportunities. This is a good time to introduce children to new ideas and group activities. Clairvoyant faculties could be stimulated during this period, and the individual may have opportunities or new ideas concerning speculation or investments in corporate financial affairs.

Transit Sun Sextile Neptune

This transit stimulates the individual's imagination, and is therefore excellent for all creative work. The individual can gain insight into the workings of the subconscious mind during this period. This transit is helpful for meditation and intuition, and there can be an intuitive rapport with romantic partners, friends and group associates. Friends, neighbors, brothers and sisters can arouse interest in spiritual or philosophical pursuits, or the native could be instrumental in arousing such an interest in them. There could be an interest in helping others with their psychological problems or working with hospitals, institutions or charitable organizations.

Transit Sun Sextile Pluto

This transit often stimulates ideas for recycling or reclaiming discarded resources. Or it could make the individual aware of the need to discard that which no longer serves a useful purpose. Opportunities can arise for creative enterprises involving the use of corporate resources. This is a favorable period for handling matters related to taxes, insurance, corporate money or alimony, and to seek funding and financial support for projects or creative endeavors. It is a good period for the individual to embark upon programs of physical or spiritual self-improvement, and this transit provides a stimulus to the willpower so that one can take decisive action. The native could establish friendships or affiliations with people of power and authority, and this transit is also helpful in the unfoldment of the intuitive faculties and occult abilities.

Transit Sun Squares

These transits indicate a period during which the individual could try to force his or her will in whatever situation is indicated by the planet receiving the transiting square from the Sun. For this reason the native should be careful of ego confrontations, and should not allow others to coerce him or her. Neither should the native coerce others. There is often the necessity to struggle and work hard under this transit if one is to overcome obstacles and achieve goals.

Transit Sun Square Sun

This transit can indicate problems arising over ego confrontations or an attempt by the individual to force his or her will in a given situation. Overindulgence in pleasurable pursuits or excessive expenditures or speculations is also a danger. This is not a good period for romantic or social activities. Care should be exercised in dealing with children so as to maintain a sympathetic understanding. In romance, there could be a breakdown of the relationship caused by resentment on the part of one or both parties. Constructively used, this transit can be a stimulus to ambition and positive achievement. But care and diplomacy should be exercised in dealing with superiors or those in positions of power and authority. If the Sun is afflicted in the natal horoscope, precautionary measures are especially important.

Transit Sun Square Natal Moon

The individual's conscious will and subconscious desires could be at cross purposes during this period. This transit can indicate difficulties in family, domestic or financial affairs, and problems can arise with family members or the opposite sex. This is not a good time to ask for money or favors from those in positions of power and authority or from family members or the opposite sex. Nor is it a good time for financial speculation, expensive social activities or dealing with real estate and home products and services. Emotional issues and difficulties could arise with children, unwanted pregnancies can occur and discordant emotional issues can interfere with romantic relationships. During this period the native should be careful of diet and digestion, because the vital energies often are at low ebb.

Transit Sun Square Mercury

During this transit the native is apt to experience difficulties in communication with brothers, sisters, neighbors or coworkers. The ego can stand in the way of an objective impartial view of reality. Often, personal pride can distort the ability to reason impartially. These difficulties are especially emphasized if the Sun and Mercury are afflicted in the natal horoscope. Care should be exercised while on short journeys, telephoning, writing or other forms of communication. This is a period to be wary of false, inaccurate or incomplete information, and caution should be exercised while communicating with superiors or those in positions of power and authority as it is easy to be misunderstood at this time. This is not a good period for communication with romantic partners, dealing with children or engaging in important social activities because of the potential for misunderstandings, misinformation and wrong decisions. If the Sun is afflicted in the natal horoscope, the native could be tempted to speak untruthfully in order to protect personal pride and ego.

Transit Sun Square Venus

This transit can bring emotional and financial problems connected with romantic relationships, creative endeavors, social activities or business dealings. Overindulgence in social activities, sexual excess or financial expenditures on luxury items can create problems. The feelings of those with whom the individual is dealing, especially in close personal relationships, can be easily hurt. This often arises out of ego sensitivity on the part of one or both natives. Care and diplomacy should be exercised in partnerships and in romantic and marital relationships. During this period, the native should avoid the role of a prima dona who demands personal attention. Self-centered attitudes could cause problems in social situations during this period. Unwise pursuits of pleasure could be used as an escape from personal emotional difficulties. If the Sun is afflicted in the natal horoscope, the native could demand personal favors or neglect the needs of others. Properly used, this transit can be conducive to social conviviality or artistic creativity, and can be especially helpful to those who are normally shy and retiring.

Transit Sun Square Natal Mars

This transit can bring out aggressive, competitive and egocentric attitudes. The individual is apt to try to force his or her will on others in order to achieve personal desires. This attitude will arouse resentment and, in extreme cases, it could result in a physical confrontation. Thus, this is not the time to get into a disagreement with the boss or those in positions of power and authority. Care should be exercised and all safety regulations observed in handling machinery, chemicals and all other things that could be potential health or fire hazards, and the native should avoid impatience that could lead to impulsive acts that he or she would later regret. Strife because of ego confrontations with children or romantic partners or those in positions of power and authority could cause upsets and problems. Sports and other competitive games are apt to become rough or dangerous during this transit. Physical or emotional overexertion can pose a danger to the native's heart or head. If the Sun is afflicted in the natal horoscope, the desire to force one's will on others can emerge strongly at this time.

Transit Sun Square Jupiter

This transit tends to emphasize overconfidence and extravagant tendencies. There is a tendency to use religious, philosophical and cultural traditions and institutions for one's own selfish purposes. Seemingly altruistic actions and attitudes on the individual 's part can be based on a desire for personal importance or other ulterior motives. This is not a good time to engage in financial speculation or gambling, and the native should avoid indulging in unwise or excessive pursuit of pleasure. Self-deceptive escapist tendencies can be activated by this transit, which calls for realism and wisdom in the bestowal of help and sympathy to others. Dogmatic and fanatical religious and cultural attitudes should be avoided, especially if these are used as subconscious ego defense mechanisms. If the Sun is afflicted in the natal horoscope, the native could express an unrealistic view of his or her self-importance during this transit. This egotism and desire for personal attention could manifest as pretended humility and piety.

Transit Sun Square Saturn

This transit can stimulate attitudes that are rigidly overcautious or conservative. If carried to excess, the native could become dogmatic and authoritarian in treating those under his or her authority, while at the same time being rigidly subservient to superiors. This is not a good time to seek favors or promotion from those in established positions of power and authority. It is best to maintain the status quo and to avoid making drastic changes. Negative attitudes may be motivated by fear of disgrace or loss of status, and enterprises started under this transit require hard work and discipline in order to succeed. This is not a favorable time for engaging in romantic or social activities because the native is likely to lack self-confidence. The could also be rebuffed or considered too conservative or drab by others. Problems could arise with children stemming from insufficient or overly severe discipline, and the native could lack emotional warmth or understanding in dealing with children under this transit. Speculative investments made at this time will not work out satisfactorily. If the Sun is afflicted, caution should be exercised to avoid rigid authoritarian attitudes used as ego defense mechanisms.

Transit Sun Square Uranus

This transit can bring sudden upsets in financial dealings and speculation, romantic relationships, social activities, friendships, groups or relationships with children. The individual could be unpredictable, headstrong or egocentric. This is not a favorable time for involvement in new friendships, organizations or group activities as they will be temporary. There can be attitudes of personal freedom at all costs while disregarding the rights of others or agreements made with them. Fascinating but short-lived romantic attractions can come into being during this period. Upsetting occurrences arising out of inconsistency in dealing with children or rebelliousness on their part can upset the native. Gambling and unwise speculation can be disastrous during this period, especially if the Sun is afflicted in the natal chart. The native's vitality can be erratic and unpredictable, and this transit can cause palpitations and erratic heart actions afflicting the motor nerves of the body. This is not a good time to engage in dubious occult practices or to be involved in groups or cults engaged in such practices. If the Sun is afflicted in the natal horoscope, inconsistency and dogmatic attitudes can present problems at this time.

Transit Sun Square Neptune

This transit can arouse all types of subconscious emotional distortions that can make the native susceptible to psychic influences and abnormal impulses. This influence encourages tendencies toward escapism and self-deception, which can occur through alcohol, drugs or overindulgence in pleasurable pursuits. The individual could be deceived or deceive others in romantic relationships. Gambling and unwise financial speculation can have disastrous consequences at this time. The native must take extra care to be clear and precise in dealing with children, at the same time being on the alert for deception or evasiveness on their part. If the Sun is afflicted in the natal horoscope, this period could bring out any tendency for abnormal behavior in order to get attention from others. Self-deception and avoidance of responsibility can also show up in the native's behavior. This transit can also encourage delusions of grandeur to prop up the native's ego and desire for importance.

Transit Sun Square Pluto

This transit stimulates a desire for power and dominance. If carried to excess, it can tempt the native to use ruthless or destructive tactics to fulfill a need for power. The native is apt to force his or her own will regardless of the consequences to associates or environment. These actions could affect the native's reputation and professional status. Coercion in corporate and business dealings is always a danger with this transit, especially if the Sun is afflicted in the natal horoscope. Care should be taken so as not to dominate others or allow oneself to be dominated. Reformist tendencies should begin with the self and then by influencing others through example. Attempts at remaking the romantic partner or imposing unnecessarily harsh disciplines on children could have adverse affects for the native. Joint finances or corporate dealings may need revision under this transit. This is not a good time for dealing with joint finances, taxes, insurance or goods of the dead. Dubious occult practices should be avoided during this transit. If the Sun is afflicted in the natal horoscope, the native could be tempted to use ruthless and coercive tactics on others for personal power and aggrandizement.

Transit Sun Trines

These transits are favorable for all types of creative self-expression in romantic, social, artistic, educational and philosophical activities. They are also helpful in dealing with children and their education. The native has an easy flow of self-expression and manifests energy, expansiveness and self-confidence in the affairs ruled by the planet receiving the trine from the transiting Sun.

Transit Sun Trine Sun

This transit gives energy, vitality and greater self-confidence. There is a strong impulse toward creative self-expression in areas related to art, music, entertainment, social activity, romance, children, education and personal leadership. The houses and signs that the natal and transiting Sun occupy and rule and also the fifth house can benefit from this creative impetus. This is a favorable transit for sports, entertainment and speculation providing the Sun is not afflicted in the natal chart. This transit also has a beneficial effect on the native's health and vitality, and can help the individual to gain a more positive self-image. This transit can bring opportunities for cultural, spiritual, educational and religious advancement and enrichment. It is also a favorable time for travel, pleasure trips and the broadening of one's self-expression.

Transit Sun Trine Moon

This transit is favorable for family, domestic and financial affairs. It is a good time for relating to the opposite sex, whether in terms of business, romance or pleasure. There is greater harmony between the native's subconscious desires and the conscious will. During this transit the individual is capable of being both receptive and active in personal self-expression. It is an excellent time for family get-togethers or social gatherings. During this transit, the native could take an interest in cooking. This is a good period for dealings in real estate, food, home and domestic products and services. One can approach those who are prominent and important concerning business matters or matters pertaining to education, philosophy, religion or long-distance travel.

Transit Sun Trine Mercury

This transit is favorable for matters related to communication, writing, education, philosophy, long- and short-distance travel and helping with the education of children. Romantic relations are helped by an easy flow of communication with the partner. Friends and those in positions of power and authority can be instrumental in expanding and helping the native to realize his or her goals and objectives. This transit can stimulate effective ideas in artistic, musical, literary, educational and entertainment fields of activity. This transit is favorable for communicating with superiors concerning work, employment and ways of improving the work environment and work efficiency. This transit has a beneficial effect upon health and the native could develop a greater interest in achieving a snappy personal appearance that is socially and romantically attractive to others. The native becomes aware of the need for correct diet and other necessary health procedures.

Transit Sun Trine Venus

This transit is favorable for business and romantic activity. It encourages a happy optimistic, cheerful disposition and a sense of friendliness and social grace. This is a good time to ask for a raise or favors from those in positions of power and authority. It is also a favorable period for dealing with children because the native will have a sympathetic rapport with their needs and feelings. The individual will be more inclined to be generous, sympathetic, kind and cooperative toward others. This is a favorable time for artistic, musical and theatrical expressions and activity. The native can be successful in handling business and legal partnerships and agreements. This is a fine time for pleasure trips, social activities, musical events, romantic encounters and the sale or purchase of art objects and luxury items. A marriage opportunity could present itself at this time, providing other transiting aspects concur.

Transit Sun Trine Mars

This transit is an impetus toward constructive, creative action. This action usually involves some form of physical activity such as sports, construction, dancing or the performing arts. The native will project with greater determination and self-confidence during this period, and often assumes a role of leadership in initiating action along business, professional, social or political lines. This is a good time to initiate programs for working with children, especially in physical activities such as sports and youth clubs. The native will have the courage and initiative to put creative ideas into constructive action. It's a good time to enlist the aid of those in positions of power and authority to help carry out these plans. There is also apt to be an interest in programs of physical fitness and self-improvement.

Transit Sun Trine Jupiter

This transit stimulates strong interests in educational, religious, philosophical and cultural activities. The individual has an optimistic, benevolent and generous attitude toward life and others. Often, the native can gain prophetic insight into cultural changes and future events based on an intensified awareness of the overall cultural context. It is a favorable time for business, seeking favors from those in positions of power and authority, seeking admittance to institutions of higher learning or engaging in religious or charitable activities. This is an excellent time to embark on a long journey or to have dealings with people in foreign countries or faraway places. This is an easier time for the native to get along with children and help them with their moral, cultural and spiritual unfoldment. Cultural and social gatherings of all types are favored by this transit. Romantic opportunities can arise through affiliations with educational, cultural or religious activities.

Transit Sun Trine Saturn

This transit is favorable for professional advancement through hard work and good organization on the part of the individual. It is an excellent time to organize professional, business, political and legal affairs and activities. It is also good for self-improvement through patience, discipline and practicality. This is a good period to approach those with power and authority concerning serious, important matters. The individual can work with older people successfully at this time, and also with children, helping them to build structure into their lives. Something in the native's past can be of benefit at this time. This transit brings the necessary organization and discipline that will put creative endeavors into practical manifestation, and brings easy flow along these lines. During this period a past romantic tie could reappear on the scene or an opportunity for romance with an older or mature person could arise.

Transit Sun Trine Uranus

During this transit, the intuitive faculties are stimulated. The individual will manifest greater individual and unique talents in fields such as art, music, entertainment, science, philosophy and occult pursuits. There is a greater willingness to experiment with new lifestyles and ways of doing things. A sudden and exciting romantic contact could be made at this time. This is an excellent transit for developing new friendships and group associations. It is also favorable for financial speculation or corporate enterprises, especially if these are of a scientific nature. This is a good time for sharing unusual and exciting experiences with children or for introducing them to scientific or metaphysical concepts.

Transit Sun Trine Neptune

This transit is favorable for all creative, artistic, musical and theatrical endeavors that require creativity and imagination. It is also a good time for meditation and an inner spiritual search. There will be increased intuitive empathy in dealing with children and romantic partners. This influence can help the native to have greater self-confidence in the expression of intuitive inspiration, and the native could be intuitively guided in his or her choice of speculative investments. It is a good time for religious activities, long journeys and cultural pursuits, especially those of an esthetic or spiritual nature. Valuable guidance could be received from a spiritual teacher, or the native may become such a teacher to others. This is a good time to gain insight into the workings of the subconscious mind. Romantic opportunities could arise through cultural, religious or spiritual activities, but att this time the native is inclined to be idealistic about love and romance.

Transit Sun Trine Pluto

This transit brings out the native's willpower and positive determination to improve self and environment. There is a greater sense of one's own identity as a spiritual being in command over destiny and circumstances, and because of this awareness the native will communicate with greater self-confidence and strength. The native will become creative in finding new uses for old or discarded items. This is a favorable time to initiate reasonable financial speculation with regard to corporate business affairs. It is also a favorable time to take charge of matters related to joint finances, insurance, taxes, inheritance and corporate money. This is also an excellent time for spiritual self-development through personal efforts in fields such as meditation, metaphysics, yoga or other spiritual practices.

Transit Sun Oppositions

These transit oppositions often bring ego conflicts and confrontations. These can arise in relationship to games, romance, financial speculation or social activities.

Transit Sun Opposition Sun

This transit can bring ego confrontations in relationships of importance to the native, so it is best to have a democratic attitude in dealing with others. Conflicts over authority are especially likely to arise with children, romantic partners and those mutually engaged in competitive games and creative artistic projects. The native should neither allow himself or herself to be dominated or seek to dominate others. When properly used this transit can stimulate the native's willpower, self-confidence and creative ability.

Transit Sun Opposition Moon

This transit can bring ego confrontations and emotional difficulties in dealing with members of the opposite sex or with family members. The native could be overly ostentatious and extravagant in parties, expenditures in beautifying the home or other social gestures. This can be a delicate psychological period in relationships with romantic partners. There could also be a temporary disequilibrium in the native's vitality and digestive processes. Children may demand special attention or be emotionally difficult. Care should be exercised in speculative financial investments made at this time.

Transit Sun Opposition Mercury

This transit can bring much intellectual activity and discussion. The native or those with whom the native is communicating may have fixed dogmatic ideas regarding issues at hand. This inflexibility of mental attitude can sometimes result in verbal ego confrontations. It is important for the native to keep an open mind since he or she may not have all the facts. If this transit is properly handled it can be good for games of mental skill, social communication and working with the education of children. One should be careful in signing contracts and formulating agreements. It is also wise to exercise tact and diplomacy in speech and communication, especially in dealing with people in positions of power and importance or in communicating with a romantic partner or while attending social gatherings. This is a good time for engaging in literary pursuits related to art and entertainment.

Transit Sun Opposition Venus

This transit can bring about emotional upsets in romantic and marital relationships. These upsets often result from one partner trying to dominate the other. Properly handled, it can also mean much mutually pleasurable sharing and emotional enjoyment. Often there could be involvement in some form of art, music or entertainment. In some cases, the native may be tempted to ostentatious social competition and unnecessary extravagance in parties, entertainment or other social gestures. Children experiencing this transit could be very demanding of time, attention and affection. The native must be careful not to hurt the feelings of others, especially where children are involved. In some cases the native could have an exaggerated opinion of his or her desirability that could appear ludicrous to others.

Transit Sun Opposition Mars

This transit can bring about conflict over authority that in extreme cases can even result in physical confrontation. The native is apt to disregard the rights and feelings of others in the effort to satisfy personal desires. This aggressiveness toward others can result in conflict and consequent problems. This is not a good time to engage in rough physical sports or strenuous physical exercise to which one is not accustomed. People often become foolishly or overly competitive under the influence of this transit. The exercise of patience, consideration, tact and diplomacy can help to overcome many difficulties and avoid potential conflicts. The native should be careful in business transactions and financial speculations at this time.

Transit Sun Opposition Jupiter

This transit tends to make people foolishly over-optimistic and over-confident. The native can go to excess in social activities, financial speculation, gambling or attempting to be a king-pin in some religious, cultural or educational activity. The native is apt to become overly ego identified with his or her particular cultural, religious and philosophical views to the point of being biased or prejudiced. There is often a certain lack of humility or an exaggerated sense of one's own importance. This can cause difficulties in relating to other people, especially if the native acts in a condescending manner.

Transit Sun Opposition Saturn

This transit usually brings a time when heavy demands are made on the native in terms of responsibility and work. It can be a difficult time for those engaged in creative or artistic projects or work. This is not a good time to approach people in established positions of power and authority for favors or recognition. It is also a difficult time for romantic relationships, for dealing with children or engaging in speculative ventures. It is best to wait until another time to stage a party or social gathering. Heavy work or professional responsibilities often stand in the way of romance or other pleasurable pursuits. The native could be overly severe or unsympathetic toward children or young people. Children or young people experiencing this transit may resent the authority of the adults in charge of them. In general, this transit can dampen the native's vitality, enthusiasm, sparkle and self-confidence. Positively used it is a spur to constructive ambition, good organization and worthwhile accomplishment.

Transit Sun Opposition Uranus

This transit often triggers the native's rebellion against the status quo in whatever affairs are ruled by the signs and houses which transiting Sun and natal Uranus occupy and rule. There could be a severance of old friendships and organizational ties and an initiation of new ones. The native or those with whom he or she must deal may become unpredictable or unreliable.

The native should avoid a double standard of expecting freedom for self while at the same time expecting others to do his or her bidding. Such one-sided attitudes are bound to arouse resentment and opposition in others. On the positive side, unexpected and exciting developments could arise in friendships, social activities, creative endeavors and in dealing with children. Children could become rebellious and hard to manage during this transit. The native should avoid rash impulsive acts and decisions, especially if they affect matters of major consequence or importance.

Transit Sun Opposition Neptune

This transit often indicates a time of intensified imagination, which, if not properly directed, can make the native prey to distortions of the subconscious mind, delusions of grandeur, a persecution complex or other psychological aberrations. These will not be serious unless the natal horoscope reveals a propensity to mental illness. There can be confusion, misunderstanding or deception in romantic or social relationships or in dealings with children, artistic endeavors or speculative enterprises. For a mature and well-balanced person, this transit can be a stimulus to the creative imagination. There is also the danger that the native will seek psychological escape through ill advised pleasurable pursuits such as gambling, excessive alcohol, drug abuse or indiscriminate sexual overindulgence. Children undergoing this transit should have careful, watchful supervision. The native could be disappointed as a result of unrealistic romantic expectations. In general the native can fail to see important relationships as they really are. Tendencies toward self-deception should be carefully watched and avoided.

Transit Sun Opposition Pluto

This transit indicates a time when the native could attempt to remake or reform others while neglecting to reform himself or herself. This could lead to resentment and conflict. The native should not allow himself or herself to be coerced nor should he or she attempt to coerce others. Care and discrimination should be used in exercising the will, especially with respect to the rights of others. There can be a tendency for the native to sever old relationships that he or she no longer considers to be useful. Unwise or dangerous occult practices should be avoided at this time. Correctly used, this transit is an impetuous to creative effort. Relationship problems could arise over matters pertaining to insurance, inheritance, taxes, affairs of the dead, corporate money, joint finances, alimony or sexual relations.

II

Transits of the Moon

The Moon, swiftest of the planets and luminaries, takes approximately two and a half days to transit a sign or house and is productive of the most rapidly changing astrological influences in our daily lives. Although lunar transits by themselves are not normally generative of events of major or lasting importance or significance, they do act as timing or triggering factors for other synchronous and more important transits in the horoscope of an individual. For this reason allusions are often made to the Moon as the "second-hand on the clock of destiny." Lunar transits are usually indicative of day-to-day and hour-to-hour alterations, modifications or variations in the mood, emotional disposition and vitality of an individual.

The effects of lunar transits through the signs are often seen through objective observation of mass psychological manifestations or public mood. For example, the transit Moon in in Aries will cause people to become generally more impulsive, aggressive, impatient and self-assertive while at the same time more enterprising, active and self-confident. In contrast, the Moon transiting Cancer will orient the public toward issues of domestic and family importance, notably the acquisition and usage of food, and will incline them toward displays of sympathy and kindness. The exhibition of greater emotional and sentimental sensitivity may also become evident. Transit Moon through Libra would in turn provide the bases for greater sociability.

In the life of an individual, the sign and house position of transit Moon are indicative of the direction of family and domestic concerns. Its house position will be particularly descriptive of the practical affairs of life which will temporarily become a family issue. For example, should the transiting Moon fall in the ninth house of an individual's horoscope, it could incline the native to organize and embark upon a family vacation, trip or outing or to encourage family attendance at a religious ceremony.

The Moon's exaltation and accidental exaltation in Taurus and the second house, respectively, will often relate the affairs of the house of the Moon's transit to family financial matters, expenditures and efforts to acquire wealth or money.

The Importance of Lunar Phases

When inaugurating any new venture or project, it is important to consider the lunar phases. This is a fact of particular importance to those endeavors entailing gatherings of people, particularly those requiring participation such as classes, social gatherings, performances and advertising.

The period from New Moon to Full Moon is favorable for the initiation or commencement of such enterprises or for making new contacts concerning any project or activity. During the waxing Moon people are generally more extroverted and outgoing. Thus, such undertakings are more likely to succeed and endure if initiated during this period.

Likewise, the period of the waning Moon, from Full Moon to New Moon, favors the completion of old projects and tending to unfinished business. During this period people are inclined to exhibit their more introverted and introspective tendencies.

Transit Moon Through the Signs

Sign positions of the transiting Moon are important to the demarcation of periods, usually of about two and a half days duration, of general public mood and mass psychological inclination, knowledge of which if properly understood can be used to great advantage.

Transit Moon Through Aries

This transit is indicative of a period during which the public mood is oriented toward intense activity, emotional impulsiveness, competition and aggressive self-assertion. People are likely to be enterprising and overtly self-expressive. Those who are shy or timid can assert themselves with greater strength and confidence.

Should the Moon make adverse contacts while transiting Aries, short tempers can lead to outbursts of anger and there is the ever-present danger of accidents and fires. Thus, care should be taken to avoid situations of physical peril and to consider the rights of others under such affliction, or conflict is likely.

Transit Moon Through Taurus

Transit Moon through Taurus marks a time of general concern with practical financial affairs. Attendance to business and concern about the acquisition of material wealth and property for themselves, their homes and families will be of primary importance to natives during this period. A placidness and evenness of temper can also be expected.

However, should the Moon make adverse transiting aspects during this period, it could give rise to stubborn, emotionally unyielding and materialistic attitudes in the native's approach to budgetary and other financial needs, demands and desires.

Transit Moon Through Gemini

This transit denotes a time of much public travel by automobile, as well as by other means of transportation. Telephone, email, Internet and postal usage will show a marked increase. Concern about new events and their effects upon the public will lead to increased interest in intellectual discussions and correspondence, reading and visits to and from family friends and neighbors.

Adverse transiting aspects of the Moon in Gemini can evoke prejudiced viewpoints and vicious gossip. Transportation foul-ups, communication delays and confusion and the transmission of erroneous information can also be expected under such afflictions.

Transit Moon Through Cancer

Transit Moon through Cancer indicates a time of concern about family issues and domestic affairs. People, particularly women, are emotionally sensitive, psychically inclined and attuned to family emotional interactions. There will be less traveling about and a tendency to remain at home. Natives will manifest a general concern about cooking and diet, and will tend to indulge themselves in food. This is a favorable period in which to visit parents (particularly the mother) or relatives, to purchase home and domestic products or to look for an apartment or real estate. During the period of this transit, one generally is searching for emotional and domestic security.

Afflictions during this transit, until they are resolved, often witness the resurfacing of past emotional incidents and subconscious memories, creating difficulties in family relationships and frequently causing overindulge in food consumption. Family budgetary or financial problems and related indulgences may come to light at this time.

Transit Moon Through Leo

Transit Moon through Leo denotes a period of greater creativity, exuberance and expressiveness, with a general tendency for the public to appreciate colorful, dramatic ways of life. This may surface as active interest in the theater, art, entertainment and other manifestations of creative inspiration. Romantic and pleasurable pursuits may likewise be energized by this particular transit. Natives will exhibit the ever-present desire to seek the limelight or personal attention, and are apt to become assertive in their thirst for pleasurable and romantic activities. Inclinations toward bossiness and attempts to exert or extend personal authority or dominance are likely to be evidenced, and should these be carried to excess, ego confrontations may occur.

Afflictions of the Moon during this transit often touch off minor altercations or skirmishes between individuals that when reinforced by other transiting aspects may lead to more serious personal conflict. Self-righteous assumption of authoritative positions those involved only worsens such situations. Speculative ventures may suffer minor setbacks or a reshuffling of assets and liabilities, particularly when these involve partnerships or other corporate means for their realization. Romantic pursuits may fizzle or there may be a lovers spat. Subconscious memories or past conditioning may plague efforts to express one's true consciousness or identity.

Transit Moon Through Virgo

This transit inclines the public to be concerned about matters of diet and health. People will express a business-as-usual attitude toward occupation, business and other practical everyday responsibilities. Dietary matters, accentuated by this transit, may assume utmost importance in the minds of many because there is a greater awareness of the effects of diet upon health at this time. This transit manifests a general tendency to become more concerned with detail, efficiency, hygiene and personal mannerisms. Thus this period often brings house-cleaning activities, organization of practical affairs and improvements in the efficiency of work methodologies. Food, clothing and health items can be purchased with greater awareness of economy, practical value and usefulness.

Adverse transiting aspects of the Moon in this sign can indicate hypercritical attitudes in a native's views of detailed methodologies, efficiency, hygiene and personal modes of behavior, often to the irritation and annoyance of others. The native's communication and interpersonal relationships with family friends, neighbors, brothers and sisters, and even parents and relatives, will show the most marked effects of such a disposition. Health may suffer under such adverse transits of the Moon in Virgo. Minor physiological upsets and ailments, combined with a tendency to feel physically ill-at-ease, can, when such afflictions are reinforced, result in illness or other recurrent health problems. Difficulties in the maintenance of proper perspective, organization and orientation in relationships between occupational and domestic affairs and related endeavors are also likely to be encountered under such afflictions.

Transit Moon Through Libra

Transit Moon through Libra marks a period of increased social interaction and concern about psychological issues and public relations. A general tendency toward gracious, polite and cooperative conduct in the handling of marital affairs, legal matters and close personal relationships will be evidenced during this transit, as well as a greater degree of refinement in the appreciation of social interaction and manifestation of individual artistic creativity. Artistic and musical pursuits are thus favored by this transit.

Afflictions of the Moon while transiting Libra will tend to create problems in a native's close personal relationships and social activities. Under severe affliction, the native could be unsociable, boorish and uncouth, and lack sensitivity. Such adverse transits may cause hypersensitivity or a lack of psychic attunement to a partner's true intentions, or there could be withdrawal from personal participation in general social intercourse. Marital affairs may suffer from psychological difficulties or debilities, blockages and a basic inability to come to practical grips with the emotional love nature. Under such adverse transits, one should remain calm and proceed in a practical and rational manner (Saturn's exaltation in Libra) in the handling of day-to-day affairs. Legal affairs should be deferred to some future time, as should all matters of importance to marital or romantic affairs and partnerships.

During the period of this transit, people should drink large amounts of water to flush the excretory system and as a help to avoid potential kidney problems.

Transit Moon Through Scorpio

Transit Moon through Scorpio denotes a period of industriousness and constructive effort toward the improvement or regeneration of existing conditions in the home, domestic environment, corporate business and financial affairs and the joint financial sphere. A great deal of energy released consequent to this transit can, if properly directed, be of great assistance to a native in cleaning up loose ends around the home and in corporate business matters. Unfinished home improvement projects and work on business matters can often be successfully completed during this period. People are likely to dredge up emotional resentments resulting from previous sexual and financial dealings. Thus, emotional confrontation based upon these considerations is a definite danger. This is not a favorable period in which to undergo surgery, nor to buy or wear new clothing or jewelry.

Afflictions of the Moon during this transit can give rise to a vindictive desire to repay past unkindnesses or to participate in secret plots for any number of reasons. Financial problems dealing with the interrelationship of personal and business money may thwart a native's attempts to improve his or her personal standing, and may block the expression of individual creativity. Financial speculation is apt to be problematical at best and may even, under reinforced affliction, have disastrous results. The initiation of any new projects is not advised during this period. Instead, a native should use this transit to clean up old business both at home and at work.

Transit Moon Through Sagittarius

The Moon transiting Sagittarius produces increased interest in educational affairs, cultural activities, foreign countries, international politics and foreign cultures, particularly where these affect the native's home and immediate environment, practical values and personal financial concerns. This transit also designates a period in which people are more inclined to embark upon journeys, engage in family outings and attend religious services. They will want to deal with one another in a more open, honest and ethical manner and, through this, foster a spirit of unanimity, of oneness, within the social and cultural contexts of society.

Afflictions of the Moon during this transit, particularly when these either trigger or reinforce other adverse transiting aspects, can give rise to difficulties in home and domestic affairs. Legal problems can create a state of nervous tension in the home, often by complicating a native's personal financial picture. Subconscious memories and past conditioning may surface and pose obstacles to an individual's proper cultural, legal or professional orientation, often leading to use of deceptive tactics and practices to assure one's position or avoid the loss of that which has already been secured or what the individual expects to gain. Foreign involvements or international political dealings, whether on a personal or national level, may adversely affect a native's domestic sense of security under such affliction.

Transit Moon Through Capricorn

Transit Moon through Capricorn denotes a period of general concern about public affairs and business activity. There is a general inclination to act upon or perform that which is practical and profitable, resulting in the native's display of greater reserve and formality in personal interactions related to these activities. Thus, the practical organization of business affairs is particularly favored by this transit. Positive actions to alleviate concerns about old age and security can likewise be taken at this time.

One should also be aware of the danger of negative or depressed emotional states during this transit. Under afflictions of the Moon and reinforcement by adverse transiting aspects, this transit could result in a dismal or gloomy emotional outlook, and possibly as a result of the native's despondency, withdrawal from career, professional and business activity. Financial complications of a professional nature are possible under lunar afflictions in Capricorn. Although these will have direct effect upon a native's home and immediate environment, they will be only of minor significance unless they are reinforced by other adverse aspects. Partnership and close personal relationships, particularly those that involve professional or career activities, status and position, are apt to suffer minor setbacks from lack of or proper allocation of funds.

Transit Moon Through Aquarius

The transit Moon through Aquarius inclines people to become more friendly and humanitarian in daily activities. It gives rise to a public willingness to accept new ideas and engage in unusual activities.

Visits to and from friends and the pursuit of group and organizational activities are favored by this transit, as are the purchase of electronics and the investigation of new inventions and technological innovations.

Should the Moon be afflicted in its transit of this sign, people will exhibit a more erratic and unpredictable behavior and thus tend to be unreliable in their fulfillment of practical responsibilities and obligations.

Transit Moon Through Pisces

During this transit people tend to adopt an introverted stance in their performance of and response to daily activities, often exhibiting a strong preoccupation with their internal psychic processes and, should the Moon be afflicted, neuroses. There is greater general susceptibility to psychic influences, subliminal impressions and stimulations subconsciously reminiscent of past experiences. Likewise, this transit will confer a greater awareness of beauty and artistic creativity in the immediate environment and the home.

Afflictions of the Moon, particularly when reinforced, can cause the heightening or intensification of emotional hypersensitivity and neurotic tendencies aroused by this transit.

Transit Moon Through the Houses

Transit Moon through the houses of an individual's natal horoscope is indicative of the manner in which the native is subjected to emotional changes and increased family and domestic activity in the practical affairs of life. Affairs ruled by both the house in which the transit Moon is posited and the house or houses in which the sign Cancer is found will manifest the effects of these emotional fluctuations and increased family and domestic involvement, particularly where aspects are formed by the transit Moon to any of the natal planets of an individual's chart. Such changes are often effected through the agency of family members, women and daily contacts.

Transit Moon Through the First House

Generally, this period is an emotionally volatile one, consequent to the Mars connotation of such a first house transit. The native is inclined to express greater emotional sensitivity and self-consciousness regarding the opinions of others, which, if improperly handled, can result in the native irritating others by his or her impatience and extremes of emotional reaction. Weight gain is often experienced as a result of the native's indulgence in the consumption of food and beverages at this time, and this transit confers the native with the inclination to personally initiate change and activity in the family and domestic environment.

Family strife is often the result of adverse lunar transits to natal planets while in the first house.

Transit Moon Through the Second House

The native is normally motivated by concern for the financial security of home and family. In view of the Moon's accidental exaltation here, the native will be able to further these desires toward completion through attendance to business and financial matters, especially those enterprises dealing with the home, food, domestic services, farming, real estate or products used in the home. Favorable transits of the Moon to natal planets while in this house provide auspicious periods in which to invest in jewelry, art, fine clothing and products used in the home.

Should the Moon make adverse contacts while in the second house, the native is apt to manifest greediness or emotional, materialistic attitudes toward finances and personal possessions.

Transit Moon Through the Third House

This transit denotes a period of considerable communication and short-distance travel with family members and neighbors. Guests or visitors to the native's home may include individuals from the immediate community or neighborhood or family relatives and friends. Favorable transits of the Moon to natal planets while transiting this house are conducive to mail, phone communication and short journeys or trips, as well as the proper organization of family affairs.

However, should the Moon make adverse contacts while in the third house, the native is apt to talk incessantly about matters of inconsequential or trivial importance. Likewise, the native may become nervous and irritable because of an inability to resolve, or even cope with, the confusion and restless activity existent in his or her immediate environment.

Transit Moon Through the Fourth House

The period of this transit is often accented by emotional involvement in family and domestic affairs. Visits to the family home or parents and endeavors to improve the domestic scene in some way are typical of this transit. The native will exhibit a heightened emotional sensitivity to family relationships and to those matters concerning possessions, home, family or family finances. People experiencing this transit become more domestically oriented, inclined toward cooking and family care.

Adverse transits of the Moon while in the fourth house can cause the native to become emotionally hypersensitive over issues affecting family affairs or domestic security.

Transit Moon Through the Fifth House

Transit Moon through the fifth house of the horoscope inclines the native to seek out pleasurable pursuits, attend parties and social functions, organize family social gatherings and pursue romantic opportunities. Romantic attachments will be the subject of a great deal of sentimentality. This transit, unless the Moon is heavily afflicted, evokes the native's innate maternal instincts toward children and is a favorable period in which to attend to their needs.

Should the Moon make adverse transits to natal planets in its passage through this house, then the native should avoid impulsive financial investments and speculation.

Transit Moon Through the Sixth House

Household cleanliness and order, family hygiene and diet will be of concern to the native when the Moon transits the natal sixth house. An increased consciousness of household chores and practical family responsibilities may dispose the native to see a physician for a routine medical checkup or to embark upon a shopping trip for necessary food, clothing or household items.

Adverse transits of the Moon's passage through this house often lead the native to feel overburdened with household responsibilities. Emotional upsets under such affliction can frequently cause an adverse effect upon the native's physical well-being. The native should thus guard the health, especially where hazards of a dietary, digestive or occupational nature are likely to arise.

Transit Moon Through the Seventh House

Transit Moon through the seventh house of the natal horoscope emphasizes relationships, both public and personal, as the subject of immediate concern to the native. An increase in the emotional susceptibility of the native to others will yield an increased sense of companionship and interpersonal warmth. A great deal of contact with the public can be expected, particularly within the context of business and social activities. Marital issues concerning family and domestic affairs are likely to assume emotional significance in the native's life at this time.

Should the Moon make adverse contacts to the natal planets while transiting this house, personal relationships may become a source of emotional upset or confusion to the native. Marital quarrels over family and domestic affairs may also be expected under such affliction.

Transit Moon Through the Eighth House

Transit Moon through the eighth house heralds a period of concern about business and financial affairs, particularly where these involve joint funds or investments. The family budget may come up for discussion with the native's spouse or other household members. Matters in regard to wills, legacies and inheritances are also likely to be the subject of concern during this period. Psychic experiences and a general increase in the sex drive are also associated with this transit.

Adverse transiting aspects of the Moon in its passage through the eighth house can give rise to quarrels with family or household members over joint finances, inheritance, insurance matters or alimony. Should such lunar afflictions augment or reinforce other heavy eighth house influences, there may even be news of the death of a close friend or relative to the native.

Transit Moon Through the Ninth House

Transit Moon through the ninth house will incline the native toward the incorporation of cultural and religious values into family and domestic life. This often includes family trips or outings to landmarks of historical or cultural significance or attendance at religious functions. Visits to the native's home by individuals from distant places or foreign countries may spark interest in foreign cultures and religious viewpoints. Contact with universities, cultural organizations and individuals connected with such institutions may provide the native with a viable set of standards upon which to base a strong sense of family cultural awareness.

Adverse transits of the Moon while in this house can cause the native to experience difficulties in adjustment to religious or cultural biases inherent to his or her family background. Under such affliction, the native may even entertain prejudiced or biased cultural or religious opinions that are based upon family conditioning.

Transit Moon Through the Tenth House

Transit Moon through the tenth house confers the native with an increased awareness of professional and business ambitions. The native will be disposed to work harder and with diligence to achieve social prestige and financial security for self and family. Personal interaction with one or both parents is often related to this current professional drive. Business dealings conducted during this transit are likely to involve real estate, food and domestic products and services.

Adverse transits of the Moon through the tenth house often give rise to conflict between the native and his or her parents, employer or other authority figures. Areas of domestic and professional responsibility may clash, forcing an adjustment of the native's attitudes toward the importance and significance of each. Such afflictions may also result in an air of family pride or snobbishness.

Transit Moon Through the Eleventh House

Transit Moon through the eleventh house tends to increase the intensity of the native's interaction with friends, groups and organizations. The native will adopt a more humanitarian outlook and express a greater amiability toward strangers and public contacts at this time. Thus, entertainment and organizational meetings conducted in the home are not uncommon to the period of this transit, and frequently such affairs and other activities of intellectual or scientific interest will entail a degree of family involvement.

Should the Moon form adverse transits while passing through the eleventh house, conflict could arise over matters of organizational management and friendship, although such encounters are usually of no great consequence. Disagreement in these areas are often the result of erratic, unpredictable, emotional responses to which the native is subject during this period; thus, no major significance should be attached to the outcome of such confrontations. Under such affliction, the native's family may voice a lack of appreciation or approval for the native's friends, or the native may express personal disapproval of their acquaintances and associates.

Transit Moon Through the Twelfth House

Transit Moon through the twelfth house will incline the native to become more quiet and retiring than usual because at this time he or she is more impressionable, introspective and psychically aware of self and environment. Meditative disciplines practiced during this period will often unlock deeper levels of consciousness, thus eliciting the native's enhanced sensitivity to subtle beauty in physical surroundings and the expression of a more sympathetic nature toward those less fortunate.

Afflictions of the Moon during this transit can cause the resurfacing of emotional memories of early childhood conditioning, often resulting in periods of inexplicable neurotic behavior. The native may even be forced to deal with the psychological problems or to care for family members who are experiencing periods of hardship or confinement.

Transit Moon Conjunctions

Transit Moon Conjunction Natal Sun

This transit will elicit the native's expression of physical and emotional vitality and lend an air of personal authority and self-assurance. Personal initiative and creative activity will be constructively directed by the native toward the improvement of family and domestic circumstances. Inclinations to plan social activities or to entertain in the home are not uncommon to natives experiencing this transit. Artistic or creative endeavors designed to embellish the home environment are often initiated during this period. Interest in and concern about children and their welfare is often accentuated by this transit.

Should this conjunction remain unafflicted by natal or other transiting planets, sensible, practical financial investments can be contracted at this time, especially in such fields as art, entertainment, real estate, food, commodities and home and domestic products and services. Such, an affliction-free transit can also be advantageously employed by the native to approach those in positions of power and authority.

Afflictions to this conjunction can, on the other hand, cause the native's self-expression to be self-righteous and egotistical, often offending those with whom the native comes into contact and interfering with the positive expression of the native's creative drive. Ventures of a highly-speculative financial nature should be avoided under such adverse influences, lest they tend to financial loss.

Transit Moon Conjunction Natal Moon

The period of this transit is likely to find the native occupied with family and domestic affairs, particularly where these relate to practical values in day-to-day circumstances. There could be concerns, both business and personal, dealing with food and home and domestic products and services, or a trip to the grocery store. Methods of food preparation, cooking and other culinary concerns are apt to catch the native's interest during this period. Business and financial affairs handled during this transit are likely to be influenced in some way by women.

Should the Moon be afflicted by either natal or other transiting planets at this time, the native should avoid emotional extremes of temperament and exercise diplomacy in dealings with women and family members. Moodiness should also be avoided because under such affliction, painful memories of the past could resurface.

Transit Moon Conjunction Mercury

This transit often brings messages and visitors to the native's home. Mail, calls and visits by family members, friends and neighbors can be expected. Frequently, the native will show an active interest in household order and cleanliness, proper diet and personal and family health and hygiene at this time, leading the native to embark upon shopping trips to purchase commodities and other necessary items for the home.

A great deal of stimulating conversation may occur during this transit, but if the transiting Moon and natal Mercury are in any way afflicted, care should be taken to avoid any tendency for idle gossip or chit-chat about inconsequential matters, particularly when the native is at work.

Transit Moon Conjunction Venus

This transit marks a favorable time for parties, dates and entertaining in the home. Sentimental moods and romantic feelings are often aroused, lending a more affable and harmonious atmosphere to social relationships, especially those with women. Closer and warmer ties can also be expected between the native and family members during this transit. Beautification of the home and business activities dealing with art, music, entertainment, public relations, food and home and domestic products and services can be successfully handled or inaugurated at this time.

Should the Moon and Venus be afflicted by natal or other transiting planets, the native could suffer emotional upsets that lead to displays of maudlin sentimentality. The native may indulge in the pursuit of sensual pleasures, food consumption, alcohol, etc.

Transit Moon Conjunction Mars

This transit can bring a period of emotional upset in the native's life, often manifesting as discord in family relationships or difficulties in dealings with women. Such stress frequently gives rise to gastric pains or indigestion, further complicating the native's mental state. The native should thus avoid hasty decisions and rash acts, in view of his or her emotional state (especially in finances and purchases) and apply the energies to domestic concerns, work around the house and do-it-yourself projects, with the provision that adequate safety precautions are observed.

Should this conjunction be afflicted, the native must exercise extra care not to lose his or her temper over trivial matters; the exercise of patience and self-control can avoid much emotional misunderstanding, conflict and, later, regret.

Transit Moon Conjunction Jupiter

This transit denotes a period of increased optimism, inclining the native to show greater kindness and consideration for others, women and family members in particular. Family outings and cultural, educational and religious activities are favored by the native's participation at this time, as are business and public relations endeavors. Religious and patriotic feelings are often aroused by this transit, especially those instilled by early childhood conditioning and parental upbringing.

Afflictions to this transiting conjunction by either natal or other transiting planets can cause the native to assume a great deal or take too much for granted, and thus become foolishly over-optimistic and extravagant in the use of personal resources. Resultant problems and difficulties will be reflected in the home and immediate environment.

Transit Moon Conjunction Saturn

This transit often brings a period of emotional depression, when painful memories based upon the native's early family upbringing or other unpleasant past experiences latent in the subconscious mind are aroused and manifest themselves as obstacles to professional progress or problems in the family and domestic environment. Thus, dealings in financial affairs, public relations and delicate family emotional issues or with women should be postponed to some future time. Heavy family responsibilities may temporarily place an emotional or financial burden upon the native. This could lead to depressed moods and a lack of sensitivity to the feelings of others. Should this conjunction be afflicted, the aforementioned difficulties are likely to aggrieve the native that much more.

On the positive side, this transit can incline the native, through the application of self-discipline, to view and handle family, professional and financial responsibilities in a much more serious and practical manner.

Transit Moon Conjunction Uranus

This transit often brings sudden and unexpected events affecting the home or family affairs. Friends or group associates may drop in without notice, or the normal family routine may be disrupted by the abrupt and precipitous action of a friend, the native or another family member. There is the possibility of some unexpected financial gain or loss during this transit, and relationships with women could take some unusual turns. Thus, regardless of the good or bad import of this transiting aspect, it will definitely break any monotony in the native's life and make it far more interesting.

Under afflictions to this conjunction by any natal or other transiting planets, the native should exercise care in the use of electrical appliances around the house. The native should also avoid erratic, uncontrolled, emotional behavior and realize that dealings with women are not apt to proceed in a smooth and predictable manner.

Transit Moon Conjunction Neptune

During the period of this transit, subconscious emotional factors within the native or other household members are likely to be stimulated or activated. This transit may also indicate the heightening of the native's esthetic, imaginative, creative ability and spiritual awareness.

However, should this conjunction be afflicted, the native is apt to withdraw into a private dream world or experience a period of psychological confusion, delusion or disorientation. Usually this means nothing more than the inclination to daydream or let the imagination run free, leading to a lack of practicality and efficiency in handling daily affairs and relationships. In rarer cases, though, where this transit triggers a simultaneous transit, the effects may be that much more serious and significant to the native's life.

Transit Moon Conjunction Pluto

This transit denotes a period during which the native is emotionally activated and infused with energy that, if wisely directed, can lead to worthwhile accomplishment in the search for inner spiritual values. Women are likely to have some significant effect upon the native at this time, often by pressuring him or her to change or improve daily routines in some manner. Temporary involvements in corporate financial affairs, insurance or tax matters, inheritance or family business matters are not uncommon to those experiencing this transit.

Should this conjunction be afflicted, the native is apt to assume a belligerent and emotionally overbearing manner in relations with others, or to be subjected to such treatment.

Transit Moon Sextiles

Transit Moon Sextile Sun

This transit of the Moon will tend to boost the native's physical vitality and confer a more outgoing nature. Thus, the native will be inclined to participate in social activities, to meet with friends and to attend group activities. New friendships may be established with members of the opposite sex, or there may be a furtherance of romantic objectives with one already within the native's circle or the offer of mutual participation in pleasurable activities. Business activity and public relations work are assisted by this transit, often through communication or short-distance travel in connection with such endeavors.

Transit Moon Sextile Moon

This transit can bring increased closeness in family activity and contact. Improvements in the native's ability to communicate with or relate to women and/or other family members will enhance their combined activities and permit the mutual direction of energies toward family goals and objectives. Although this transit may often mean nothing more than attending a family dinner party or sponsoring one for friends, it will usually incline the native to take a more active interest in culinary concerns, domestic and home improvements and other practical daily affairs that affect the immediate environment and those around the native.

Transit Moon Sextile Mercury

This transit of the Moon usually produces an increase in the native's communication and short-distance travels, often related to family matters. There is apt to be much telephoning and mail involving family members or family affairs. Advertising and public relations work in connection with the native's business endeavors can be actively and successfully pursued at this time. This is a good transit for handling business correspondence. It is also a favorable time for practical communication with others in the working environment to improve efficiency.

Transit Moon Sextile Venus

This transit of the Moon confers a cheerful disposition and a refined social and artistic sense. Music and other creative artistic endeavors can be particularly appreciated at this time. This transit has a soothing effect on the native, endowing him or her with a pleasant attitude toward others and inclining the native to show greater kindness and consideration in dealing with others. There is likely to be a great deal of social communication and interaction with friends, family members and those of the opposite sex. Romantic activities or opportunities arising in the native's social sphere of activity can be successfully pursued by dating or other methods furthering such interests. Likewise, business endeavors, shopping excursions and purchases of art or luxury items by the native are favored by this transit.

Transit Moon Sextile Mars

This transit will energize the native, inclining toward the pursuit of exercise, outdoor activity and physical exertion of all kinds. Because of the intellectual nature of the sextile, this transit of the Moon will provide the native with the ability to plan actions intelligently, thus avoiding waste of effort through the use of intellectual foresight and awareness of the effects of such personal initiative. The native will display an enterprising, energetic attitude toward business and money-making efforts, often at the insistence of a woman. The native will be encouraged to expand his or her energies in constructive efforts toward the correction or improvement of the home or domestic environment.

Transit Moon Sextile Jupiter

This transit stimulates a sense of optimism and good will and remembrance of and belief in religious principles and cultural values, especially those instilled by family upbringing. The native is thus apt to display a more generous attitude and to express interest in assisting those less fortunate. In general, kindness and consideration shown by the native to those in the immediate environment will be returned in kind by those with whom the native has close personal contact. Family participation in cultural and religious activities is encouraged by this transit, as well as the native's engagement in business endeavors that are often productive of some financial gain.

Transit Moon Sextile Saturn

During the period of this transit, the native will assume a more conscientious, introspective and cautious air. The native is likely to act in a more reserved and conservative fashion than usual, leading to a generally quiet period. If used properly it can lead to solid, worthwhile accomplishments. This transit gives rise to the urge to set one's house in order and to organize the practical affairs of life, particularly where financial, domestic and professional matters are concerned. Older, more mature individuals, especially women, and often the native's mother, are likely to give the native good advice at this time.

Transit Moon Sextile Uranus

The native's intuitive and psychic faculties are enhanced by this transit, favoring this period as a time to pursue scientific, occult or astrological activities. Sudden and unique ideas arising at this time will often lead to changes and improvements in the native's home and family life. Group activities may be conducted or friends entertained in the comfort of the native's home during this transit. Often, unexpected visits or communication from friends or family members will alter or upset the daily routine. A friend may be instrumental in breaking the monotony of daily life and injecting a note of something positive and exciting.

Transit Moon Sextile Neptune

This transit is usually indicative of a period of increased psychic ability and impressionability. The imagination is stimulated, and should the natal chart reveal the potential, the native could realize some form of conscious telepathic awareness at this time. Playing hunches in the purchasing of material goods or in the handling of business communication is often manifested by those experiencing this transit. Meditative disciplines and other paths toward inward, spiritual unfoldment may also be successfully considered and practiced at this time. The native's heightened sensitivity to the needs of others as related to this transit will manifest in the expression of greater sympathy for those less fortunate or in need of help and encouragement. Family members or friends in places of confinement or seclusion are likely to be visited or contacted by the native during this period. Likewise, the native's capability for artistic appreciation will be enhanced, inspiring participation in creative endeavors and activities.

Transit Moon Sextile Pluto

This transit will confer the native with increased energy and resolve to determine and implement changes necessary to the proper and effective handling of everyday affairs. Interest will be directed toward the improvement of business, home and family matters. Thus, the native is apt to become involved in joint finances or in handling or resolving business matters dealing with taxes, inheritance, wills and insurance. Gains made in these areas will naturally be beneficial to the family and domestic environment. The native could revamp or dispose of that which no longer useful in the domestic environment. Potential psychic abilities may be momentarily realized during this transit, often through the mental and imaginative stimulation of a woman. Without further reinforcement by other major transits or the native's study, discipline and practice of these faculties, the psychic stimulation of this transit will not be significant.

Transit Moon Squares

Transit Moon Square Sun

This transit indicates a period in which the native is apt to feel emotionally upset and out of phase with the environment, often the result of fatigue, frustration, indigestion or ill health. Dealings with the opposite sex or involvement in romantic or social activities could prove difficult. Financial speculation should be cautiously avoided or, at least, curtailed. Capriciousness or impetuousness in assertive action can often lead to petty ego confrontations with family members or others with whom the native maintains a living relationship. Thus, it is in best interest to cultivate a calm, conservative and status-quo attitude during the period of this transit.

Transit Moon Square Moon

This transit often manifests itself as a period of petty emotional upset or moodiness in the native's handling of day-to-day affairs. Dealings with women or their emotional problems tend to compound the native's difficulties and should be carefully avoided at this time. Confrontations with family members are frequent, but they are not usually of serious import unless heavily reinforced by other natal or transiting afflictions. Care should be exercised in dietary measures, lest indigestion or related disorders and their accompanying abdominal pains arise to further afflict the native. This transit could give rise to financial difficulties. Thus, the handling of real estate matters or the purchase of commodities or other goods for the home should be, if possible, delayed until more favorable transits are in evidence.

Transit Moon Square Mercury

This transit is usually evidenced as a period of mental confusion and is often indicative of a temporary lack of organization in household affairs, appointment scheduling, communication, etc. It inclines the native or those around him or her to gossip or incessant chatter, often to the point of annoyance. Misunderstandings between the native and family members, friends, neighbors, brothers and sisters and those with whom he or she has business dealings often give rise to confusion. Emotional reactions to confusion, distractions and petty annoyances can interfere with the native's reasoning and sound judgment. Family planning sessions, written correspondence and important telephone conversations should be postponed, and the native should curtail local trips and excursions, lest he or she become lost in unfamiliar territory or surroundings. Communication with women in particular should be temporarily delayed because there is likely to be a great deal of difficulty and misunderstanding at this time.

Transit Moon Square Venus

This transit inclines the native to be overly sentimental and emotional. Thus, the native's feelings will be particularly susceptible to injury, especially in cases of romantic disappointment or family misunderstanding. Excessive self-indulgence in food, drink, sex and social activity is often manifested during this period, as well as a tendency toward extravagant spending on unnecessary luxury items. Social behavior and esthetic preferences are unlikely to exhibit the native's best tastes. Consequently, the native should delay or postpone to some future time the participation in important social activities. In some cases, this transit may cause the native to adopt a hypocritical stance toward those in close personal relationship, believing that by disguising his or her true feelings, any social unpleasantness can be avoided.

Transit Moon Square Mars

This is a rather disagreeable transit, disposing the native to exhibit severe symptoms of emotional hypersensitivity, irritability and, thus, a volatile instability. Consequent upsets will often convey to those about the native the impression of one who has a "chip on his shoulder"; for one so inclined, family squabbles, emotional confrontations, impatience, carelessness, digestive disorders and related gastric pains are often the end result. Only through the exercise of patience and self-restraint is it possible to avoid much of the difficulty engendered by this transit. Important business or romantic dealings with women, as well as the handling of joint finances and matters of insurance, taxes, inheritance and alimony, should be deferred to a more favorable time to receive proper attention. Likewise, care should also be exercised to avoid danger in the home caused by the native's ignorance of or failure to observe appropriate safety precautions.

Transit Moon Square Jupiter

This transit often fosters a period of foolish overoptimism in the native's attitudes toward matters affecting the home and domestic environment. This can manifest as a deep-rooted sentimentality, interfering with sound practical judgment, or as simple laziness. In either event, it would be in the native's best interests to defer to some later time any shopping trips for household goods, commodities, groceries or other related items, or real estate matters that require the rational application of one's faculties to arrive at an appropriate decision. There is poor judgment in the selection of proper goods and materials. A tendency to overeat and an inclination toward extravagance in financial expenditures is associated with this transit; caution is advisable. This transit often subjects the native to the particular prejudices and biases of his or her religious, cultural, family and national upbringing. Much sentiment in this vein is likely to be expressed at this time, but little practical action can be expected to back it up.

Transit Moon Square Saturn

Effects of this transit upon the native are generally of strong but negative import, giving rise to feelings of melancholia and periods of emotional depression. The native feels rejected by others and so is apt to withdraw from outside contact or to act in a cold and unresponsive fashion to external stimuli. Painful memories of negative past experiences, latent in the subconscious, could be temporarily reactivated and surface to plague the native adversely, influencing the home environment and daily activities. Family, professional and financial responsibilities, should they arise at this time, are likely to be a serious, although temporary, source of worry. Sluggish digestion is common for those experiencing this transit. Difficult though it may be, the native should try to cultivate a positive, optimistic outlook during this period. Business affairs or dealings with women should be postponed until a more propitious period is in evidence, and heavy foods should be avoided.

Transit Moon Square Uranus

During this transit the native is likely to experience sudden and unpredictable emotional changes, often leading to eccentric behavior in an attempt to surprise, shock or otherwise evoke some emotional reaction from others. Likewise, the native may be subjected to a similar display by members of his or her household, often in an abrupt and rather rude manner. Friends of the native may drop in at inopportune moments, annoying family members, or conversely, friends of family members may make a nuisance of themselves or become a source of anxiety to the native. Important group or organizational activities, especially those conducted in the home, should be postponed to some future date, and the native should curb any impulsiveness or extravagant tendencies in spending. Caution should also be exercised when using appliances or working with electricity in the home.

Transit Moon Square Neptune

This transit disposes the native toward daydreaming. Subconscious memories during this period are apt to evoke emotional responses inappropriate to present circumstances, so the native tends to lack a sense of practicality in handling everyday responsibilities and family, business and financial affairs. For this reason the native is apt to appear withdrawn into a private dream world. Even if the native does not exhibit these tendencies, it is possible that he or she will have to deal with others who do. In any event, this transit does not favor the native's participation in psychic practices, for it is a deceptive one. Difficulties will arise in the attempt to distinguish between subconscious wishes and bona fide intuitive guidance, and, should the native choose to engage in such activities he or she will run the additional risk of exposure to the perils of undesirable astral influences that are often damaging to the psyche.

Transit Moon Square Pluto

This transit possesses the potential of arousing strong and, in extreme cases, violent emotional reactions. Thus, during this period, the native should seek to maintain an attitude of equanimity, avoiding any tendencies to emotionally dominate or reshape others. The native's unnecessary subjection to similar treatment or the harboring of any kind of emotional resentment should be avoided. This transit often gives rise to family disagreements over inheritance, joint finances, insurance, taxes and alimony, and may cause conflict over the handling of corporate business affairs and in dealings with women on important matters. Caution should be exercised in all financial dealings and wherever there may be participation in psychic practices. This transit is often associated with a period favorable to social and romantic activity. At this time the native is most apt to experience improvement in physical vitality and an enhancement of his or her sense of self-confidence and emotional self-assurance that will inspire confidence in others. Thus, dealings with the opposite sex, business affairs, matters of reasonable speculation, the devotion of attention to children, culinary efforts and the native's participation in family games and social activities can be successfully entertained and are likely to yield highly favorable results.

Transit Moon Trines

Transit Moon Trine Sun

This transit often indicates a period favorable to social and romantic activity. The native is most apt to experience improvement in physical vitality and an enhancement of his or her sense of self-confidence and emotional self-assurance that will inspire confidence in others. Thus, dealings with the opposite sex, business affairs, matters of reasonable speculation, the devotion of attention to children, culinary efforts and the native's participation in family games and social activities can be successfully entertained and are likely to yield highly favorable results.

Transit Moon Trine Moon

This transit notes a period generally favorable to family, domestic and everyday business affairs. The native will exhibit stable emotional equilibrium. Thus, matters of cooking, housework, family relationships and shopping for the home can be properly and expediently handled and, should the native be searching for an apartment or involved in real estate maneuvers or transactions, these will also show the positive effects of this transit.

Transit Moon Trine Mercury

This transit confers the native with a rational view and approach to practical problems affecting work, health, home and family and the ability to arrive at intelligent solutions. Manifestations of this are apt to include stimulation of the native's interest in improving family diet, hygiene and household cleanliness, order and neatness. Study, intellectual activities and writing and correspondence can be successfully carried out at this time. There is apt to be considerable telephone conversation between the native, friends and family members. Advertising, shopping trips, short journeys and household affairs are favored by this transit.

Transit Moon Trine Venus

This transit denotes a time of increased social involvement and pursuit of pleasurable activities. The native will manifest a happier and more outgoing disposition, showing kindness, consideration and emotional sensitivity and sympathy to others. It will thus be easier to attract money, romantic partners and social benefits and to deal with or seek favors from women during this transit. Business affairs in the artistic, musical and entertainment fields as well as those dealing with food and home and domestic products and services will benefit by this transit. This is a favorable time for social events and family gatherings.

Transit Moon Trine Mars

This transit produces a period of increased energy and initiative directed toward the furtherance of domestic and business objectives. Programs for personal self-improvement through exercise, sports or other physical exertion as well as house cleaning and do-it-yourself projects and all types of strenuous physical activity can be auspiciously inaugurated at this time. Often the movement of the native's residence or rearrangement of the home is related to this transit. A great deal of energy will be injected by the native into professional money-making activities, and this transit could even trigger a concerted drive for professional prominence and honor. However, the more important of the above changes must be reinforced by other similar influences. For those who are timid or shy, this transit will help encourage more open, honest and straightforward communication in the expression of personal feelings and viewpoints.

Transit Moon Trine Jupiter

This transit will dispose the native toward a more positive and optimistic outlook on life. Constructive religious, cultural and educational values instilled during one's upbringing will be stimulated and brought to the fore at this time, leading to the expression of greater kindness and sympathy toward others, especially those less fortunate. This transit marks an excellent, although short, period for family participation in religious and cultural activities as well as family outings and journeys. The educational needs of children can be properly handled at this time, and favors or cooperation can be more easily sought of women. Business affairs dealing with real estate, food and home and domestic products and services as well as fund-raising activities for charitable or religious institutions will receive positive assistance from this transit.

Transit Moon Trine Saturn

This transit inclines the native to adopt a more cautious and conservative approach to the handling of practical everyday affairs. Greater reserve is also apt to be displayed in reaction to and behavior toward those in close personal relationships. Approaches to and discussions with older individuals, parents and those in positions of power and authority will often be profitable and, adeptly handled, the native is likely to take special pains to organize financial affairs and to set his or her house in order. This transit also denotes an excellent period in which to tackle problems that require emotional control and sobriety, and also for the conservative management of business dealings, real estate and home and domestic products and services.

Transit Moon Trine Uranus

This transit provides a period of exciting and constructive change to break the daily routine. Group meetings or activities are likely to be conducted in the home. Family members or group associates are apt to drop in unexpectedly. Relationships with women are invigorated by an exciting and unusual flair. Public relations activities launched at this time are certain to possess some form of unique appeal. The native could receive unexpected intuitive guidance that will direct improvement of home, family and domestic affairs or matters related to friends and group activities. A flash of inspiration could awaken the native to new and unusual ways to make money that could lead to new financial and business matters.

Transit Moon Trine Neptune

This transit indicates an introspective period in the native's daily life. Whatever psychic abilities the native may possess are stimulated at this time. Psychological difficulties and unconscious motivations based upon past conditioning can be more easily understood and handled. Thus, this transit marks an excellent period for personal meditation and the pursuit of inner spiritual growth. Intuition, empathy, sympathy and understanding of others is enhanced by this transit, and the native may find it easier to relate to women about sensitive emotional issues. The creative imagination is inspired by this transit, favoring artists, entertainers and musicians.

Transit Moon Trine Pluto

This transit denotes a period that is excellent for the elimination of unnecessary and superfluous matters from the native's emotional, family, domestic and business affairs. An increased willingness to confront emotional problems and subconscious conditioning will spark the necessary courage and willpower to drop destructive habits and negative automatic daily routines. Latent psychic abilities often come to the fore under this transit. Thus, the native is apt to gain intuitive insight into both female and mass psychological orientation that will enable him or her to transform and improve environmental conditions. There will be greater resourcefulness in the accumulation and expenditure of financial assets. The native will discover new uses for old and discarded items, old furnishings or household items that can either be repaired or refurbished. The initiation of a fast or purgative dietary regime can be successfully undertaken at this time. Family situations are apt to exhibit the benefits of this transit through improvement of relationships.

Transit Moon Oppositions

Transit Moon Opposition Sun

This transit gives rise to emotional conflicts and disturbances involving authority or ego-oriented issues, often leading to relationship difficulties between the native and those of the opposite sex as well as those in powerful or authoritative positions. Such outbursts may even pose a threat to or interfere with the native's vitality and health. Family members, especially children, are likely to annoy or fail to cooperate with the native. Likewise, the native may also confuse or confound others, creating an atmosphere of distrust. Entertaining or planning social gatherings should be postponed until a more propitious time. Business or speculative financial investments should be avoided during this transit, and the native should guard against undue extravagance.

Transit Moon Opposition Moon

This transit tends to produce emotional confrontations over issues related to financial partnerships, personal money and possessions and may often lead to conflict over family and domestic matters. Women or mother figures are apt to become a constant source of annoyance or disturbance to the native. Should the native overeat to escape problems, indigestion is likely to be the result. This transit requires the native to practice diplomacy in family relationships. Emotional conflicts arising out of relationship problems involving women or family members could make the native moody and ill at ease and perhaps interfere with health. Care should also be exercised in handling family finances.

Transit Moon Opposition Mercury

This transit usually produces confusion in the native's handling of practical everyday matters. Written and telephone communication are apt to be garbled, misunderstood, misinterpreted or overlooked, resulting in annoyances, confusion and inefficiency. Tendencies of the native or others to gossip incessantly about inconsequential or trivial matters are likely to arouse personal antagonism. Thus, the native should avoid unnecessary idle conversation, especially while on the job. Improper dietary habits will often give rise to digestive difficulties and intestinal upsets. The native should avoid unnecessary exposure to germs, infections and unsanitary conditions. Sloppiness in household organization, personal hygiene and appearance will, likewise, adversely affect relationships with others. At this time the native should take special pains to exercise diplomacy and consideration in dealings with brothers, sisters, neighbors and coworkers.

Transit Moon Opposition Venus

The native or those with whom the native has a close personal relationship are apt to be emotionally hypersensitive and easily hurt during this transit. Difficulties in romantic and marital relationships are likely to be experienced and those with women and family members in particular are especially delicate at this time. Consequently, kindness and gentleness should be shown in dealing with those individuals where emotional considerations are important. Others could entice the native to be excessively self-indulgent in food, alcohol and social and sexual activities. Likewise, the native may be guilty of similarly influencing others. Extravagance on luxury items, entertainment and other pleasure-oriented pursuits should be kept within reasonable bounds. Expenditures on artistic and other items for home decoration in particular should be carefully reviewed before purchase during this transit.

Transit Moon Opposition Mars

This transit is apt to coincide with emotional confrontations between the native and family members or others living under the same roof. Emotional impatience will induce a tendency in the native to be irritable and easily upset, particularly if natal Mars is afflicted. Thus, restraint should be exercised to curb emotional desires and habits that could arouse such conflict. Social situations conducive to such irritation or annoyance, whether the native's own or on the part of others, should be avoided. Relations with women should be most delicately handled to avoid any roughness, impulsiveness or inconsideration. Care should be taken to avoid the potential danger of fire, injury or accident in the home at this time. Likewise, the ingestion of hot, spicy foods may give rise to indigestion, gastric pains and related distress during this transit. Impulsiveness in business dealings and financial expenditures should be checked or kept within reasonable bounds during this period.

Transit Moon Opposition Jupiter

This transit could bring a period of excessive sentimentality and misdirected sympathy in the native's handling of day-to-day affairs. Emotional prejudice about religious, ethnic, cultural or political views instilled by family upbringing are apt to surface at this time, giving rise to the native's adoption of extremes of attitude in regard to such matters. The native is also prone to be misguided during this transit, so participation in any religious, cultural or educational groups and organizations, though their intentions may be good, should be carefully scrutinized. Long-distance travel, journeys and extravagance in financial expenditures should be cautiously avoided during this period. This transit may also incline the native to overeat or indulge in rich foods that are not only fattening, but adversely affect the liver.

Transit Moon Opposition Saturn

Periods of loneliness or emotional depression are often related to this transit. This is frequently the result of oppressive family burdens or responsibilities that the native is forced to shoulder. Professional, domestic and financial problems often add to such difficulties. Painful subconscious memories are likely to be aroused, causing the native to adopt a negative and limited emotional outlook on life. This period is thus not conducive to relations or communication with older individuals, those in established positions of authority, parents or women, particularly elderly women. During this transit it is best to involve oneself in matters that will uplift the spirit. Cooperation is the key word here; through effort and the adoption of a positive emotional attitude the native can accomplish a great deal.

Transit Moon Opposition Uranus

This transit often produces instability and sudden disruptive developments in the native's domestic affairs and family relationships, frequently as a result of the actions or activities of friends and group associates. The native or those with whom he or she has everyday contact are prone to behave in an unusual and provocative manner, thereby upsetting the home environment. Women, especially, with whom the native must deal could conduct themselves in an unpredictable and uncooperative way. Unexpected factors are likely to upset or overturn any previously laid plans and expectations. Thus, new business ventures and dealings in matters of joint finance, taxes, inheritance, insurance and alimony should be postponed to a more favorable time. Dealings with eccentric friends and organizations should, likewise, be delayed, especially if such matters involve the use of the native's home or money.

Transit Moon Opposition Neptune

Relationship difficulties experienced under this transit are usually caused by vagueness, confusion, indecisiveness and distortions of the subconscious mind. The native is prone to being absorbed in a private dream world, creating a gap or barrier between self and others, often rendering the native oblivious to proper handling of practical everyday affairs. The pursuit of psychic practices or the entertainment of impractical emotionally-oriented religious notions should be avoided. This transit requires the exercise of a realistic outlook and practicality in relationships, especially those with women, to realize its potential. Alcohol, drugs and non-nutritive foods should be avoided during this transit, for they are apt to cause digestive discomforts.

Transit Moon Opposition Pluto

This transit often produces a period of emotional confrontation between the native and family members, women and others with whom he or she has everyday contact. This is often the result of attempts to remake the emotional attitudes of others. Such ego conflicts can be caused by the native's efforts to force his or her will upon others, or vice versa. Problems and emotional issues may also arise over joint finances, insurance, taxes, inheritance, alimony or corporate money, and financial difficulties consequent to these matters are likely to have an adverse effect upon the family and domestic environment. A desire on the part of the native to start anew or eliminate old negative conditions could, under this transit, be carried to extremes without really resolving the basic issues or causes of such circumstances or solving the root problems. Temporary estrangement from family members could result from these attitudes. Psychic and occult practices should be avoided during this period, lest the native run the risk of falling victim to negative astral influences.

III

Transits of Mercury

Transits of Mercury are usually of short duration because, relative to any transiting body except the Moon, Mercury is the most rapid in its orbital progress. Such transits are usually effective for one or two days unless Mercury is retrograde or stationary in its zodiacal motion.

Regardless of their brevity, however, the influence of these transits is of great importance in astrological charting and prediction. The passage of transiting Mercury through the houses of an individual's horoscope and consequent aspects to the natal planets will determine the nature and orientation of important communication both sent and received. This transit often times the advent of important decisions and the birth of ideas critical to the future destiny of the native in question. Thus, Mercury's transits can provide important clues to the day-to-day development of the native's thinking processes. When we realize that no important action can be taken without prior thought, the importance of Mercury's transits can thus be comprehended, for they explain a great deal of the comings and goings of the native and the reasons for this activity.

Such transits are vital to students, writers, lecturers and those who work in or with communication media of any form, and they are important to any native's work, job relationships and health. Variations in the native's involvement and functional diversity in friendships, groups and organizational activities can be observed through close scrutiny of Mercury's transits, its passage through the houses and aspects made to natal planets. Such house transits are indicative of changes and developments in this sphere of activity. This is due to Mercury's exaltation in Aquarius, the sign dealing with such affairs.

Also influenced by this sign of Mercury's exaltation will be the native's realization of goals and objectives (an eleventh house function) for all desired ends and the means by which they are effected originate in thought, with which Mercury directly deals. Thus, if thoughts or ideas are acted upon, there can be the realization of goals. Mercury's nature as a neutral planet, however, will cause any thoughts to be colored by the strongest aspect made to or by Mercury in the natal chart and the nature of the planet receiving aspect from its transit.

Retrograde, Stationary and Direct Periods of Mercury

On an average of three times yearly, Mercury, as seen from Earth, turns retrograde, passes through a stationary period, then returns to direct motion. These particular motions of Mercury have profound significance upon mankind in terms of the flow of communication and the unfoldment of plans and ideas. When Mercury turns to retrograde motion, there is a slowing of communication which is often accompanied by confusion, changing plans, indecisiveness and unexpected factors that make work and communication difficult to handle. This tendency often becomes manifest in situations of mail slowdowns and telephone breakdowns, transportation problems, misprints and late shipments in industry that frequently result in production delays and the like. This is especially true of the electronics industry, where the lack of small parts can hold up a whole production line. Uranus' rulership of electronics and the sign Aquarius, in which Mercury is exalted, is often the reason for such hindrances.

Illness, labor strikes, equipment breakdowns and failures in negotiations can hold up progress during a retrograde period of Mercury. Thus, this is a poor period in which to sign contracts or launch new projects. The native should wait until Mercury is once again direct in motion and has passed the degree at which it first went retrograde before making any important decisions, signing contracts or handling important negotiations.

Retrograde Mercury will have a greater impact upon natives ruled by it or those engaged in Mercurial professions such as teaching, writing, lecturing, negotiating, communication media, medicine or travel.

Mercury's stationary period is usually one of reconsideration in the native's views on important decisions and a time for the gestation of new plans and ideas. The results of this, however, are not immediately apparent and may not become so until Mercury has passed that position in the zodiac in its forward motion where it previously turned retrograde. Should Mercury make an important aspect to a natal placement during its stationary period, effects associated with this particular body will have a profound influence upon the future development of the native's plans. Again, this may not be apparent until Mercury, again in direct motion, reaches the same position it held before turning retrograde. Transits made by Mercury during this retrograde period often necessitate the reorganization or modification of plans and procedures.

Until Mercury has reached the position of first retrograde motion, the effects of its retrograde and stationary periods have not been fully felt, for these periods of Mercury make it possible to carefully consider, at leisure, all of the possible ramifications of actions and decisions.

Through this, many factors can come to light which enable the native to make choices or decisions that are wiser or safer in the long run. For this reason, the seemingly frustrating experience of such retrograde and stationary periods can be a blessing in disguise.

Retrograde periods of Mercury can be utilized to dispose of unfinished tasks and business affairs that were started during a direct period. During the retrograde or stationary period, the native can consciously direct effort toward introspection and thus draw knowledge and guidance from deeper levels of consciousness.

When Mercury is direct in motion, communication, travel, decisions and business affairs can proceed rapidly. Thus, the native can progress with confidence in planning new activities and endeavors.

Transit Mercury in the Houses

Transits of Mercury through the houses indicate which practical aspects of the native's life will appeal to his or her mental attention at a particular time. Thus, affairs ruled by the house through which Mercury is transiting are be the subject of much thought, communication and traveling about. Brothers and sisters, neighbors, coworkers and others associated with the native's work, correspondence and general communication are apt to play an important part in these matters.

The native will make plans and decisions about the affairs ruled by the house transited, and these concerns will be connected in some manner with the house ruled by Mercury in the natal horoscope and the house and sign occupied by natal Mercury. This will include all of the planets strongly aspected by Mercury in the natal horoscope, the natal house in which Aquarius is found and the natal planets found in Gemini, Virgo and Aquarius.

Should Mercury be in retrograde motion or stationary while in a particular house, the affairs of that house could become subject to confusion, delay or changes.

Should Mercury make adverse transits to natal placements while passing through a house or be heavily afflicted in the natal horoscope, the affairs ruled by the particular house may exert an unfavorable effect upon the native's health or capacity for work. Often, interference with the efficiency of the native's work will be caused by mental distractions or the needless waste of time in useless talk or non productive activities. Much depends of course upon the aspects made to Mercury while transiting a specific house as to the nature of its effects upon the affairs ruled by that house, whether it be good or bad news, a wise or poor decision.

As transiting Mercury passes through each house, its nature as a neutral planet will cause the thought processes of the native to assume the coloring of each as indicated in the natal horoscope.

Transit Mercury Through the First House

Mercury's transit through the first house produces a period in which the native devotes more thought to personal self-projection and related goals. The native will become more talkative and expressive than usual and show greater interest in communication and intellectual forms of self-expression.

The Aries connotation of the first house may incline the native to be mentally competitive during this transit; under adverse transits to natal planets during this passage this behavior could result in an argumentative tendency, especially when natal afflictions are reinforced by such transits.

Writers, lecturers, teachers and those whose occupations require dynamic, intellectual personal expression will particularly appreciate this transit of Mercury because it will motivate them to be outspoken in their consideration of matters related to their work. During this transit the native will become sharply conscious of matters related to dress, health, diet and personal hygiene, coupled with an interest in improving conditions of the working environment. Greater activity and communication among friends and group associations can be initiated by the native.

Transit Mercury Through the Second House

Mercury's transit through the second house points the native's intellectual focus toward concerns of a financial nature and those dealing with the acquisition of personal possessions. Often the native will become highly motivated to seek more lucrative employment during this transit. This could involve the native in occupations related to the fields of writing, publishing, news media, advertising, clothing, food, medicine and health aids. Frequently, the financial affairs of friends, groups and organizations will exert increased influence upon the native's dealings during this transit. Interest and consequent participation in vocational training or education may help to boost the native's earning ability. This transit, in general, will produce a period of much communication about personal material values, business matters and financial affairs.

Favorable transits of Mercury in its passage through this house are favorable for financial planning and business strategy. Afflictions to natal Mercury and adverse transits, on the other hand, could cause undue worry about financial affairs or serious problems in business. Such difficulties could arise because of ill health, unemployment or problems in business communication or bookkeeping. Unnecessary travel and telephone usage could cause a temporary depletion of funds. The native should seek to eliminate the sources of confusion and inefficiency and thus dispose of these problems.

Transit Mercury Through the Third House

Mercury's transit through the third house of the natal horoscope produces a period of increased intellectual activity. This is because Mercury is the natural ruler of the third house, corresponding to Gemini in the natural zodiac. Writers, teachers, lecturers and those who work in communication will find this an especially favorable transit, as will those with occupations requiring considerable travel or correspondence. Communication will flow easily and rapidly, and the native will actively express new and original ideas.

Should Mercury be afflicted either in the natal chart or in its transit through this house, the native is apt to indulge in unnecessary chatter. Gossip or difficulties in communication with friends, neighbors, brothers, sisters and coworkers could cause serious problems. Transportation difficulties and confused directions often result in delays and misunderstandings or hindrances to communication, particularly email and telephone calls, can directly affect the native's business or group activities, health or well-being. Care should be exercised under such circumstances in the signing of contracts or the formalization of agreements or promises.

This transit of Mercury will in general incline the native toward the acquisition of knowledge and other practical affairs, whether it be through reading or attending courses of an academic nature. There will also be more than the usual degree of communication about and among friends, neighbors, brothers, sisters and coworkers.

Transit Mercury Through the Fourth House

This transit of Mercury is indicative of a period in which the native is more inclined to communicate with family members and show concern for their diet, health and personal hygiene. Family necessities may even motivate the native to seek more lucrative employment and thereby alleviate such anxiety.

Interest is apt to arise in the intellectual solution of everyday, practical household problems, often leading the native to introduce educational and intellectual activities into home and family affairs. The family library could be expanded at this point, and there is apt to be some form of family participation in literary activities or cultural organizations. Home improvement projects may flourish, particularly where these relate to the native's health, diet, personal hygiene, sanitation, crafts, improved food production methods or other practical ventures.

Transits of Mercury through the fourth house will often bring news, mail, visits, telephone calls or packages from family members in other localities. Changes in employment during this transit could necessitate relocation of the native's household.

Should Mercury make adverse transits to natal placements while transiting the fourth house or be heavily afflicted in the natal horoscope, the native may fall victim to illnesses contracted from family members or be forced to assume direct responsibility for the care of an ill family member. Such afflictions are also apt to create confusion and misunderstanding between the native and those in the immediate domestic environment.

Real estate contracts should not be negotiated or concluded under adverse transits of Mercury in the fourth house, nor should home improvement projects of any kind be initiated or undertaken. All appropriate rules of household sanitation should also be carefully observed at this time.

Transit Mercury Through the Fifth House

Mercury's transit through this house inclines the native to express greater interest in children and their education and to appreciate and experience pleasure in the pursuit of intellectual studies, travel, lectures, reading materials and games of skill. Occupational endeavors and study and attention to diet and health will also be valued by the native at this time. Attraction to intellectual types of individuals is likely, and the native may even meet a romantic partner while traveling, attending school or engaging in studies or projects. In any event, the receipt of mail, telephone calls or news from children or romantic partners will show a marked increase during, and may even highlight, this transit. Those involved in creative fields, hobbies or other pursuits will find this to be a particularly favorable transit because it will inspire them with original ideas.

Should Mercury favorably transit any natal placements while passing through this house and be favorably aspected in the natal horoscope, there arises the good probability of financial gain through some carefully planned and executed speculative venture. In the opposite extreme, though, should Mercury be afflicted, utmost caution should be exercised in this regard.

Adverse transits of Mercury in its passage through the fifth house can give rise to misunderstandings in romantic relationships and financial losses through unwise speculation. Such afflictions could also cause the native, through the pursuit of excessive or unwise pleasurable activities, to neglect work and health and thus suffer the consequence of such neglect.

Transit Mercury Through the Sixth House

The period of Mercury's transit will demonstrate the native's application of intelligence toward improving work and health and conditions contributing to these. The native will become markedly conscious of the need for efficiency in work performance and thus will be apt to advance and develop original ideas for increasing proficiency and productivity. Educational and training programs for career advancement, as well as those for studying diet, health, medicine and hygiene, are likely to appeal to the native during this transit. In any event, the native will exhibit a particular and cautious nature where these matters are concerned. During this period, communication will be devoted primarily to matters of work and health, attitudes which will be displayed in his or her concern about order, neatness, dress and personal appearance.

Adverse transiting aspects of Mercury while in this house could cause the native to experience problems in areas of health, diet and work. Communication difficulties could arise with employers or coworkers. Late shipments of parts, flaws in the production process or excessive chattering while on the job could interfere with efficient productivity. Work-related situations and their inherent problems could become complicated or difficult to understand. Overwork or occupational hazards may threaten the native's health, which should be guarded when under such affliction.

Transit Mercury Through the Seventh House

This transit of Mercury is indicative of a period in which the native will demonstrate an increased curiosity about psychology, human relationships and the mental processes of partners and close personal friends, and there is apt to be much communication with the public, friends and partners in this regard. The native is apt to be attracted to intellectual or scholarly individuals during this transit. Thus, marital attachments contracted at this time are likely to be of an intellectual nature.

Favorable transits of Mercury while in this house make this an opportune period for the pursuit of public relations work, advertising and the negotiation of contractual agreements, as well as for the resolution of problems in work or business affairs and the handling of legal matters.

Afflictions of Mercury during its seventh house transit can cause misunderstandings and disagreements in partnerships, often manifest in legal difficulties or problems associated with business and occupation. The native could become involved in arguments, disputes, debates or lawsuits with open enemies.

Transit Mercury Through the Eighth House

The period of this transit is apt to be one when important communication is received about matters of finance, wills, inheritance, alimony, death, taxes or joint finances. Important pieces of information, significant concepts regarding occult matters or intuitive revelations of scientific import may become available to the native at this time. Unsolved mysteries, police probes and other secret investigations will be of strong appeal, especially if these concern life-and-death matters or sexual intrigues. Sex and its psychological, sociological, medical and spiritual implications is likely to be a topic of major interest at this time. This transit in general is a period in which the native should examine his or her motives in the handling of eighth house affairs and try to understand the spiritual significance inherent to these matters.

Favorable transiting aspects of Mercury during its passage through this house are conducive to the study or investigation of occult subjects and the planning of future business strategy. Aspects of this type to the outer planets of Pluto, Neptune and Uranus could indicate communication with deceased relatives and friends or discarnate beings.

Should Mercury make adverse transits in its passage through the eighth house, the native may manifest interest in death, sex and business and political intrigues. Confusion, conflicts or disagreements could also arise over joint finances, corporate business affairs, inheritance, taxes or insurance, or there could be delays in business and financial communication or contracts.

Transit Mercury Through the Ninth House

This transit of Mercury marks a time in which the native's interest in religion, philosophy, higher education and travel will be reawakened and encouraged to develop. The native may desire to investigate broader aspects of the prevailing social order, which may give rise to an interest in foreign countries, their histories and cultural patterns. The native may even receive news from relatives or friends in faraway places or distant countries encouraging travel to see these exotic places. In general, this is a good period for serious contemplation, writing and engagement in other scholarly pursuits. Generally during the period of this transit, the native should seek to maintain a calm, practical attitude while pursuing higher intellectual and spiritual goals.

Under favorable transits while passing through this house, Mercury's influence may induce the native to seek admission to universities or institutions of higher education or to embark upon long journeys to distant regions. Such propitious transits will particularly favor writers wishing to approach publishers so that their work may obtain a wider distribution.

Should Mercury form transiting afflictions while in the ninth house, difficulties could arise around the native's studies at a university or delays and problems could be experienced in travel or communication with or from distant places. Unexpected hindrances or disappointments may prevent the native from seeking or gaining admission to colleges or universities, or there could be a tendency to pursue foolish religious or educational ambitions. Hypocrisy in the handling of these matters may even become evident.

Transit Mercury Through the Tenth House

This transit of Mercury will incline the native to seek knowledge or education for the advancement or furtherance of career status or position. The native will be more disposed to evaluate ideas on the basis of their practical value in relation to career ambitions and desires. Friends or group and organizational associations of the native may play an important role in professional activities. An intellectual interest in politics and political figures could develop and may lead the native to become involved in political organizations dealing with these matters. Communication with government agencies, officials or individuals of position and status is likely at this time. The native's occupational endeavors will become subject to the close scrutiny of his or her employer during this transit. It would thus be to the native's benefit to exercise extra care and caution while maintaining a high level of efficiency in the handling of job responsibilities.

Favorable aspects of Mercury while transiting the tenth house will further the native's efforts toward seeking employment or favors from those in positions of power and authority. If the native is ensconced in such a position of responsibility, he or she may be required to resolve important issues concerning subordinates.

Transiting afflictions of Mercury in the tenth house can create difficulties in communication with the native's employer or others in capable or official positions. Poor choices and decisions are also apt to be rendered where profession or career is concerned.

Transit Mercury Through the Eleventh House

During the period of this transit the native is apt to experience frequent communication with friends and organizational associates, often in reference to new ideas, philosophies and humanitarian projects. Original, intuitive thinking stimulated by this transit may spur the native's interest in studies of a humanitarian, occult or scientific nature. Greater interest in human understanding coupled with a willingness to communicate with individuals from all walks of life will often result in new friendships and group associations. Close personal fellowships may be established with coworkers or those the native meets through the occupation. In some cases there can be an active involvement with labor unions during this period.

Should Mercury make adverse transits while passing through this house, there are apt to be misunderstandings or communication breakdowns with friends. Thus the native may become subject to unwise advice in dealings with these people, and may also be inclined under such affliction to expound upon impractical, Utopian ideals.

Transit Mercury Through the Twelfth House

This transit of Mercury denotes a period in which the native is apt to reflect upon and act in a more secretive manner about personal thoughts and feelings. This can result in an increased interest in meditative disciplines and may even lead to an inner spiritual quest. The native may become the secret confidante of friends, coworkers, brothers, sisters or neighbors, and because of this may be drawn into secret schemes and plots of various sorts. Writers and artists will benefit from the imaginative stimulus conferred by this transit, and they and others are apt to express greater interest in mystical and occult studies and manifestations of the same.

Favorable transits of Mercury during its passage through the twelfth house could lead the native to acquire valuable insights and guidance through intuitive faculties.

Should Mercury make adverse transits while passing through this house, the native may fall victim to mental depression or psychological aberrations arising from the subconscious mind. The desire to escape practical responsibilities, manifest in tendencies to dwell upon past events, could interfere with health and occupational duties. Secret enemies could delay information or messages or deliberately misinform the native.

Transit Mercury Conjunctions

Transit Mercury Conjunction Sun

This transit of Mercury denotes a period in which the native can develop a great degree of mental creativity in ideas about art, entertainment, writing, financial speculation, children and their education, as well as social and romantic affairs. It is a time of increased self-confidence in verbal and mental expression and for the development of individual ideas and points of view. A spirit of intellectual competitiveness endowed by this transit can lead to the native's interest in games of mental skill such as chess. This transit brings an increased desire to perform constructive work and to care for personal health and hygiene. This conjunction in general will incline the native toward intellectual energy and creativity, thus rendering it a propitious transit for teachers, writers, students and others whose professions require intellectual achievement and communication.

Afflictions to this conjunction by either natal or other transiting planets can cause the native to adopt a selfish attitude. The outcome of this is often mental bias favoring the native's point of view without any degree of necessary personal objectivity.

Transit Mercury Conjunction Moon

This transit of Mercury often brings mail, telephone calls or communication of some sort from other family members, and may even require the native to render important decisions on matters affecting the home or family affairs. A critical review of dietary habits, particularly from the point of proper health and hygiene, can be advisably undertaken at this time; necessary improvements and reforms in eating habits and personal hygiene will reflect in the native's better health, vigor and stamina. The status of sanitary conditions in the home may come up for review, resulting in propitious home improvements or a thorough house cleaning. Financial and business affairs of the native that are emphasized at this time will usually relate to food products or domestic services, often involving business correspondence, communication, inventory and accounting procedures in these areas. Employers undergoing this transit will take pains to review the performance of their employees, and will hire, fire and make necessary changes in accordance with their conclusions. Communication with women is apt to revolve about the native's possessions, business or family and domestic affairs.

If this conjunction is favorably aspected to the natal chart or by other transiting planets, events affecting the above areas will proceed smoothly, resulting in notable improvements.

Should this conjunction be afflicted, however, difficulties are apt to be experienced in these matters. There could be problems with health or digestion that tend to interfere with the native's work. Illness among employees could slacken business production. In any event, under such adverse transits the native should avoid making decisions based upon emotional considerations.

Transit Mercury Conjunction Mercury

This transit marks a period of intensified intellectual activity. Communication with brothers, sisters, neighbors, friends and business, professional and organizational associates at this time may force the native to render important decisions affecting relationships with these individuals, health and occupational endeavors. Enhanced intellectual originality and creativity, as conferred by this transit, will assist the native in this process by focusing attention upon life goals and objectives and revealing their means of accomplishment. The curiosity will be intensified, leading to the native's investigation of subjects of interest. The native is thus apt to correspond, formulate ideas, engage in studies and scientific inquiries and embark upon short trips.

Should this conjunction be afflicted by either natal or other transiting planets, indiscriminate speech, problems in communication, nervousness and ill health could delay or present obstacles to participation in such efforts. Difficulties are also apt to arise in relationships with siblings, neighbors, friends and occupational associates.

Transit Mercury Conjunction Venus

This transit of Mercury often brings increased participation in business and social communication and intellectual interest in and consequent discussion about art, music and matters of esthetic, cultural value. Thus, students and creative writers involved in these fields will derive great benefit from their efforts during this period. Serious communication or discussion with romantic or marital partners or with others in close personal relationships is likely at this time. Attendance to social affairs sponsored by friends, groups and organizations may require short-distance travel, but often provides! the native with business, romantic and artistic opportunities. Writers, entertainers and those engaged in advertising or public relations will find this a propitious period in which to further their career ambitions, as it will be for those seeking employment in fields dealing with art, music, entertainment and related business affairs. During this transit the native is apt to develop a curiosity about human psychology, social activity and the responses of others. On the positive side, this can lead to demonstrations of greater sympathy and understanding in communication with those needing emotional encouragement and support. Speech will be graced with a dynamic, kind and charming quality, aiding sociability and improving romantic opportunities. Jewelry, fine clothing, perfume and other personal adornments are of great appeal during this transit, and such items will make the native and his or her surroundings more attractive to self and others.

Should this conjunction be afflicted by natal or other transiting planets, gossip or idle chit-chat while on the job could interfere with the native's efficiency in occupational endeavors and give rise to difficulties. Extravagant expenditures or the tendency to make promises that cannot be fulfilled could also present a source of difficulty. Often, insincerity and hypocrisy can be used as a means to avoid unpleasantries when this conjunction is adversely aspected.

Transit Mercury Conjunction Mars

This transit of Mercury is indicative of a period of mental aggression and forceful communication on the part of the native. Accumulated mental irritations will be voiced in a forcible manner which, in extreme cases, could result in violent verbal clashes. Much communication and short-distance travel can be anticipated in regard to business affairs, particularly where these deal with matters of engineering, industrial production, insurance, taxes or large-scale corporate enterprises. However, during this period, the native should exercise caution when driving, especially if this conjunction is afflicted. Failure to do so in this latter instance can result in accidents endangering life and limb. Tendencies toward nervous impatience while on the job can also result in difficulty, accident or injury during this transit. The native must make conscious effort to exercise consideration and diplomacy in dealing with coworkers, employers and employees. Energetic progress, on the other hand, can be made through organization and enterprise during this period. Ambition and competition in work, business and intellectual activities can further the native's career and professional goals. Valuable insights may give rise to improved methods of initiating new enterprises, solving problems and increasing efficiency and productivity. This transit, on the whole, will help the native to overcome indifference and inertia in the performance of necessary tasks, obligations and responsibilities.

Should this conjunction be afflicted by natal or other transiting planets, the native will be inclined toward embroilment in intellectual battles and disputes, often leading to caustic or sharp words.

Transit Mercury Conjunction Jupiter

During the period of this transit, the native will be drawn to educational, philosophical and religious interests. This is thus an excellent transit under which to commence a program of higher education or to apply for admittance to or employment in universities or academic institutions. Religious or philosophical instruction may be gained from conversation, discussion or tutelage under the auspices of a minister, teacher or guru. Curiosity about foreign countries and their history, language, religion and culture may lead the native to communicate with those in distant places or to actually embark upon long journeys to study or experience the realities of these interests. Profound insights into the forces molding public opinion and influencing cultural developments within society may be perceived by the native during this transit. Thus, this is a propitious time for involvement in professions related to writing, teaching, editing, publishing, advertising, communication, media, travel, politics, law and public relations. Contract negotiations, promotional advertising and legal affairs can be auspiciously handled during this period. The native's optimistic air of confidence, as conferred by this transit, will inspire the confidence of others and help to mold and shape their attitudes in a positive direction.

Afflictions of this conjunction by either natal or other transiting planets could cause the native to become unduly overconfident or to take too much for granted, often resulting in serious disappointments or setbacks. There is also the danger of unrealistic thinking because of a lack of practical experience.

Transit Mercury Conjunction Saturn

This transit of Mercury bodes a time of serious decisions, often dealing with the native's professional affairs and public reputation. Practical assessments of work and responsibility will be forced by this transiting conjunction, particularly where these relate to the native's realization of his or her own ambitions. Decisions reached during this period will often involve the native's responsibilities to others; this is because of Saturn's exaltation in Libra and Mercury's rulership of communication. Thus, when others are involved, the native should openly and frankly offer to discuss the realities of the situation and through mutual agreement arrive at the best practical solution beneficial and fair to all concerned. The native will initiate contact with older, established friends during this period, and is likely to impart or receive serious counsel that will in some manner directly involve friends or group associates and professional affairs. A frequent consequence of this transit is criticism from professional associates or superiors. This can cause the native to adopt an unsympathetic or harsh attitude toward subordinates or employees. Overwork, in turn, can lead to ill health or mental exhaustion. Contracts and agreements concluded during this transit will be permanently binding. Thus, they should be appraised with caution and serious deliberation before settlement is reached. In this case, retrograde Mercury will cause delays and frustration in complying with the terms of the accord. Conservative dress and guarded speech in the native's disposition will be notable at this time. Sufficient rest, adequate diet and deep breathing are prerequisites for the maintenance of vitality during this transit.

Favorable aspects to this conjunction by either natal or other transiting planets constitute this period as a propitious time for deep thought and study, scientific investigation, mathematical endeavors and business and professional planning.

Afflictions, on the other hand, can cause the native to be beset by worries and may even lead to the adoption of a negative, pessimistic or extremely unsympathetic attitude. This will create difficulties in attempts to communicate with others, often resulting in loneliness and frustration.

Transit Mercury Conjunction Uranus

This transit of Mercury will confer the native with many intuitive and original ideas and with a greater curiosity about unusual, occult, scientific or sociological events. Stimulating new interests will often be aroused by friends and group associates. The native may be drawn toward unusual group activities or friendships. Unexpected and exciting communication, mail and telephone calls are apt to influence the native's life. Sudden and unexpected short trips or coming and goings can be expected during this transit. The native may in some manner abruptly change his or her occupation, dietary habits or manner of dress, and even the basic mental outlook.

Favorable aspects to this conjunction could lead to the effective implementation of new and innovative procedures in the native's work, dress, health, personal hygiene or communication.

Afflictions could incline the native to make snap judgments and decisions without due consideration of all the facts or possible consequences of such moves. Such aspects may even result in victimization by those advocating eccentric ideas and ill-considered schemes.

Transit Mercury Conjunction Neptune

This transit indicates a time when the native is disposed toward mental introspection. In general, the native will manifest a high degree of psychic attunement, although he or she could also be subject to the aberrations of the subconscious mind. Revelations may be realized through clair-voyant experiences or prophetic insights consequent to this transit. In some cases, the native will be able to sense the thoughts and feelings of others, either on a subconscious, subliminal level or through conscious mental telepathy. In any event, the native will experience a height-ened awareness of subtle, subliminal clues.

Should this conjunction be favorably aspected by natal or other transiting planets, the creative imagination will be enhanced, conferring the native with intuitive inspiration in artistic, musical and literary endeavors and in efforts to resolve problems related to work or health.

Afflictions will likewise evoke the negative aspects of the native's introspective nature, result-ing in absent-mindedness, indifference to work or dress or daydreaming. Also inherent to such adverse aspects is a tendency toward deception in communication and important relationships; should Neptune be further afflicted in the natal horoscope, neurotic or psychotic experiences are possible.

Transit Mercury Conjunction Pluto

This transit of Mercury is indicative of a period in which the native's thoughts are directed to-ward serious and profound issues, often relating to the inner, occult mysteries of life. Large-scale economic and corporate affairs or matters of life and death will draw his or her at-tention. A strong desire to solve mysteries, ferret out secrets and investigate the obscure and the unknown will manifest during this period. If the natal chart alludes to his capacity for such, this transit could endow the native with profound psychological, scientific or occult insights, often the result of intuitive, clairvoyant experiences. This can be a favorable transit under which to improve and regenerate work methods and habits and thinking and communication processes. Decisions and negotiations may be required to alleviate conditions affecting joint finances, in-heritance, taxes, insurance or corporate financial affairs.

Favorable aspects to this transiting conjunction by natal or other transiting planets can involve the native in some form of research or investigation, often requiring the utmost secrecy. The na-tive is apt to become privy to confidential information or communications at this time.

Afflictions to this conjunction, on the other hand, could dispose the native to mental domination or control of other individuals and the danger of fanatical adherence to dogma or beliefs.

Transit Mercury Sextiles

All sextiles are ascribed a Mercury connotation because of their intrinsic nature as third house (Gemini) or eleventh house (Aquarius) influences (respectively, the rulership and exaltation of Mercury). Therefore, transit sextiles of Mercury are indicative of opportunities for intellectual mental expression in the fields, areas or departments of life affected by the planet aspected.

Transit Mercury Sextile Sun

This transit of Mercury imparts an impetus toward creative self-expression in communication, whether it be in speech, writing, bodily expression or manifestations through artistic media.

Public speaking, literary pursuits and communication with important individuals are particularly favored at this time, and there is likely to be considerable travel in connection with social, romantic and educational activities. Games and pleasures requiring mental skill will be of great appeal. The Sun's exaltation in Aries will motivate the native to implement new ideas and procedures in work methodology, health regimen, diet and relationships with friends, brothers, sisters, neighbors, groups and organizations. This transit, in general, will result in the native's expression of greater confidence and surety in speech and articulation of thoughts and ideas.

Transit Mercury Sextile Moon

This transit denotes a period of increased mental expression by the native in his or her home. Intellectual endeavors, studies, literary readings and activities involving groups and friends directed toward intellectual enlightenment are likely to find concrete manifestation in the native's domestic environment. Occupational or business efforts are apt to be conducted in the home, even if this simply means bringing work home. Greater interest will arise in the maintenance of proper diet, personal hygiene, sanitary conditions and order in the native's home. Steps could be properly undertaken at this time to correct any deficiencies in these departments. Much visitors, mail and telephone calls can be expected during this period, and there will be a marked increase in the native's communication with his or her mother or women in general. Family members may become involved in a great deal of short-distance travel. In any event, the native can anticipate more than the usual comings and goings during this transit. Considerable business communication, particularly that involving buying and selling through the mail or Internet, can be handled at this time, and may lead the native to make a practical appraisal of the value of possessions or stock on hand. Valuable insights into his subconscious conditioning and the instinctual aspect of the native's nature, often consequent to this transit, can provide the native with a foundation or framework for future progress in these areas.

Transit Mercury Sextile Mercury

This transit of Mercury heralds a period of increased intellectual activity and communication. The native's intellectual curiosity and inclinations toward scientific inquiry will be highly stimulated by this transit. Increases in the rapidity of thinking processes and in the conception of original ideas engendered by this transit make this an excellent period for those engaged in writing, teaching, lecturing and work with the communications media. Valuable new ideas realized at this time can lead to improvements in the efficiency of the native's work, diet, health regimen and activities related to groups, organizations, transportation and communication. Considerable travel or communication with brothers, sisters, neighbors, friends and organizational associates can be expected during this transit. Improved communication abilities with coworkers, employers and employees can lend a degree of smoothness to occupational operations and can lead to advancements in scientific work, business, investigations and studies.

Transit Mercury Sextile Venus

This transit of Mercury is indicative of a time of increased communication and short trips in regard to social activities, friends, group associates and business partners. The native will also develop an intellectual curiosity about art, music and other aspects of cultural refinement. The native will exhibit greater consideration and diplomacy in speech and communication at this time, and is likely to converse and travel with romantic or marital partners or close friends. Venus' exaltation in Pisces will move the native to encourage others in a happier and more optimistic outlook upon life. Through the establishment of amicable lines of communication and relationships with coworkers, employers or employees, the native will discover difficulties in the working environment, take steps to improve these conditions and thus beautify the occupational setting and make the work situation more pleasant. Advertising and public relations endeavors will be favored during this period. In general, the native's health and disposition will show positive signs of improvement and harmony at this time, consequent to a confident, constructive mental outlook.

Transit Mercury Sextile Mars

This transit denotes a time of increased communication and travel related to engineering, corporate business and military affairs and to physical activities, sports and other forms of muscular exertion. Self-confidence in the expression of the native's ideas or personal beliefs can be expected, but this may lead to debates over politics or other controversial issues. Those whose jobs require physical and mental action to seek information will find this an exceptional transit for performance in occupational endeavors. The native will have original ideas that will improve the efficiency of professional work and actions, thus making this a propitious time to initiate new industrial or professional projects. Work involving friends and group associates can be effectively implemented during this period to bring about needed changes and constructive action. This transit will generally confer the native with greater initiative and enterprise in study, teaching, writing, engineering or any other occupation.

Transit Mercury Sextile Jupiter

This transit of Mercury heralds a period of mental optimism and expansiveness in the native's outlook. Writing, teaching, publishing and the handling of legal affairs are favored at this time, as are the signing of contracts and concluding of agreements; but the native should take pains to avoid foolish overoptimism in these latter affairs. This transit is also conducive to long journeys and the pursuit of education in institutions of higher learning. However, due to the short duration of Mercury transits, this period could be most advantageously used to apply for admittance to a university or to submit a manuscript to a publisher. Messages and communication from others in faraway places can be expected at this time, often giving rise to the native's curiosity about foreign countries, cultures, histories and religions. Philosophies, too, might have appeal for the native during this period. Valuable insights are often realized that provide the native with a more practical view of the prevailing social order and its institutions.

Transit Mercury Sextile Saturn

This transit marks a period of constructive mental concentration and discipline useful to the effective furtherance of professional ambitions. The native will be inclined to study and tackle serious projects and engage in literary, mathematical and research endeavors. Particularly favored by this transit are tasks of a mathematical nature or those where a sense of structure of exact measurement is required. Thus, architects, skilled craftsmen, machinists, opticians and others whose work entails great precision will find this a propitious transit for their occupational endeavors. Business and professional correspondence and bookkeeping can be properly organized and handled at this time. Valuable insights may be forthcoming from past experience in the native's work, research or professional involvements. Communication with older, mature individuals or those in positions of established power and authority is likely during this period. Old friends and group associates may reenter the native's life, or there may be communication regarding them. All of this will help the native to realize long-range goals and objectives. In general, this transit will dispose the native toward greater care and conscience in areas of health and occupation.

Transit Mercury Sextile Uranus

This transit will endow the native with intuitive flashes of mental inspiration and insight. Surprising and unusual methods suggested by the native will, when applied, increase efficiency and productivity in the occupational environment. This will be particularly noticeable if the native is involved in scientific, electronic or metaphysical work, research or study. This is thus an excellent transit for scientists, researchers and inventors. The repair of electrical gadgets, wiring and the purchase of electronics are favored at this time. Insights gained of the subtle, superphysical forces of nature make this an excellent period for the native's engagement in astrological work, study and prognostication. Student teachers, lecturers and others in communication occupations will find this a propitious transit because of the original, mental insight it affords. Also indicated by this transiting sextile is the native's involvement in considerable short-distance travel or communication related to friends and group and organizational associates.

Transit Mercury Sextile Neptune

This transit stimulates the native's imagination and heightens the level of intuitive awareness, thus providing the native with valuable insights into the workings of his or her subconscious mind. Should the natal horoscope indicate the potential for such ability, the native could experience clairvoyant revelations or telepathic communication with others. The native's capacity for actual visualization of objects and places related to inner awareness is enhanced by this transit. Thus, artists and designers will be particularly favored at this time; but it does require discipline to express such ideas in an objective, physical manifestation (and this must be supplied from elsewhere in the chart). Creative writing is also favored by this transit. Often during this period, the native will become the repository of secret or private information relayed by friends and relatives. An innate curiosity about mystical and occult subjects can bloom in the native's study of such esoteric material and participation in organizations dealing with the mysterious side of life. Institutions or places of retreat may be visited by the native during the period of this transit.

Transit Mercury Sextile Pluto

This transit is indicative of a period in the native's life when he or she will express an increased curiosity about the occult or hidden side of life, often as a result of some clairvoyant experience or inexplicable communication with discarnate human beings. This could arouse an intellectual interest in life after death or reincarnation. Study in scientific fields, parapsychology and related subjects is favored by this transit. The native may also be inclined to improve or reshape procedures and methodologies dealing with work and health. This could include refinement of techniques of spiritual healing or the implementation of new scientific advances in the healing arts. Decisions and communication regarding corporate finances, insurance, taxes, inheritance and the goods of the dead can be properly handled at this time. This transit will, in general, incline the native's receptivity toward the acquisition of profound occult or scientific insights.

Transit Mercury Squares

Transit Mercury Square Sun

This transit of Mercury indicates a time when the native's ego is apt to interfere with the ability to think clearly. Primary emphases in communication and most other activities will center upon the native's own point of view, and will thus lack necessary objectivity. Authoritative attitudes in speech and communication are likely to annoy others. Overindulgence in social and romantic activity could interfere with work, study and health. Excessive socializing while on the job is apt to result in inefficiency in the native's occupational endeavors or strained relationships with coworkers and employers. Communication with romantic partners is apt to experience difficulties and obstacles. Efforts toward artistic or creative self-expression will often be blocked by an inability to resolve practical details. This period is not a favorable one for the conclusion of contracts involving financial speculations or investments. Students experiencing this transit may find it difficult to concentrate on their studies. Communication with family members, and particularly with children, is apt to be difficult, at best.

Transit Mercury Square Moon

This transit is indicative of distinct difficulties in the family and domestic sphere of activity. Communication with family members has a tendency to break down, often as a result of disagreements over cleanliness in the home, personal hygiene, dress modes and dietary habits. Annoyances caused by delays in mail or other messages will usually affect the home in some manner. Professional worries and responsibilities are apt to interfere with harmony in family life. Subconscious emotional problems stemming from childhood and family upbringing could surface to distort the native's judgment and thus obstruct his proper use of objective practical reasoning. Social functions planned in the native's home should be deferred to a later date because visitors or friends are likely to disrupt family affairs. Delays in transportation and misunderstandings are also apt to interject a note of chaos into the family schedule. Illness contracted by one family member could be passed on to others, interfering with occupational, educational and other normal responsibilities, and even standing a good chance of depleting the family budget. The purchase of household items should also be postponed because such acquisitions are likely to contain various inherent defects. Clothing purchased during this transit may contain imperfections or flaws, or may even be beyond the native's ability to pay.

Transit Mercury Square Mercury

This transit of Mercury can bring a period of difficulty and confusion in the native's work, communication and friendships. Delays in messages or the receipt of erroneous information could give rise to circumstances forcing the native to alter a decision or change his or her mind about important matters. Thus, the native may be required to rework or adopt a less acceptable plan of action in these affairs, disposing him or her toward nervousness and irritability. Misunderstandings on either the native's part or the part of others can create difficulties in relationships with family members, colleagues, brothers, sisters, neighbors, friends or organizational associates. Problems in communication with coworkers, employers or employees can lead to a drop in production and interfere with occupational efficiency; delayed shipments of essential parts and equipment or idle social gossip while on the job will only add to this decrease in productivity. A temporary illness could result in a lapse in occupational projects and time-dependent fulfillment of obligations. Any short-distance travels are likely to be beset by traffic jams, car troubles, confusing directions, detours or the native's just plain getting lost. Petty annoyances, particularly the accidental omission of necessary items, clothing, etc., are also likely to interfere with the native's work and travel at this time.

Transit Mercury Square Venus

This transit is likely to cause misunderstandings and difficulties in the native's communication with romantic, marital and business partners. Meaningless and unwarranted social gossip can give rise to problems in relationships with friends, neighbors, family and coworkers. Socializing while on the job should be cut to a bare minimum or eliminated altogether to avoid problems with the native's employer or superiors. Emotional problems of others will draw little sympathy from the native at this time. Indeed, the native may annoy others by constantly referring to his or her own emotional difficulties. In any event, such factors are more than likely to interfere with the use of sound judgment and consequent arrival at practical decisions. Business and financial plans of the native may be subject to outside intervention or disturbances. This is definitely not a propitious time for the sale or purchase of art or luxury items. Overindulgence in sweets, improper dietary habits and excessive social activity could result in the native's ill health or clash with occupational responsibilities.

Transit Mercury Square Natal Mars

This transit of Mercury is indicative of a period of difficulty in the native's work, health and communication connected with professional, corporate or financial affairs. Cooperation with friends, coworkers or business and professional associates is likely to be problematical, at best. Conflicts and disagreements are apt to arise over joint finances, taxes and the like. During the period of this transit, the native's critical, irritable, self-centered attitude will incline toward involvement in arguments or verbal encounters with others, and may make the native prone to rash and impulsive decisions. Likewise, the native's ideas are likely to be met by opposition and resistance from others, particularly in areas of professional responsibility. Thus, the native should await a more favorable time to present them. Endorsements of contracts or papers should be postponed to some future date, especially if these deal with insurance, taxes, corporate finances, business partnerships or professional or corporate affairs. This is not a propitious time to hold conferences, make public appearances or present speeches or lectures. Neither is it favorable for the pursuit of advertising, promotional endeavors or the conclusion of important sales or purchases. The native's susceptibility to inflammations of the body and infectious diseases may interfere with occupational responsibilities. There is the additional danger of industrial or automobile accidents or damage to tools, clothing or equipment.

Transit Mercury Square Jupiter

This transit often indicates an attitude of over-optimism in planning, decision-making and self-esteem. Ideas and suggestions presented at this time are apt to be noticeably lacking in practicality and realism, reflecting an inherent inability, consequent to this transit, to properly apply knowledge gleaned from experience. Aroused interests in philosophy, religion and education are apt to falter for lack of necessary discipline and common sense to practically utilize and apply such new-found knowledge. This transit often gives rise to the native's indifference toward work responsibilities. Although the native may be searching for a practical field of endeavor, the tendency to pursue distant or illusive goals will frequently cause a neglect of responsibilities. This transit is not conducive to a change of occupation, long journey or application for admission to an institution of higher learning. Generally speaking, it would be wise to practice moderation during this period and to maintain a sense of practical realism, if possible.

Transit Mercury Square Saturn

This transit introduces difficulties and obstacles into the native's occupational sphere. Vital business communication is likely to be slowed or delayed, particularly if Mercury is retrograde. Those involved in manufacturing are apt to experience delays and frustration due to late shipments, strikes, equipment failures and other problems. The native may be called upon to shoulder a greater degree of responsibility on the job, although he or she may be too conservative in thinking or lack inspiration to find solutions to these problems. Health problems, weariness and even exhaustion are often the result of such taxing demands upon the native's mind and body. Sluggish digestion or other illness could interfere with work performance. The native may even be faced with the responsibility of caring for others. The native or those with whom the native must communicate, may adopt a negative, unsympathetic or pessimistic outlook. Thus, problems and difficulties are apt to arise in relationships with partners, friends, coworkers and group associates. Applications for future employment, discussions with employers, handling of legal matters and requests for an audience with individuals in established positions of power and authority should be deferred until some future date. Students experiencing this transit can expect a heavy work load and a lack of sympathy from their instructors. Short-distance travels can be held up or detoured by traffic jams and other annoyances. During this transit, it is generally best to try to maintain the status quo and await a more auspicious time to attempt progressive change.

Transit Mercury Square Uranus

This transit indicates a time when the native is apt to be rash and impulsive in decision-making. Although natives will express interest in new and original ideas, these ideas are likely to be impractical under current circumstances. Careful thought should be given to the ideas of others before accepting whimsical notions that could have unexpected results. Friends and group associates of the native may come to regard him or her as eccentric and uncooperative, and could give the native well-meant but impractical advice or the native could come to view friends or partners as unreliable or peculiar. Caution should be exercised while dealing with electrical appliances, driving, traveling and traveling partners. Unexpected difficulties are apt to arise in the native's occupational endeavors, forcing the native to adjust to a new set of circumstances. Short of a lack of choice in the matter, the native should not seek to change employment at this time. It is generally wise to allow adequate time during the period of this transit for careful consideration of the situation before concluding important decisions or subscribing to important documents or agreements, especially if these relate to corporate business affairs, inheritance, taxes or insurance.

Transit Mercury Square Neptune

This transit of Mercury is often indicative of a period of mental confusion in the native's life. Subconscious forces or biases will tend to interfere with the native's capability for factual and rational comprehension. Under this transit, there arises the tendency to withdraw into a private dream world, and thus neglect work, communication or practical responsibilities. Communication is likely to be delayed or muddled in some way. Individuals experiencing this transit who possess the potential for serious mental crises and related illnesses are apt to manifest symptoms at this time. In extreme cases, this may even result in a hospital visit for treatment or recuperation. The native could, conversely, visit a friend or relative in a medical or mental institution who exhibits these same tendencies. The use of drugs or medication without a doctor's prescription should be especially avoided during this period. Employment changes, the handling of important correspondence and the conclusion of contracts or agreements should be deferred to some later period. Mental preoccupation or drinking while driving could result in a jail or hospital stay. Daydreaming while on the job can cause inefficiency in the native's work. Difficulties are apt to be experienced while on short journeys or trips, whether it be due to automotive troubles, improper directions or simply losing one's way. During this transit the native is apt to say the wrong thing or divulge secrets to the wrong people. Friends, relatives or neighbors may become a source of annoyance or difficulty because of their confusion and psychological problems. This is especially true if the native is called upon to listen to sob stories or assume the role of an amateur psychiatrist or confessor.

Transit Mercury Square Pluto

This transit denotes a period in which the native is confronted by mysteries and difficult decisions, particularly those dealing with joint finances, corporate money, taxes, inheritance, insurance or alimony. The arrival of unfavorable news concerning death could cause the native to become disturbed or perplexed about the possibility of life after death, reincarnation, psychic experiences and occult influences. Concern about the world economic situation could give rise to the native's efforts to help solve ecological problems, most notably in terms of the peaceful use of atomic energy and the recycling of industrial wastes. Difficulties in relationships with friends, employees or employers may result from dictatorial attitudes on the part of the native or others. Coercion, forcefully applied, can lead the native to adopt an approach to work that is wholly unacceptable or it could result in a breakdown of relationships with friends and group associates. This transit often gives rise to health problems that necessitate a complete revision of the native's diet or personal grooming habits. Generally, the native experiencing this transit is likely to be drawn into arguments, secret intrigues and intellectual power struggles. The native could be forced to relinquish some cherished ideas and illusions in the face of cold, harsh reality.

Transit Mercury Trines

Transit Mercury Trine Sun

This transit of Mercury heralds a period of creative, mental inspiration in the native's life. Clarity in the native's expression of ideas will project confidence to others and thereby inspire faith and trust in others. The period of this transit is a propitious one for vacation trips and all social and educational activities, as it is for seeking audiences or favors from those in positions of power and authority. Thus, students, teachers. lecturers, writers and performing artists will be particularly favored at this time. The writing of theses and school papers and the handling of correspondence and journeys planned in the pursuit of knowledge or pleasure may provide the native with further opportunities for advancement in creative endeavors. Often, the native will frequent health spas or be involved in physical fitness programs, while at the same time expressing increased interest in games of mental skill. The native can enjoy intellectual activities with friends and group associates, providing additional opportunities for intellectual creative self-expression.

Transit Mercury Trine Moon

During the period of this transit the native can expect improvements in communication with family members and may even embark upon short journeys or trips to visit them. Important messages and visitors are apt to be received in the home, particularly those relating to the native's occupational or business affairs and family educational activities. Favorable changes can be expected in the home environment in terms of cooking and dietary improvements, or the purchase of articles providing efficiency and comfort to domestic living. It is a favorable time to start home improvement projects and to broaden the scope of available family reading material and the introduction of social, religious and cultural activities into the family context. In this latter case, the native's home is likely to become a meeting place or center for social activities of groups and associations. Attendance at family outings and get-togethers and the proper handling of family and business correspondence will engender an air of accomplishment in the native's view of his or her own actions. This transit confers the ability to communicate harmoniously with women and family members. This transit, in general, will render the native the ability for constructive, scientific self-education in such matters as diet, personal hygiene, household health and ecological practices.

Transit Mercury Trine Mercury

During the period of this transit the native will be disposed toward constructive, intellectual activity, often manifested in efforts toward self-education in areas of health, diet and hygiene and in endeavors designed to improve occupational opportunities and capabilities. The application or implementation of original and constructive ideas in communication will lead to a more effective personal link between the native and brothers, sisters, neighbors, friends and work and group associates. The pursuit of academic programs, travel, writing and study are highly favored by this transit. Thus, this is a propitious period to submit manuscripts for publication, endorse documents and negotiate and formulate agreements. This a good time to seek other employment or to hire employees to fill vacancies and the native is also apt to introduce new concepts in on-the-job methodologies that will increase the efficiency and productivity of the whole.

Transit Mercury Trine Venus

This transit of Mercury provides for harmonious social communication and activities involving the native's friends, work associates, brothers, sisters and neighbors. Romantic opportunities may arise through the native's engagement in intellectual, educational, occupational, group and organizational activities, and considerable travel can be expected in connection with these and other social functions. Here, the native will be presented the opportunity to combine business with pleasure. This is an excellent time to purchase fine clothing and other personal adornments conducive to an image of personal refinement. Diet and personal hygiene are also often altered by the native to project a more attractive image. Advertising and the handling of public relations will thus be easier to carry out. The native could develop an intellectual curiosity in art, music and other cultural refinements, and could also seek to beautify the working environment and to establish more harmonious relationships with others in the work area. This is an excellent period in which to plan parties and social gatherings and to compose business letters that must be handled in a tactful and diplomatic fashion or to design greeting cards and artistic creations.

Transit Mercury Trine Mars

This transit of Mercury favors the native's energetic application of knowledge and skills in pursuit of business and professional goals. The will be endowed with the ability to express ideas with greater forcefulness, self-confidence and authority toward these ends. The native will undoubtedly discover new methods which, when properly implemented, will improve productivity and efficiency on the job by organizing the production processes and promoting their effectiveness. Thus, this transit favors the efforts of engineers, designers, technicians, skilled craftsmen and those engaged in investigative careers, scientific research and business market analysis. The native's engagement in political debates and campaigning or literary endeavors at this time will be rewarded. Physical fitness programs and exercise schedules initiated during this period will generate improvements in the native's health that will favorably influence the future. This transit, will in general, confer the native with an honest and forthright manner in the expression of attitudes and opinions.

Transit Mercury Trine Jupiter

This is an excellent transit for travel, literary endeavors, pursuit of academic goals, engagement in lecture tours, religious studies, handling of legal matters, negotiation and endorsement of contracts, application for employment or study at universities, submission of articles for publication or involvement in matters of public relations or advertising. Through the development of a more positive and constructive mental outlook, and an often concurrent acquisition of valuable and profound insight into prevailing business and cultural trends of society, the native will be able to further goals and objectives and likewise expand business, occupational and professional affairs. Group and organizational activities dealing with philosophical, educational and religious studies and investigations will be of great appeal to the native during this transit, and he or she will demonstrate a more compassionate and humanitarian mental outlook toward others. The period of this transit is a prime time to travel. The native will develop a strong curiosity about distant places and their cultures, histories and religions, and is likely to receive communication from or dispatch messages to foreigners or friends in faraway places or countries. Visits by these individuals will only serve to increase the native's desire to embark upon such foreign travels. Business dealings with foreign countries or distant regions is also a likely possibility. This transit denotes a favorable period in which to seek the advice of spiritual counselors and teachers, as well as to deal with hospitals and institutions.

Transit Mercury Trine Saturn

This transit of Mercury ushers in a period of progress in the native's handling of practical affairs concerning business, profession and health. This is often accomplished through the ability to selectively assimilate valuable ideas and concepts from past experiences, friends and work associates who are older and more experienced in areas of concern and subsequently apply them to further his or her own professional and career advancement. This transit's endowment of a greater capacity for disciplined, sustained, organized concentration favors the native's pursuit of serious mathematical and scientific studies. It can also lead to the development of an increased sense of practical organization in job-oriented methodologies. The establishment of lasting and legally binding contracts and the consolidation of financial affairs are particularly encouraged by this transit. Designers, architects, engineers, skilled technicians and craftsmen will find this an auspicious transit for their occupational endeavors because of the mathematical precision, patience and sense of structure provided by this Mercury-Saturn combination. In general, this is a favorable transit for the practical expression of ideas and communication.

Transit Mercury Trine Uranus

This transit betokens a period in which the native will be inspired with original, intuitive ideas, particularly where these deal with the application of modern scientific methods and techniques toward efficient labor and work practices. Uranus' exaltation in Scorpio, the natural eighth house sign and ruler of insurance matters, designates this as a propitious time to contract on an insurance policy, especially health insurance. This is also true of transit trines of Mercury to Mars and Pluto. This is the "brain-storm" transit, when the native is apt to receive flashes of intuitive insight that reveal solutions to problems that have been of concern for a considerable period of time. Thus, there are likely to be sudden revelations or periods of unusual perception during which the native will discern unusual methods by which he or she can make significant gains in corporate business affairs or matters of joint finance or thorough study and research in the scientific, technological, electronic, occult or astrological areas. This transit marks an excellent period in which to join or expand one's participation in these and related humanitarian organizations. Reading, writing, lecturing or teaching in these fields will lead to substantial improvement in the native's orientation toward life goals and objectives. The native may very well establish new and exciting friendships during this transit, and is apt to either receive communication from or dispatch them to friends, organizations, work associates, near relatives or neighbors. Visits can be expected during this transit, whether they be to or from the native. Intuitive insights, friends, groups or organizations could provide the native with important scientific information about health and diet. Natives possessing clairvoyant potential frequently experience conscious mental telepathic communication during this transit.

Transit Mercury Trine Neptune

This transit of Mercury increases and enhances the native's imagination and capacity for creative visualization. Should the natal horoscope reveal an inherent ability in the native for clairvoyance, this transit will produce experiences of this nature. Prophetic insights into the future, telepathy and paranormal phenomena may surface as manifestations of this capability. During this transit the native will be able to tap knowledge and wisdom latent or dormant in the subconscious mind, and through this can acquire valuable insights into the workings of his or her own subliminal processes and thus gain a greater degree of self-awareness. Secret information or privileged knowledge may be confided to by others, and this may offer the native an advantage of some sort. An increased interest in mysticism and religious philosophies could lead the native to embark upon both long and short journeys in search of spiritual teachers and advisors. Readings or writings on subjects of this nature are favored by this transit. Writers, poets, musicians and entertainers will find this an excellent transit for the furtherance of their endeavors. Visits to hospitals or other institutions will be planned to attend and converse with those confined there or for thorough diagnostic checkups for ailments of a nature that is either unknown or difficult to identify. The native may even develop a strong interest in spiritual healing and the impact of mental energies upon food assimilation and body chemistry.

Transit Mercury Trine Pluto

This transit is indicative of a period in which the native will seek to acquire insights into the mysteries of creation and human consciousness. Thus, the native is apt to expend a great deal of energy in the pursuit of studies of a metaphysical, religious, philosophical, occult, parapsychological or advanced scientific nature. On a mundane level of experience, this transit can provide for the native's progress in communication dealing with corporate business affairs, joint finances, taxes, insurance or inheritance. Often, this will stem from important intuitive insights. The native is likely to have a mental realization of the importance of sound dietary, health and ecological practices on a personal as well as a social level. Recycling endeavors, particularly those dealing with industrial waste products and sewage, will be of interest. Advanced scientific techniques are apt to be introduced by the native in efforts to reuse discarded materials and thus improve efficiency and production in occupational efforts. Communication with brothers, sisters, neighbors, friends, group associates and coworkers will exhibit distinct signs of improvement or renewed interest during this transit. Travel connected with the native's pursuit of academic or scientific knowledge may provide information and sufficient bases for the initiation of mass programs designed to utilize this understanding.

Transit Mercury Oppositions

Transit Mercury Opposition Sun

This transit of Mercury is often productive of verbal ego confrontations between the native and his friends, work associates, organizational colleagues, brothers, sisters and neighbors. Difficulties are thus apt to arise in romantic and social communication and relationships. Unfortunately, this is usually due to a lack of understanding in the native's or another's interpretation of the real meanings and intentions of what is said. This is not the best time to request either an audience with or patronage from those in authority, for they are likely to be preoccupied, unsympathetic or indifferent to the native's suggestions or pleas. Difficulties are likely to arise in connection with lectures or public appearances, and petty confrontations are apt to erupt over games of intellectual skill. Pleasure trips and vacations should be postponed until some future time because of the native's lack of agreement with others as to their direction or purpose. Petty annoyances are also likely to waylay plans because of automotive troubles, confusing or impossible directions, delayed communication and the like. Difficulties experienced in study, work or research will often result from environmental distractions caused by others. To protect and guarantee good health, the native should avoid overwork and overindulgence in pleasurable pursuits. Patience must be exercised in the native's dealings with children, yet with the objective of maintaining correct rules and procedures. This transit will, in general, force the native to recognize and reckon with others and their points of view.

Transit Mercury Opposition Moon

Emotional factors springing from the native's subconscious mind or family conditioning are apt to interfere with the capability for clear and concise judgment and communication during the period of this transit, particularly in work, family and business relationships. Environmental distractions in the home are also likely to disturb concentration in work or study. A lack of practical judgment due to established emotional conditioning and habits can often lead to indiscriminate attitudes in the native's views on diet, health, dress and personal hygiene. The end result of this is frequently a disorderly personal environment, an unkempt personal appearance or overindulgence in the wrong types of food. Problems in the home could result from water leakage, poor plumbing or ill health in the family. Emotional factors will tend to arise as obstacles to effective cooperation can strain relationships between the native and family members, coworkers, friends, organizational associates or neighbors. Idle social gossip and annoying telephone calls about inconsequential matters could adversely affect the native's well-being or efficiency in work. The native or those with whom the native must deal may be prone to talk incessantly to the point of annoyance. Difficulties in work or in communicating with women or the public associated with this transit render this a poor time for the native's involvement in advertising or public relations endeavors.

Transit Mercury Opposition Mercury

This transit of Mercury indicates a time when the native is apt to be burdened with an inordinate amount of detail in work and communication. Nervousness and ill health are liable to be a source of difficulty in personal relationships, occupational endeavors and related communication; because the opposition aspect deals expressly with relationships, differences of opinion are apt to arise between the native and others as to the proper handling of mutual affairs. Misunderstandings and misinterpretations of meaning and intent are often the cause of such problems. Delays or confusion can be expected in the delivery of correspondence or in the receipt of shipments that are essential to the native's work. Difficulties will be experienced in efforts to coordinate travel schedules with others. Thus, it is best to await a more favorable period in which to endorse legal papers or formulate contracts or agreements. During this transit the native should try to be flexible and amenable to change, especially where ideas and methods are concerned because the native is not likely to possess all of the factual information necessary to reach a proper and just final judgment.

Transit Mercury Opposition Venus

This transit is indicative of difficulties and misunderstandings in the native's social communication. Venus' rulership of Libra, and thus its direct relation to the opposition aspect, confers this transiting aspect with other effects that are not necessarily of an adverse nature. Often, the establishment of friendships and social relationships or activity concerning them is indicated by this Mercury-Venus opposition. The native could become involved in business and financial negotiations, often dealing with art, music or entertainment. Cultural, artistic and social activities will bring the native into contact with the public. However, the native must recognize and be constantly aware of the importance of diplomacy, dress, personal mannerisms and tactful speech and their bearing upon personal reputation and popularity. Foolish and frivolous expenditures should be avoided during this transit. The native will be sympathetically aware of emotional factors affecting close friends and associates, but must escape the tendency to become involved in petty emotional issues. The native should be cooperative and polite in communication with coworkers, group associates, friends and family. Meaningless chit-chat and gossip can create misunderstandings that lead to more difficult problems and may interfere with efficiency at work. Overindulgence in rich foods at this time could adversely effect the native's health.

Transit Mercury Opposition Mars

This transit often indicates a period of conflict and difficulty in professional and business relationships. This is frequently characterized by open verbal battles that can affect the native's reputation. At best, the native is likely to exhibit irritability and a short temper. Speeches, public appearances, the negotiation of contracts and agreements and the handling of important business transactions should be deferred to a later time. Statements or accusations made by or to the native can give rise to anger and heated exchanges. Caution should also be exercised when writing or in conversation. Ego-identified points of view can be a source of trouble for the native, who should instead try to maintain an attitude of impartiality because all of the pertinent facts may not be available. Breakdowns of equipment, transportation difficulties and late shipments could interfere with occupational endeavors. Conflict or breakdowns in communication with work and professional associates can also give rise to such problems. The native could be subject to infectious respiratory diseases, and should work involve potentially dangerous equipment, impatience, nervousness and irritability will increase the danger of industrial accidents. Care and patience should also be exercised while driving to avoid the possibility of accidents. Frustration and impatience may become a common feeling because the native's ideas are not likely to be either implemented or acted upon immediately. However, should the native feel aggravated by or anger toward another individual, remarks should be carefully considered before being verbalized because caustic comments uttered during this transit are likely to result in unpleasant consequences.

Transit Mercury Opposition Jupiter

During this transit of Mercury, the native is likely to express an overly optimistic view of plans and projects. Grandiose ideas may be entertained, while at the same time the practical details necessary to implement them are neglected. The native's tendency to overexpand work commitments could cause him or her to tackle more than can be safely handled. At this point, confusion about practical details could result in missed appointments reflecting poorly on occupational responsibilities. This transit may even give rise to a tendency to make promises one has no hope of keeping. Conversely, the native may become indifferent toward work and study responsibilities, ignoring necessary endeavors. Travel and long-distance communication are apt to be less than satisfactory, and confusion could arise in communications between the native and family members over domestic affairs. Serious doubts are likely to surface in the native's mind about religious and philosophical ideas, but attractions to unsound religious cults and concepts will not help the native resolve these questions. This is not a favorable period in which to deal with publishers, universities, religious organizations, hospitals or institutions. The native's overindulgence in rich foods or drink could adversely affect the health, especially the liver.

Transit Mercury Opposition Saturn

During the period of this transit, the native will be forced to make difficult decisions that can have a great effect upon career and reputation. Information, sometimes of a scandalous nature, can be brought to light that will adversely affect the native's status and honor, especially if he or she holds a position of leadership and responsibility. This is not a favorable time to push for the acceptance of ideas by those in positions of established authority, nor is it conducive to public relations, writing, lectures or public appearances. Legal matters, particularly contracts and agreements, should be postponed to a more favorable time because the native is apt to become involved in troublesome and costly disputes over these affairs. Court appearances associated with such legal difficulties are apt to interfere with work responsibilities and thus cause occupational problems. This transit will, in general, tend toward a worrisome and pessimistic outlook.

Mental anxiety and overwork can adversely affect health and vitality; at the same time, negativity and lack of sympathy for others' ideas and communication can result in loneliness and unpopularity. Temporary estrangements can be expected from friends, brothers, sisters, neighbors and occupational, professional or organizational associates. During this transit it is best to maintain the status quo and to avoid initiating any major changes or making any important decisions.

Transit Mercury Opposition Uranus

This transit marks a period of uncertainty. New facts or ideas brought into focus by others may force the native to revise or at least reexamine personal thoughts, decisions and life direction. Difficulties are apt to arise in communication with friends, neighbors, group associates and co-workers, as well as in scientific and technological endeavors. The native may revolt against work and daily responsibilities as a sort of declaration of independence from these affairs. Thus, this transit would not be a propitious period in which to handle business affairs related to corporations, insurance, taxes or inheritance, nor to seek a change of employment unless forced to do so. The native may come into contact with friends of an eccentric, unstable or unreliable nature who will give poor but well-intended advice. Conversely, the native may act in the same manner or may suddenly have a change of mind for no apparent reason. Interest expressed in occult, metaphysical or astrological subjects may be real but will lack the sound approach necessary to understand, comprehend and utilize these precepts. During this transit the native must be open-minded and cooperative in a sensible, practical fashion in order to realize goals.

Transit Mercury Opposition Neptune

This transit of Mercury indicates a time when the native's subconscious mind and uncontrolled imagination can interfere with the ability to communicate and perceive the ideas of others, especially in friendships, work associations, family relationships and organizational contacts. This is not a favorable time to deal with hospitals or institutions, nor to seek medical diagnoses. In the latter case, such analysis is likely to be erroneous or inconclusive. Deception in friendships or other close personal relationships is a distinct possibility during this transit. The native may become either the recipient of or the perpetrator of misleading gossip or so-called inside information. In some cases this transit will cause the native's withdrawal into his or her own private, subjective world, thus making communication difficult. Daydreaming and a general lack of awareness of environmental circumstances are often associated with this transit. Should the native become upset by disturbing dreams or psychic experiences or unduly sensitive to the thoughts and feelings of others, the mental processes will suffer. Symptoms of illogical behavior evidenced during this transit are occasionally indicative of tendencies toward mental illness. Confusion is apt to arise in the receipt or dispatch of communication, the scheduling of appointments and the proper use of directions when traveling.

Transit Mercury Opposition Pluto

This transit often produces disagreements and subsequent difficulties in the decision-making process regarding business and financial relationships, particularly those dealing with joint finances, corporate affairs, insurance, taxes and inheritance. The establishment of better lines of communication or a revision of personal thinking processes may be required to handle work responsibilities. This is thus not a favorable period in which to endorse contracts or formulate agreements dealing with these matters. Such contracts will constantly be subject to amendment or alteration, creating a state of nervous tension. The native may become mentally preoccupied with thoughts of death or the occult worlds at this time, and the native may even receive news of the demise or illness of a friend, coworker, neighbor, associate or sibling. The native's witness of the abuse of nature can lead to the native's painful personal awareness of ecological problems. Indeed, if this mistreatment is related to the native's occupation, it may become a threat to health or life. Suspicions are apt to surface about the thoughts, ideas and motivations of others. In extreme cases the native may resort to spying, secret intrigues or attempts at mental manipulation to at least keep abreast of, if not control, the situation. Conversely, the native may become the subject or victim of such actions on the part of others. This could be an extremely dangerous time for travel or secret communication. Overall, during the period of this transit, the native should try to cooperate with others and through mutual effort improve occupational and health conditions. Permitting or perpetrating the use of coercive tactics to extract information should be avoided.

IV

Transits of Venus

Transits of Venus are significant in their influence upon the romantic, marital, financial, business and partnership affairs of the native concerned. Artistic inclinations are also apt to surface, finding concrete expression in music, painting, sculpture, drama and other refined art forms.

The native will become increasingly concerned about the maintenance of harmony in close personal relationships, particularly those involving the opposite sex. Affairs are likely to be influenced in some meaningful fashion by women, especially those who are young and attractive, wealthy or engaged in a great deal of social activity.

Transiting Venus will motivate the native to acquire objects of beauty, refinement and luxury, and the native will express interest in lucrative business endeavors, particularly those related to art, music, entertainment and luxury items. Expenditures on jewelry, perfume, fine clothing, home decorations, artistic expressions, social activities and entertainment are common to Venus transits, as is the native's attendance at concerts, gallery showings and other public displays of refined artistic endeavor.

Natives experiencing these transits direct a general interest toward the maintenance of peace and harmony in the affairs ruled by Venus in transit, in the natal horoscope and by the planet or planets transited in the birth chart.

Adverse transits of Venus tend to promote the native's extravagance, foolhardiness and overindulgence in food, pleasures and sensual gratifications. There could even be involvement in ill-advised romantic affairs under such afflicting transits.

Retrograde Venus

Retrograde periods of Venus will cause the affairs ruled by the house, sign and natal planets aspected by Venus' passage to be subject to more careful evaluation and greater introspection by the native. This propensity is that much more accentuated if Venus is retrograde in the natal horoscope. Caution in social, financial and romantic matters will become apparent. The native may expect to experience a general decline in social, romantic and business activity.

Venus in the Houses

The affairs ruled by the house through which Venus is transiting will be subject to financial change, social activity, artistic expression and the direct influence of women.

Should Venus make favorable transiting aspects to natal planets in its passage through a particular house or be well-aspected in the natal horoscope, financial or social gain can be expected through attending to the affairs ruled by that house. Such gains are apt to be acquired through the assistance or influence of women in the native's life who often bring increased opportunities for social activity and romantic involvement.

Transits of Venus confer greater peace and harmony to the affairs ruled by the house in which Venus' passage is noted.

Transit Venus Through the First House

Venus' transit through the first house is indicative of a period in which the native becomes socially outgoing and active in efforts to initiate social activities. Personal mannerisms will develop a refinement and charm that will be more pleasing to others and confer greater social grace, while at the same time permit and even encourage the native's expression of individuality within the social context. Natives experiencing this transit will express greater interest in personal adornment through their acquisition of fine clothing, jewelry, cosmetics, perfume and hairstyle. This is particularly true where women are concerned. Men undergoing this transit often purchase new clothing, exhibit slight alterations in hair style and buy more or different cosmetics. Creative self-expressions in song, music, painting, acting and other modes of artistic representation are common to this transit, making this a favorable period for singers, artists, sculptors and other professionals utilizing their abilities.

Transiting afflictions involving Venus in the first house can cause the native to lack taste and refinement in social activities or in efforts toward artistic self-expression. This may arise from or give rise to a sense of social or romantic competition in the native's life. Self-indulgence in the pursuit of sensual pleasures can also be expected under such adverse transits.

Transit Venus Through the Second House

This Venus transit presents the native with the opportunity to gain financially through businesses related to art, music or luxury items. Financial favors from banking institutions, employers and people of wealth and means, particularly women, can be successfully sought. The marketing and purchase of art and other luxury items can be successfully and profitably concluded. Natives are apt to display greater sensuality in the physical pleasures of life, acquiring jewelry, fine clothing, perfume, art, luxury items for the home or possessions representative of opulence and wealth. Venus' transit through this house of its accidental rulership makes this an ideal time for painting, sculpture, music and other forms of refined artistic expression.

Should Venus make adverse transits to the natal planets while transiting this house, the native may exhibit a tendency to be extravagant in the expenditure of resources on unnecessary luxuries.

Transit Venus Through the Third House

Venus' transit through the third house is indicative of a period of active social communication between the native and brothers, sisters, neighbors or business associates. Interest may also arise in the native's use of communication to establish friendly social relationships. Grace, tact and diplomacy in speech, writing and other forms of communication will be evidenced in the native's correspondence and phone conversations with friends, which will further his or her social aspirations. The native may be inspired to write a romantic interest and social contacts. Interest may arise in poetry and varied forms of artistic illustration. Singers, artists and performers can make particularly advantageous use of this transit to express themselves through the media. Short pleasure trips and social excursions are common to this transit. Natives experiencing this transit may also feel prompted to beautify or upgrade their personal means of transportation.

Adverse transiting aspects of Venus while in the third house can cause the native to dissipate time, energy and money in non-productive chit-chat and unnecessary trips and telephone conversations.

Transit Venus Through the Fourth House

Venus' transit through the fourth house is indicative of a period in which the native is motivated to use the home as a center for social activity, romantic courtship and/or artistic expression. This transit is also conducive to the establishment of greater harmony within the home, particularly among family members. Natives experiencing this transit often bring friends or individuals into their homes whom they wish to help in some way. Business activities, especially those related to artistic pursuits, may find positive expression in the native's home environment. There is apt to be a strong urge to beautify the home or immediate environment of the native, often involving expense in the acquisition of new furniture, kitchen utensils or art, or in lavish social entertainment.

Transiting afflictions of Venus in the fourth house can incline the native toward unnecessary financial expenditures for domestic luxuries and entertainment or over-indulgence in eating habits.

Transit Venus Through the Fifth House

Venus' transit through the fifth house is indicative of a period in which the native will experience an active and expanding social life with many and varied pleasurable pursuits. It is a favorable time for the native to host parties and other social events. Romantic opportunities often enter the native's life during this Venus transit, and this is a favorable time to seek favors from those of the opposite sex. Women who wish children are more apt to become pregnant during this transit. Those working with children or organizing games and social activities are likely to achieve a greater degree of success in their efforts. Artists, musicians, actors and performers are favored by this passage of Venus through the fifth house, and the native's sense of beauty, refinement and creative ability in pursuit of these goals is enhanced.

Favorable transits of Venus through this house to natal planetary positions, when combined with a well-aspected Venus in the natal horoscope, can favorably affect financial investments or speculative ventures, especially those related to the field of art, entertainment, music and luxury items.

Adverse transits of Venus through this house can result in an unwanted pregnancy or could lead to the native's loss of time and money through excesses in the pursuit of pleasure and sensual gratification.

Transit Venus Through the Sixth House

Venus' transit through this house is indicative of a period in which the native will express increased interest in food and dietary habits, personal grooming, dress requirements and the occupational environment. Opportunities for engagement in social activities and can often arise from the native's participation in occupational endeavors and health programs. Acquaintance with individuals encountered in food stores and supermarkets, as well as other businesses dealing with practical everyday activities can also blossom into close personal relationships or a mutual social involvement. The native may introduce music, art or decorations into the occupational environment and thus make working conditions more pleasant and enjoyable. Relationships with coworkers and employers will, in general, show distinct improvement, thus favoring the period of this transit as time to seek improved working conditions or request a salary increase. Concerns about health, diet and programs of exercise will be of great interest to the native, particularly where improvement in these areas will enhance attractiveness to the opposite sex.

Transiting afflictions of Venus in its passage through the sixth house, when combined with adverse aspects to Venus' position in the natal horoscope, can cause inefficiency to be a stumbling block to the native's career advancement. This is often the result of excessive socializing in the office or on the job. Under such afflictions the native's health may also suffer from overindulgence in sweets and other rich foods.

Transit Venus Through the Seventh House

Venus' transit through the seventh house portends a period of increased social contact with the general public. The native will behave in a more sociable, outgoing and considerate manner toward others, and thus is apt to attract others and become engaged in close relationships or partnerships. This is a favorable period for marriage or approaching a potential marriage or business partner. Public relations related to business affairs can be handled with ease, particularly if such matters pertain to art, music, entertainment or luxury items. Social events such as gallery exhibits are apt to show great promise if the native is an artist. During this transit, women are likely to assume an important role in the native's affairs.

Afflictions to Venus in the natal chart, when combined with adverse transits of Venus in this house, can cause the native to dissipate time, energy and money in pointless social activity. The native may also react in the opposite extreme, becoming weary of social activities that hold little or no meaning for him or her.

Transit Venus Through the Eighth House

Venus' transit through the eighth house can bring the native gifts, inheritances or financial gain through business partnerships, marriage or other close personal relationships. The native may even be offered an opportunity in a business or corporate relationship of some kind. Sympathetic inclinations in the native's attitudes may lead him or her to be called upon to console those who have lost relatives or dear friends. The native may be attracted to a relationship introducing him or her to the world of the occult or related forms of art and music.

Should Venus be afflicted in the natal horoscope and make adverse transits while in this house, sexual overindulgence is a danger.

Transit Venus Through the Ninth House

Venus' transit through the ninth house is indicative of a period when the native is apt to travel for pleasure, hence making this an excellent time to take well-deserved vacations or embark upon a honeymoon. Interest in foreign cultures and art forms may rise to prominence during this transit, as may the native's interest in religious art and music. The native will adopt a more philosophical attitude toward partnerships and marital and romantic relationships. Social and romantic opportunities may arise from interest and participation in religious functions, institutions of higher learning, travel or philosophical pursuits. Close friends or romantic partners are apt to encourage engagement in matters related to collegiate academics, philosophy, religion and foreign cultures. Often, a close friendship or romantic attachment is established with one who is either of foreign birth or associated with academic institutions. The native may even be visiting a distant place or country when this occurs.

Adverse transits of Venus in the ninth house can cause the native to spend money foolishly or unwisely on unnecessary travel. There is also the danger of neglecting scholastic responsibility to pursue social pleasures.

Transit Venus Through the Tenth House

Venus' transit through the tenth house indicates a period when the native's social status and prominence are enhanced. It is a favorable time to seek favors from those in power and authority and, should Venus be well aspected in the natal horoscope, this is a propitious time for the native to request a raise in salary. Wealthy or prominent women can assist the native's advancement in career, business affairs and status. Transactions of business matters dealing with art, music and entertainment are particularly favored by this transit, as is the native's participation in social functions. Business partnerships and financial transactions fare favorably during this transit, thus displaying the native's greater ambition to acquire material wealth and social status.

Should Venus make adverse transits to the natal planets while passing though this house, the native is apt to develop an aristocratic or snobbish attitude toward others.

Transit Venus Through the Eleventh House

Venus' transit through the eleventh house is indicative of a period in which the native will look forward to and actively establish new friendships and social relationships. Participation in co-operative efforts and ventures with friends, groups and organizations will offer increased opportunities for social and romantic involvements. Women of beauty or social status or wealth could be attracted to the native at this time. Renewed interest and participation in musical and artistic groups and organizations could lead to the establishment of close friendships with esthetically-inclined individuals, artists, musicians, sculptors and others. The native's sociability, sympathetic inclinations and understanding toward friends will attract those people who can help the native achieve his or her goals and objectives. Harmony among friends, groups and organizations will be the key to success in achieving these hopes and wishes.

Adverse transits of Venus to the natal planets could lead the native and his or her friends to the mutual dissipation of time, energy, and money in the idle pursuit of pleasure.

Transit Venus Through the Twelfth House

Venus' exaltation in Pisces, corresponding to the twelfth house, imparts great significance to this house transit. The native experiencing Venus' passage here will develop a kinder and more generous outlook toward those less fortunate. Cognizance of one's inner spiritual sources of beauty and enrichment will encourage the native's furtherance of profound spiritual understanding and thus increase awareness of beauty. Social inhibitions are apt to fall by the wayside, permitting the native's expression of hidden artistic talents, often in painting, music and other art forms. The native' participation and cooperation with others in matters related to retreats, places of seclusion and medical, religious and educational institutions may give rise to opportunities in the social and romantic spheres of life. Creative, artistic self-expressions of the native may also receive support from these same institutions. Generally, this transit encourages the native's deeper appreciation of beauty, sympathy and compassion for others.

Should Venus make adverse transits to the natal planets while transiting this house, the native is apt to be involved in a secret romance.

Transit Venus Conjunctions

Transit Venus Conjunction Sun

This transit notes a period of increased romantic activity, and is particularly favorable for attracting members of the opposite sex. The native will exhibit a happier, more optimistic and outgoing outlook toward everyday affairs, thus disposing him or her toward a more agreeable, sunny and smiling character in relations with others. The fifth house-Leo connotation associated with the Sun's involvement here, when combined with Venus' artistic and refined nature, makes this an excellent combination for creative work, particularly for those engaged in artistic professions such as acting, painting, music and stage performances. Should the Sun and Venus be favorably aspected in the natal chart, investments and financial speculations involving business and dealings in art, music and entertainment are apt to show profit and personal benefit during this period. The native at this time may favorably seek the assistance of those of power and authority. Children and their education can be positively and progressively directed during the period of this transit. This transit is generally favorable for the native's creative self-expression in social and business activity, especially where these relate to the fields of music, art and entertainment.

Afflictions to Venus and/or the Sun in the natal chart can cause the native to overindulge in pleasurable and related social activities. This can result in the unnecessary and reckless misuse of financial resources in sensual pursuit or in unstable speculative ventures.

Transit Venus Conjunction Moon

This transit marks a favorable period for the improvement of the home environment, social activities conducted in the home, promotion of family life and associated endeavors. The native is apt to behave in a more considerate and helpful manner toward other family members during this transit, encouraging harmonious interactions in this important sphere of life. Family reunions can be planned with purposefulness and will be received in a favorable light. The native is prone to expend a considerable portion of financial resources to purchase art, kitchen appliances and creature comforts designed for convenience, esthetic taste and practicality. The double Taurus connotation of this transit (Venus' rulership and the Moon's exaltation) favor the native's involvement in business and financial affairs, particularly those dealing in real estate, food and domestic products. Women are frequently associated with such matters, and may draw the native into their social world as a result. Men undergoing this transit may find themselves strongly attracted to the opposite sex and, for those already engaged in intimate contacts or marriage, there is apt to be a renewal or reawakening of romantic feelings. During this transit the native will generally exhibit a peaceful, serene and emotionally stable attitude toward everyday affairs with the added benefit of a harmonious home and family environment.

Should either Venus or the Moon be afflicted in the natal horoscope, the native may be inclined to overindulge in rich food, thus creating the possibility of digestive problems or excess weight.

Transit Venus Conjunction Mercury

This transit of Venus denotes a period favorable to the native's harmonious communication with brothers, sisters, neighbors, business associates and romantic partners. Literary pursuits, particularly poetry and fiction that require a strong Venusian esthetic sense, can find positive expression at this time. The preparation of illustrations and graphics for publication, as well as other forms of artwork, can be effectively accomplished during this period. Advertising and other public appeals, especially through the media, are favored by this transit. The native will display greater consideration and sympathy for and with those with whom he or she is communicating or working. Speech and manner of communication will find wide audience among viewers, listeners or readers with whom the native's messages come into contact. Cooperation with those in the media, the formulation of legal contracts and the handling of business arrangements can provide the native with profitable contacts. Short journeys arranged for social purposes can be a source of personal pleasure and edification. Close ties and communication with friends will experience renewed interest and mutual participation, and may lead to the addition of others to the native's circle of friends. Esthetic concern of the native about personal appearance may lead to major alterations in his or her style of dress, for this is an excellent transit under which to purchase or refresh one's wardrobe. Under this transit the native may come to view and advocate artistic modes of expression as agents that help to heal mind, body and spirit. Thus, this transit is in general favorable to activities and particularly communication related to functions of a social, business or close personal nature.

Should either Venus or Mercury be heavily afflicted, there are apt to be misinterpretations of the native's intentions and expressions. This may result from bad timing or a lack of expertise in the social graces related to daily activities. Misunderstandings in personal communication can give rise to others' mistrust of the native's social and financial motives.

Transit Venus Conjunction Venus

This transit is favorable to the native's pursuit of artistic and social activities, particularly those involving women or promoting business affairs dealing with artistic endeavors and entertainment. The native is likely to become outgoing in personal expression, thus encouraging his or her presence at social functions and activities. Close cooperation and participation in activities with friends, business partners or associates, or a spouse or romantic partner could lead to unexpected business, romantic or marital opportunities. The native will express greater sympathy and consideration for those less fortunate, and will seek to be a source of comfort to them. Financial gain can be realized through business dealings in the fields of art and entertainment and during this period the native is apt to purchase luxury items. In general, the period of this transit is a favorable one for social engagements, artistic endeavors and the pursuit of romantic fulfillment.

Should Venus be heavily afflicted in the natal horoscope, the native may be inclined to force his or her presence and views upon others at social functions, thus alienating them. The native may assume a great deal in close personal relationships with others, and thus adopt a pretentious or haughty attitude toward those with whom he or she is dealing. There is a tendency to overspend on entertainment and luxury items, leading to financial embarrassment. These tendencies will not impress friends or romantic partners.

Transit Venus Conjunction Mars

This transit produces a period of increased social, romantic and sexual activity in the native's life. The native is apt to be increasingly attracted and attractive to the opposite sex. Artists, musicians, sculptors, actors and others engaged in the pursuit of creative expression through the arts are favored by this transit. This transit denotes a favorable period for the native's participation in business affairs, partnerships and corporate finances, for there is the probability of financial gain through attendance to these matters. Financial gain can also be realized through marriage, inheritance or joint financial ventures. In general, this transit indicates increased social, personal or physical expression directed toward artistic, corporate business or romantic objectives.

Afflictions to this transiting conjunction in the natal chart could give rise to jealousy in romantic relationships. Marital or intimate romantic attachments of the native could result in an unwanted pregnancy during this period. Matters related to business partnerships, marital relationships, inheritances or situations of joint finance can become a source of conflict should Mars be afflicted in the natal chart.

Transit Venus Conjunction Jupiter

This transit indicates a period of social activity revolving about the native's contacts and affairs of a religious, academic, travel or institutional nature. Social, romantic and business opportunities are apt to arise through associations with universities, churches, religious institutions or foreign cultures. Interest in religious art and music and the artistic manifestations of foreign cultures will experience a period of expansion and development because of the increased sensitivity and appreciative ability of the native. The native is likely to express himself or herself in a happier, more optimistic and socially outgoing manner, so this is thus a highly favorable time for him or her to embark upon a vacation or to visit a faraway place in the pursuit of pleasure. Inclinations toward greater generosity and consideration in dealing with those less fortunate may motivate the native to initiate or participate in the staging of benefits to raise funds for religious, charitable or educational institutions. This period is excellent for those involved in negotiations with foreign people or transacting business with established institutions.

Should this transiting conjunction be afflicted in the natal chart or by other transits, the native may be inclined toward excessive extravagance in financial expenditures.

Transit Venus Conjunction Saturn

This transit denotes a period in which the native develops a serious attitude toward business, legal matters, partnerships and other relationships requiring attention and assumption of responsibility. The native's personal manners and social interactions will become more practical, formal and reserved. Although the native's approach may lack warmth, he or she is apt to be involved in social activities related to professional, political and business matters. This period is unfavorable for initiating new romantic relationships because of the restraining influence of Saturn. Business, romantic and marital attachments will be either consolidated or severed. Some instances of this transit will instead indicate the establishment of a close personal or business relations with an older or accomplished individual, or may even bring the reactivation of an old love relationship. This transit will in general incline the native toward a more serious and practical attitude in dealing with situations and obligations on a personal or business level. Thus, it can be a good period for business and professional affairs, provided there are no serious afflictions.

Adverse transits or aspects in the natal chart to this transiting conjunction can produce social or financial difficulties deleterious to the career or profession of the native.

Transit Venus Conjunction Uranus

During this transit the native is apt to experiment with new social, romantic and business opportunities that arise through contacts with friends and group and organization activities. Sudden romantic attachments could have an unexpected impact upon the native's life. Financial gain and business advantages could arise through marriage partnerships, friends, organizations or corporate business affairs or through inheritance, gifts or the investment of other people's money. Creative endeavors benefit from original ideas, and in general the native will be inclined toward the unconventional in his or her approach to romantic, business and social activities during this period. Should this transiting conjunction be afflicted by other natal or transiting planets, impulsiveness in the native's behavior could cause him or her to terminate an existing romantic relationship or part company with business associates to pursue matters affording greater personal freedom or other romantic interests.

Transit Venus Conjunction Neptune

This transit is indicative of a period in which the native is apt to enter into secret or hidden relationships, often pertaining to romance, business or religion. The double Pisces connotation (Venus' exaltation, Neptune's rulership) of this transiting conjunction will incline the native to express kindness and generosity toward those less fortunate than, and in the event of his confinement to a hospital or institution, the native would likewise receive sympathetic treatment. This Pisces influence could also manifest itself through the native's interest in mysticism as expressed in religious or artistic motifs because this transit often brings a time of heightened sensitivity to beauty and enhancement of the artistic imagination. Musicians, artists, dancers, actors and sculptors are likely to receive inspiration from an intuitive level in their performance or creative, original self-expression. Afflictions to this transiting conjunction by other natal or transiting planets can cause the native to be deceived in money matters, romance, close personal relationships or business matters. Secret romantic affiliations could create serious personal difficulties and, under heavy affliction, result in scandal. Should the native be institutionalized during this transit, mistreatment could adversely affect the subconscious mind.

Transit Venus Conjunction Pluto

This transit marks a period in which the native is apt to become involved in intense personal and romantic relationships. The active initiation of these and other business partnerships will incline the native to eliminate those attachments and associations no longer of purposeful value so that the native might devote time and energy to more profitable enterprises. Close personal relationships inaugurated during this period can endow the native with a deep level of spiritual insight into such relationships. Or the desire could arise to remake, reform or remold those parties with whom the native is involved. Romantic attachments established at this time are apt to result in heavy sexual involvement. Financial opportunities can arise through the native's corporate business affairs, marriage, inheritance or joint finances. Intuitive inspiration is often received by those involved in artistic or musical pursuits. Generally speaking, however, this is apt to be an emotionally tense period. Should this transiting conjunction be afflicted by either natal or other transiting planets, sexual jealousy is likely to adversely affect close personal, romantic or marital relationships.

Transit Venus Sextiles

Transit Venus Sextile Sun

This transit is indicative of a period in which the native manifests greater creativity in artistic and social expression. Profitable ideas for the accumulation of wealth may result in participation in or initiation of business pursuits dealing with various forms of artistic endeavors, musical compositions or entertainment from which the native derives great pleasure. This is a propitious time to initiate communication with those in positions of power and authority because they are apt to provide the native with opportunities for creative self-expression that can be beneficial in either a financial or social way. Attention to children and their education under this transit and the time devoted to this purpose will be well spent. Generally, the native experiencing this transit will manifest a happier, sunnier and more outgoing disposition.

Transit Venus Sextile Moon

This transit indicates a time when communication with family members and those influencing the home and family is likely to establish a harmonious, cooperative and effective link between those concerned. Social activities initiated in the home environment are favorably influenced by the native's congeniality and comfortable disposition, and may even lead to the native's use of the home as a center or meeting place for group and organizational endeavors of a refined social or business nature. There can be financial gain through business activities related to the fields of art, music, entertainment, food, real estate, home and domestic products and services. The native could become romantically involved with a friend or group acquaintance. In general this transit will confer the native with a calm emotional disposition and a refined social sensitivity.

Transit Venus Sextile Mercury

This transit is indicative of a favorable period for social and business communications, including relationships between friends, neighbors, brothers, sisters, spouses and romantic partners. Business negotiations and the formulation of contracts will be easier to handle. Skill and diplomacy in communication will bring greater harmony with coworkers, employers, friends or group associates. Intellectual pursuits are apt to flow smoothly, particularly those requiring esthetic ability. Thus, poetic composition, writing, and the preparation of illustrations, layouts or drawings for publication are favored by this transit. Advertising campaigns or public appeals can be initiated and profitably carried out through the use of communication media. Overall, the native has an interest in enhancing personal attractiveness.

Transit Venus Sextile Venus

This transit indicates a period of harmonious romantic, business and social interaction. The native will tend to be more friendly and communicative in relationships with others. Business, social or professional activities, and particularly public relations work associated with these, are favored by this transit, as are social, musical and artistic events. Opportunities for financial gain are apt to arise through these involvements or through friends, neighbors and partners. For musicians and artists this marks a period of refined, creative achievement.

Transit Venus Sextile Mars

This transit indicates a period of increased social, romantic and sexual activity. Artists, musicians, performers and sculptors, are favored by this transit, for it confers them with energy and vitality to undertake and follow through in the active manifestation of their talent. Business partnerships dealing with corporate enterprises and ventures in the arts, music and entertainment are favored by this transit. The native may even discover and initiate new approaches to the acquisition of wealth through such business involvements. The native will express a more aggressive spirit in social and romantic activities which often involve short trips in the pursuit of these ends. Friends or group associates can become lovers or romantic partners. Physical activities, notably dancing, hiking, boating and other sports, are apt to appeal to the native. There may arise a fondness for stirring or exciting music, parades, concerts and other stimulating performances.

Transit Venus Sextile Jupiter

This transit produces a period of socially-oriented communication and travel. It is favorable for vacationing, travel, religious pilgrimages and journeys of an educational or business nature. The native will be more socially outgoing, happy and optimistic in attitude, expansive and "at one" with the world. Business dealings with foreigners and the study of foreign art, music and culture are favored by this transit. These activities could lead to social or romantic opportunities. Writers and artists could have opportunity to display or publish their works, thus gaining public recognition and financial remuneration for their efforts.

Transit Venus Sextile Saturn

This transit provides the native with the opportunity to make progress in serious business and artistic endeavors. It is a favorable period for establishing a business or professional partnership. There could be financial gain through carefully studied financial investments in art, luxury items or antiques. Public relations work and diplomatic dealings with individuals of wealth and status can be successfully initiated or concluded at this time. The native's sense of decorum, tact, and patience stimulated by this transit can be helpful in dealing with partners, business contacts and those of the opposite sex. Financial dealings and business affairs will be stabilized, organized and directed toward the native's greater security. Opportunities may arise for the native's romantic involvement with an older or a well established individual. The native may even experience the return or reappearance of an old love or close friend. This transit is generally favorable for serious, important social and financial dealings.

Transit Venus Sextile Uranus

This transit of Venus is indicative of a period during which the native will experience unusual, exciting and unexpected social and romantic opportunities, often originating through friends, groups, organizations or corporate business dealings. Artists and musicians will display greater inspiration and originality in their works during this period. Others experiencing this transit are apt to develop an interest in unusual forms of art or music. Electronic gadgetry or technological innovations could be adopted as a medium for expression in the native's business, artistic, musical or social activities. Unusual, inspired and original ideas directed toward financial gain may often involve the native in these fields. New friendships are apt to be established with unusual and creative individuals. In some cases, this transit can produce sudden marriage or partnership opportunities. Unexpected short-distance travel will often revolve about the native's social, romantic or business activities.

Transit Venus Sextile Neptune

This transit marks a period in which the native is apt to experience intuitive inspirations related to the fields of art, music, social activities, public relations and related businesses. The native's sense of beauty is enhanced by a subtle level of perception and may lead to an interest in religious art, the art of foreign cultures, photography or other artistic pursuits requiring a great deal of imagination. The native will express a kind and sympathetic attitude toward others, and will often display a particular willingness to help those less fortunate. Often, this will lead to his participation or involvement in religious, medical and charitable institutions, universities or travel, from whence the native can gain romantic, social or business opportunities.

Transit Venus Sextile Pluto

This transit of Venus provides the native with opportunities in business ventures, cooperative financial enterprises, social activities or romance. Corporate business projects are apt to show progress, especially if they deal in matters related to art, music, entertainment or luxury items. This transit notes a time for personal self-improvement and regeneration. The native will adopt a more socially outgoing attitude, and is apt to develop an interest in artistic and musical efforts as a means of spiritual upliftment. Sexual activity is likely to increase, and the native may be inclined toward a more spiritual concept of love with the desire to transform conditions surrounding him or her. Intuitive inspiration in artistic, musical and other creative endeavors is possible, resulting in the native's greater appreciation for the efforts of others and motivating his or her own personal expression toward artistic manifestation.

Transit Venus Squares

Transit Venus Square Sun

This transit of Venus is indicative of a period in which the native is apt to overindulge in social pleasures. Egotistical or narcissistic attitudes toward personal appearance, attractiveness and desirability are likely to develop. Expenditures on entertainment or pleasures designed to impress others are inclined to be excessively extravagant. The native's social obsessions and unwise lack of restraint in spending may even generate problems with those in authority. Inertia and the tendency to avoid responsibilities and unpleasant tasks are often the result of this transit, and may even incline the native toward overindulgence in dealing with children. Love affairs and romantic attachments are apt to suffer the difficulties of selfish interests on the part of one or both individuals, and ill-advised romantic engagements initiated at this time will produce problems later on.

Transit Venus Square Moon

During the period of this transit the native is apt to overindulge in dietary habits, with resultant health problems and a consequent lack of energy. He or she can become lazy and avoid responsibilities. Personal emotional difficulties involving family members or individuals coming into the home could degenerate into emotional hypersensitivity, the native imagining hurts and slights he or she feels are perpetrated by others. Overprotectiveness of family members, children or others with whom the native is emotionally attached can be easily aroused. Family finances could be a source of problems due to the native's extravagant expenditures on domestic and luxury items and food. Thus, the native's propensity for maudlin sentimentality and lack of clear perception in social, romantic and family affairs makes this an unfavorable period for participation in domestic or social activities.

Transit Venus Square Mercury

This transit is indicative of a period in which the native should exercise caution in social, romantic and business communication. Difficulties encountered in the occupational environment are apt to involve the employer, coworkers or superiors. Such problems could arise from the native's excessive chattering or socializing while on the job, resulting in inefficiency or the neglect of work and its consequent responsibilities. Health can suffer from excessive or incorrect dietary habits. The personal deportment, including dress and hygiene, can vary to extremes or in some cases could be simply neglected. Preoccupation with unimportant social details can cause the native experiencing this transit to overlook important issues, ignorance of which could adversely affect him or her. Social gossip will often create difficulties in personal relationships.

Transit Venus Square Venus

This transit denotes a period in which the native is inclined to adopt extremes of opinion in views on social, romantic, financial and marital affairs. Faulty esthetic taste and judgment can cause the native to spend a great deal of money on luxury items and pleasures, adversely reflecting on home or reputation. A propensity toward overindulgence in sex and the pursuit of other pleasures can cause problems in close personal relationships. The native could, under such conditions, develop an extreme emotional hypersensitivity to his or her own needs and desires, while failing at the same time to maintain an awareness of the feelings and needs of others. Carried to the opposite extreme, this transit could also cause the native to become foolishly or unnecessarily sympathetic to the desires of others, thus exposing the native to the emotional impact of their problems as well as encouraging them to use the native to attain their own selfish objectives. The planning of social activities or expenditure of large amounts of money on pleasure or luxury items should thus be deferred or postponed to some future date, and diligent caution should be exercised in business and financial dealings.

Transit Venus Square Mars

This transit of Venus marks a period in which the native is prone to emotional slights and injured feelings or apt to experience difficulties in social, financial and romantic affairs. Tact and diplomacy will be lacking in romantic and social situations. The native's consequent overt aggressiveness in pursuit of romantic satisfaction can lead to emotional and sexual overindulgence or ill-advised sexual or romantic attachments. Such inappropriate social behavior or sexual jealousy could cause problems in established romantic or marital relationships. Extravagance in financial expenditures on pleasure, business or luxury items often stems from the native's uncontrolled desire for sensual gratification, and may frequently lead to conflict or problems over joint finances, corporate financial affairs, taxes, inheritances, insurance in business partnerships or alimony. Such difficulties may in turn adversely affect the native's public reputation and social standing.

Transit Venus Square Jupiter

This transit of Venus inclines the native toward overoptimism in financial, educational, religious and social affairs. Unnecessary expenditures and overexpansion in business affairs, social activities and pleasures should be carefully avoided during this transit, for they can deplete the native's budget and thus cause disharmony in partnerships, marriage or other close relationships. Excessive social involvement can also result in failure to accomplish work or study objectives. As with other adverse Venus transits, the native is prone to indifference and laziness in personal habits and maudlin sentimentality and misplaced sympathy. Thus, the native should not put off until tomorrow what can be done today, while taking care not to overextend himself or herself. This is not a favorable period in which to deal with churches, hospitals, universities or other institutions, nor is it a time to embark upon vacations or long journeys for they are apt to prove to be more costly than anticipated.

Transit Venus Square Saturn

This transit often indicates social, financial and romantic problems and disappointments. Business and financial affairs will experience difficulties in their anticipated progress, for there will be many obstacles to be overcome. Those in positions of established authority or involved in the field of public relations will not be favorably disposed toward the native's views and may even block or delay achievement of occupational objectives. The native is thus apt to adopt a coldness, stiffness or formality in professional dealings, an attitude that will often carry over into family matters and relationships. Feelings of rejection or being unloved can cause the native to react in a cold and unsympathetic manner to the emotional needs of others. Thus problems, even estrangements, will often be experienced in marital and other close personal relationships during this transit.

Transit Venus Square Uranus

This transit of Venus disposes the native toward involvement in ill-advised, unstable romantic and sexual relationships. During this period the native is likely to meet an individual whose magnetic personality holds great fascination. Although an attachment or affinity with another may be thoroughly enjoyed, the native's improper appraisal of his or her involvement could draw the native into a situation possessing neither good nor permanent consequences. Partnerships, friendships and romantic affiliations important to the native's well-being may be terminated under this transit, thus creating difficulties in future attempts to reestablish or reinstate such relationships. The initiation of marital or other forms of close partnership should be delayed or postponed to some future date. Friends or group associates can influence the native to engage in unwise or excessive social activity, encouraging expenditure of time and money in expansive although non-productive involvements. Corporate business affairs are likely to be beset by unforeseen factors disruptive to the native's financial plans. The unreliability of others' behavior may often result in serious setbacks to the native's professional progress and consequent advancement. Advertising, promotion and public relations work will be difficult at best. Caution should be exercised when participating in occult or psychic activities, particularly those dealing with sexual magic.

Transit Venus Square Neptune

This transit of Venus indicates a period when the native is subject to deceptive practices, either of his or her own making or on the part of others in romantic, social and business affairs. Business dealings initiated during this transit will often possess hidden flaws unapparent at their outset. This is frequently due to the native's lack of perception in his estimation of the work and expense necessary to their achievement. A Utopian, idealistic disposition generated by this transit will often lead to the native's psychological withdrawal or regression into a detached dream world. Thus, decisions on esthetic matters are likely to reflect faulty judgment and a neglect of practical business and social responsibilities. Secret love affairs during this transit are apt to have undesirable long-range consequences. Such private or personal matters could fall subject to scandal and public exposure, resulting in social embarrassment. Emotional problems involving the native and other family members are likely to surface in a more pronounced fashion, demanding the native's attention to and resolution of their underlying motivations.

Transit Venus Square Pluto

This transit will incline the native toward involvement in ill-advised sexual relationships, thus creating difficulties in close personal, and particularly romantic, attachments. Marital and romantic partnerships may often suffer the effects of sexual jealousy during this transit. A tendency to adopt a "me first" attitude and its consequent lack of consideration for the emotional feelings of others can hinder the native's social progress. Partnerships and close personal friendships must be diplomatically handled during this period to avoid a severance of their association with the native. The handling of important corporate business affairs or matters of joint finance should be deferred to some future time, and moderation should be exercised in necessary or immediate financial expenditures. Financial holdings and valuable possessions should be protected, in the event of their loss or theft. Conflict is likely to arise over insurance, taxes, inheritances or alimony.

Transit Venus Trines

Transit Venus Trine Sun

This transit of Venus enhances the native with charm, enabling him or her to cooperate in public or close personal relationships. A happier, sunnier disposition will attract good fortune and permit the native greater freedom in creative expressions. Approaches to those in power or authority will be favorably viewed and may even obtain the native favors and promotions. Involvements in business enterprises related to the fields of art, music, entertainment or children and their education are beneficially influenced by this transit. The devotion of time and energy to children and their education and social activity during this transit will be favorably rewarded. Social activities and entertaining will offer the native plentiful opportunities and provide needed contacts who will further the native's social, professional and romantic objectives. Musicians, singers, artists, actors and performers will particularly appreciate this transit because of the refined, creative spirit that enhances personal self-expression. The combination of the nature of the trine aspect (first to fifth house) and the involvement of the Sun and Venus here (Sun accidentally exalted in the first house and natural ruler of the fifth, Venus' natural rulership of the seventh) is helpful to the marriage relationship.

Transit Venus Trine Moon

This transit of Venus is conducive to the native's involvement in business affairs dealing with art, music, entertainment, luxury items, food and domestic products and services and denotes an excellent period to plan family gatherings and social activities in the home. Artistic creativity will manifest itself in the native's pursuit of various fields of expression and their associated media. The native will endeavor to beautify his or her home and surroundings with new art, furniture, decorations or kitchen utensils and gadgetry. Popularity with women is conferred the native by this transit, making this an excellent period for romance and social activity. Often, women of wealth and prominence will assist the native in business affairs.

Transit Venus Trine Mercury

This transit of Venus stimulates the native's participation in social activities and increased communication in relationships with friends, brothers, sisters, neighbors and group associates. Often, the native will travel in connection with social and romantic endeavors and opportunities. The aptitude of the native for original, creative ideas at this time makes this an excellent transit during which to pursue artistic and literary expressions and activities. Thus, efforts in the fields of advertising, public relations and the news media will be favorably viewed during this period. The desire for pleasantness and beauty in the working environment may incline the native to make improvements in occupational conditions or to ask for a raise. Relationships with coworkers will be much more pleasant because of a concern for their well-being as well as the native's own.

Transit Venus Trine Venus

This transit of Venus favors social and romantic activities. Friendship, business partnership, marriage and close personal relationships can be advantageously initiated at this time because the native attracts good fortune through kindness toward and consideration for others. Businesses related to the fields of art, music, entertainment and luxury items often flourish during this transit and, as a result, the native is apt to acquire and accumulate works of art, objects for personal adornment and luxury items of considerable value. The native's attendance at social activities, particularly concerts, parties and art exhibits, may offer various opportunities to widen and enhance the scope of his or her artistic tastes. Performances by artists, musicians, singers and actors are often of exceptional quality during this transit.

Transit Venus Trine Mars

This transit marks a favorable period for business, social, romantic and sexual relationships because the native will display greater vitality, enthusiasm and personal magnetism in pursuit of these and related objectives at this time. Actors, musicians, performing artists and others who utilize energy, expertise and enthusiasm in their work will benefit from this transit. Dancing and sports in particular, as well as other pleasurable physical activities, will be helpful at this time. Corporate business affairs and financial investments can be favorably initiated during this transit, particularly those dealing with members of the opposite sex, whether such relations be specifically business or intrinsically influence the romantic sphere. Financial gain may come to the native through gifts, inheritances, marriage or financial partnerships. Women who wish to become pregnant are more apt to become so under this transit.

Transit Venus Trine Jupiter

This transit of Venus provides an excellent period for travel, vacations and social activities related to churches, universities and other cultural institutions. Negotiations with hospitals and other institutions can be favorably initiated or concluded, particularly if these are designed to benefit those less fortunate than the native. Involvement in fund-raising activities for religious, educational or charitable causes will also produce favorable results during this transit. Businesses dealing with imported or exported items or with foreigners and foreign countries are furthered by this transit. Social and romantic activities will progress harmoniously at this time and may even afford the native additional opportunities to further his or her objectives in this sphere of activity. Young people and children are apt to play an important role in these affairs during this period. In general, this transit will witness the native's development of a happy, optimistic and philosophical outlook toward life.

Transit Venus Trine Saturn

This transit of Venus favors those involved in serious artistic pursuits, the composition or performance of classical music, professional businesses or social dealings with older or established individuals. Often, such relationships with more mature, established persons will be of a romantic or business nature. During this transit, the native will exercise an increased sense of responsibility toward the handling of money and accumulated wealth. Thus, the native is apt to acquire objets d'art, antiques and other belongings or furnishings whose value increases with age. Greater circumspection in manners and social behavior makes this a favorable period for the native to handle public relations, especially where his or her attitude and deportment directly influence business or diplomatic affairs. Business and professional partnerships will benefit from the steady and lasting progress that can be made at this time. Although the effects of this transit are neither obvious nor immediate in their import, the native, in a quiet, meditative search for beauty and happiness, does acquire positive, durable values in his or her approach to human relations, business and financial affairs. Old friendships may be renewed, as may past romantic attachments, and in marital relationships the native will display a greater sense of responsibility toward both his or her mate and professional obligations.

Transit Venus Trine Uranus

This transit of Venus presents the native with unusual and often unexpected social, romantic and business opportunities arising through business affairs, friends, occult endeavors, group activities or matters dealing specifically with modern technological innovations and techniques. This is an excellent transit for creative artists, for it confers the ability to express a great degree of originality and intuitive inspiration. Often, unusual technological approaches to art form and musical composition are inaugurated during this period. Unusual partnership opportunities often arise under this transit, for the native will manifest greater personal magnetism and a more adventuresome spirit in the search for new friendships and social ties. In establishing relationships with new, exciting and gifted people, the native may encounter sudden, stirring romantic opportunities of benefit to him or her in the furtherance of marital objectives. This transit will in general confer the native with a sparkling, joyous and convivial personality during its transit.

Transit Venus Trine Neptune

This transit of Venus indicates a period in which the native becomes sensitive to subtle spiritual and esthetic values. Imagination and perception of beauty are enhanced, and the native will be inclined to express kindness and sympathetic compassion toward others, particularly those less fortunate. Negotiations and other dealings with hospitals, institutions and religious organizations can be favorably handled and concluded during this transit. This is an excellent period for musicians and artists of all types, as well as for businesses dealing with works of art, music and luxury items, for it stimulates the intuitive imagination and confers the native with an appreciation for manifestations of the subconscious mind, and psychic faculties. Rewarding experiences often arise through partnerships and romantic relationships, and during this period an ideal love could appear on the scene. Travel, vacations and religious pilgrimages can be successfully initiated and enjoyed at this time. Karmic returns could bring the native gifts or financial rewards for past virtuous actions and confer harmony and understanding in family relationships.

Transit Venus Trine Pluto

This transit provides a period of increased intuitive inspiration in artistic, musical and other creative endeavors. The inauguration of business partnerships and involvement in business affairs, financial speculation or businesses related to art, music, entertainment and luxury items are favored during this period. Frequently, the native will become involved in business or artistic pursuits dedicated to the restoration or renovation of material objects, especially art objects, paintings and the like. New methods of earning money, accumulating wealth or handling business affairs are apt to be introduced into the native's day-to-day affairs. Needed medical and surgical treatment can be properly and successfully diagnosed and handled at this time. Partnerships, close friendships and marital relationships often assume a new and improved outlook during this transit, or exciting and stimulating romantic opportunities may enter the native's life.

Transit Venus Oppositions

Venus' benefic quality and its natural rulership of the seventh house and the sign Libra, corresponding to the natural zodiacal opposition influence (first to seventh house), behooves us to view its transiting oppositions in a more favorable light. However, these aspects still require that the native extend a willingness to cooperate and show consideration for the rights and feelings of others. Adherence to these principles will confer benefits in material and emotional ways through business, romantic and marital relationships.

Transit Venus Opposition Sun

This transit is indicative of a period in which the native is apt to enter a phase of romantic, social, business or marital involvement, but it will only be through expressions of optimism, consideration, friendliness and cooperative spirit that progressive gains can be made through such associations. Narcissistic and self-centered attitudes surfacing at this time will usually result in rejection or censure by others. Arrogant and authoritative attitudes are apt to arouse feelings of resentment and disgust. Caution should be carefully exercised in business affairs and financially speculative ventures. Extravagant expenditures designed to impress others, particularly expenses on social activities, luxury items, lavish entertainment and other liberal gestures, often result in financial depletion and less than favorable reactions on the part of others. Often, these expositions will be interpreted as expressions of personal vanity or grandiose devices patterned to fulfill some personal motive.

Transit Venus Opposition Moon

This transit of Venus necessitates the native's proper exercise of diplomacy and emotional sensitivity in family and domestic relationships. At the same time, excessive emotional displays and maudlin sentimentality must also be forgone lest they interfere or adversely influence business, romantic and social relationships. Real or imagined emotional slights and hurts, especially those involving family members, should be carefully weighed and handled in a tactful and definitive manner. Financial affairs in marital, business and family relationships will become subject to emotional conflict, and again, an attitude of cautious optimism should be employed in the native's response to such stimuli. Business and public relations efforts dealing with real estate, food, home and domestic products and services should be handled with care, as should the native's purchasing of luxury items and expensive home furnishings. Difficulties are often caused by the native's over-indulgence in food and its accompanying emotional frustration. Defense mechanisms, particularly excessive food consumption, triggered by the native's subconscious desires and emotional memories, are apt to be a source of difficulty during this transit. Thus, dealings with women during this period must be subjected to the most careful and objective scrutiny before action is taken.

Transit Venus Opposition Mercury

This transiting opposition of Venus often produces confusion and misunderstanding in the native's social, romantic and business communication. Idle gossip, particularly that arising from misquotation of the native's true intent, can cause difficulties, if not a complete breakdown, of close personal relationships. This is especially true in relations with brothers, sisters, neighbors, friends and business associates. Delays in the forwarding or receipt of mail or other communication will be a source of confusion in business activities, rendering this period a poor time to sign business contracts or conclude financial agreements. Excessive socializing while on the job can result in confrontations with the native's employer and associated inefficiency. The native is apt to be careless in matters of personal hygiene and health during this period, and may often exercise poor judgment in selection of personal attire. Thus, personal appearance is likely to suffer a lack of proper bearing. Extravagant expenditures on clothing and apparel for personal adornment may cause the native to project an image unbecoming to his or her natural character. During this transit, the native is apt to confuse directions and become lost while trying to find the home of a friend or the site of a social function.

Transit Venus Opposition Venus

During the period of this transit, the native should avoid extravagant expenditures on social activities, luxury items and other unnecessary objects or notions, for this is neither a favorable time to purchase goods nor to engage in business or personal activities related to art, music, entertainment or public relations. Marriage, partnerships and business agreements consummated at this time will be subject to the native's emotional hypersensitivity and reactions to imagined slights by others. The native's judgment is likely to be distorted by emotional factors associated with such close personal relationships. Difficulties may block the native's ability to either give or receive love during this transit, and social activities are apt to be filled with subtle innuendoes. This is a period during which the native should try to see things from the point of view of others. Unwise self-indulgence should be avoided.

Transit Venus Opposition Mars

This transit marks a period in which the native is apt to encounter difficulties in romantic, marital, sexual or business relationships. Emotional impulsiveness and uncontrolled desires can involve the native in undesirable love relationships or situations conducive to sexual jealousy. Excessive sexual indulgence will often lead to physical depletion and a lack of energy in the native's handling of everyday affairs. Marriages, partnerships and close personal relationships can experience strife and the negative effects of emotional confrontations. This is not a favorable time during which to handle important corporate dealings or to formulate business contracts, for conflict is likely to arise over joint finances, business partnerships, taxes, insurance or, in the event of a divorce, alimony, any of which can affect the solvency of the native. To achieve the most advantageous use of this transit the native must exercise emotional control, restraint and tact in dealings with others. The native is obliged to consider the principles of justice and fair play in all actions if he or she is to handle these matters in a harmonious fashion.

Transit Venus Opposition Jupiter

This transit of Venus is indicative of a period of personal excess in the native's life, whether it be overeating, overspending, sexual over-indulgence or over-participation in social activities. The native will find it difficult to say no to social invitations or to another drink or another piece of pie. Sentimentality can get the better of the native during this transit. Thus, the native is likely to lack good judgment and discrimination. This transit is not favorable for a marriage. Nor is it conducive to the native's involvement with religious matters or business promoters that promise salvation and riches in return for contributions. Excessive spending on vacations, trips, social activities or luxury items should be curbed, lest they later result in a financial pinch.

Transit Venus Opposition Saturn

During this transit the native is apt to develop a cold and harsh attitude toward the emotional feelings of others, often marking a critical period that can make or break a marriage, close friendship or business partnership. Delays and difficulties are likely to be experienced m business and financial affairs. Disagreements may even erupt into conflict in marital or business partnerships over the handling of money or financial matters. Poor or unwise past management of resources will reflect in the pinch and restriction the native feels at this time. Heavy work responsibilities could prevent or obstruct the native's participation in social or romantic activities, entailing a lack of opportunities in this sphere of action for the duration of this transit. This is not a favorable time to request the patronage or assistance of elderly, established individuals, or the native's employer or those in positions of authority; nor is it propitious for marriage or the inauguration of business or social activities.

Transit Venus Opposition Uranus

This transit marks a period in which the native is apt to be enticed into romantic and sexual relationships possessing no lasting value. Friends and business associates may draw the native into unwise social or financial activities. There is the possibility of breaks in friendships and group affiliations, and new acquaintances attracted under this transit will more than likely be unreliable and short-lived. Conflicts arising in marriage, business partnerships and other close relationships will often revolve around joint finances, corporate money, inheritance, taxes, insurance or alimony. The impulsive expenditure of financial resources will often be the cause of such problems. Infidelity and sexual jealousy could provoke the termination of a marriage or romantic relationship. The native should exercise caution in business dealings related to the fields of art, music, entertainment, electronics and other forms of modern technology, and above all, avoid involvement with those promoting get-rich-quick schemes.

Transit Venus Opposition Natal Neptune

During this transit of Venus, the native becomes subject to deception, and particularly self-deception, in marital, financial, business or romantic relationships. This is often due to the native's sentimental nature and failure to perceive reality in its true light. Thus the native is apt to lack discrimination and wisdom in well-intentioned attempts to bestow affection and kindness. Peculiar mystical groups and cults of dubious value may appeal to the native during this transit, participation in which should be carefully monitored and understood lest he or she be deceptively used by such groups to accomplish ulterior or secret motives. This is not a favorable period for the formulation of business agreements or partnerships, for there are often hidden factors coincident to such contracts that are detrimental to the native's well-being. Particular wariness should be exercised when dealing with those advocating questionable business negotiations and get-rich-quick schemes. Also possible during this transit is the native's involvement in secret love affairs that could be detrimental to his or her reputation. Although imagination and vision are enhanced by this transit, the native is apt to lack practicality or good taste in pursuit of artistic and musical interests.

Transit Venus Opposition Pluto

During this transit of Venus, the native is apt to experience difficulties in business, corporate, financial, romantic and sexual relationships. The native is particularly subjective to uncontrolled desires, which can cause an inconsiderate, selfish disposition toward the emotional feelings of others, resulting in permanent damage to the native's reputation and business relationships. This transit is not conducive to the reorganization or improvement of the native's business, social or financial affairs or relationships, for conflict is apt to arise over corporate or joint finances, insurance, taxes, alimony or business partnerships. Reformative or regenerative attempts contrived to benefit or correct existing debilities in these areas are likely to arouse the resentment and opposition of others. The native should exercise caution in business dealings and avoid those individuals of questionable moral integrity. Sexual jealousy can be a continual source of problems in marital and romantic relationships during this transit. It is advisable to shy away from large crowds and social gatherings while the native is experiencing this transit, for there is the ever-present danger of uncontrolled rowdy mass behavior injurious to his or her well-being.

V

Transits of Mars

Mars transits act as energizing, exciting, activating influences in the life of the native. These transits are usually accompanied by strong desires and an impulse to action. This Martian energy can be expressed through useful accomplishments. However, if the energy is not properly handled, it can manifest itself in outbursts of anger or violence or in willful, impulsive acts.

It is important to consider the stationary and retrograde periods of Mars. During these periods Mars can occupy a single sign or house for periods of up to six months. Major changes result in the affairs ruled by that sign or house. These affairs are, in turn, linked to the houses where Aries, Scorpio, and Capricorn are found in the natal chart.

If Mars makes important transiting aspects during one of these stationary periods, the positions often indicate decisive turning points in the life of an individual. This will be more pronounced if the transit involves a natal aspect to Mars. In any event, changes will be evident in the affairs led by the house Mars transits during its stationary periods.

When Mars is stationary while progressing from retrograde to direct motion, the native will begin a new trend in his or her actions. This becomes more noticeable when Mars once again resumes forward motion.

When Mars is stationary in progression from direct to retrograde motion, the native may be forced to delay his or her present course of action and go back to handle unfinished business. The house and natal planets experiencing the retrograde period of Mars will be subject to prolonged action and unrest.

The cycles of Mars are very important in the life of any individual. It takes Mars approximately two years to pass through all the signs of the zodiac, and during this cycle, transiting Mars forms a conjunction, square or opposition to each natal planet about once every six months. These transitory aspects touch off periodic crises in affairs ruled by the respective planets.

If Mars is natally aspected to the planet affected by transit Mars, the effects will be that much stronger, and should the natal Mars be conjunct, square, opposition or inconjunct the transiting aspect, a serious crisis will precipitate each time the natal aspect is set off.

These cycles should be observed carefully by every serious astrological student because they often mark the beginning or conclusion of important affairs in the native's life.

Transits of Mars Through the Houses

The transits of Mars through the natal houses of the horoscope show the practical affairs of life that are influenced during that period by dynamic action, motivated in turn by desire.

If Mars makes favorable transits to natal planets and is well-aspected in the natal horoscope, the native will further his or her constructive ambitions in an organized fashion and achieve worth- while goals through personal effort.

If Mars is afflicted in the natal chart and makes unfavorable transit aspects in a particular house, the native can be exposed to danger through the affairs ruled by that house. The native can pre- cipitate rash, ill-considered acts which may lead to conflict and loss in matters ruled by the house Mars is transiting. There is a tendency for the native to become impatient and lose his or her temper in dealing with such matters.

Transit Mars Through the First House

This transit of Mars is particularly important because Mars rules Aries. Therefore, it is acciden- tally dignified in the first house, corresponding to Aries in the natural zodiac. Mars in this posi- tion initiates a period of greater self-assertion and personal physical activity. The native will feel physically energetic. This energy can manifest itself in work, sports, exercise or restless- ness, if it is not directed.

If Mars makes unfavorable transits in the first house and is afflicted in the natal horoscope, the native could be exposed to physical danger, accident or injury. An overly aggressive and self-centered attitude could result, bringing resentment and conflict from others. In any event, the native will be more competitive during this transit.

If Mars makes favorable transits and is well-aspected while transiting the first house, the native can improve his or her health and vitality through exercise. The native can also conclude vital projects requiring physical exertion and take confident, positive action in self-expression.

Transit Mars Through the Second House

This transit position of Mars indicates dynamic personal action directed toward financial gain and acquisition of material possessions. The native could become involved in business related to manufacturing construction machinery, steel industries, corporate affairs and aggressive sales efforts. He or she could work with, acquire or sell property related to these things.

If Mars is afflicted in the natal horoscope and makes stress transits while in the second house, there could be conflict over money or frustration over money or possessions. The material desires of the native could bring difficulty during this period. The danger of theft or loss of money or possessions is present and the native could become angry over the mishandling of financial affairs. There is also the possibility that the native's financial aggressiveness or impulsive expenditures could cause conflict.

If Mars is favorably aspected in the natal horoscope and makes favorable transits while in this house the native can make financial gains through enterprising work and business activity.

Transit Mars Through the Third House

Mars transiting the third house emphasizes the active, energetic pursuit of knowledge and practical information. Natives are to become involved in heated discussions and debates. There could be much communication in professional and corporate affairs, although an afflicted Mars at this time would not be conducive to the settlement of contracts and legal disputes. In some cases natives with the transit become involved in secret investigations or with the news media. There is likely to be much coming and going, with particular regard to automobiles and other means of transportation.

However, adverse transits of Mars in this house increase the danger of automobile accidents due to carelessness or recklessness, along with the likelihood of traffic citations. Afflictions to transiting Mars could bring troubles with brothers, sisters or neighbors.

Favorable transits in this house mark a period suitable for the initiation of action to implement creative and original ideas.

Transit Mars Through the Fourth House

The transit of Mars through the fourth house is apt to bring upsetting circumstances or conditions in the home and family. If Mars makes favorable aspects while in this house, the native will have the motivation and energy to make necessary improvements in the domestic area. This could amount to a good house cleaning or a home improvement project.

If Mars makes adverse aspects while transiting this house, the native could be injured in the home or become involved in domestic quarrels and conflicts. Here, there is danger from fire and the breakdown of appliances. The native may have to deal with aggressive or objectionable people who come into the home. The transit of Mars through the fourth house can stir up deep psychological memories relating to family upbringing that could be emotionally upsetting for the native.

Transit Mars Through the Fifth House

Transiting Mars in the fifth house usually emphasizes the native's aggressive pursuit of pleasure, romance or creative self-expression of some kind. The native can become involved in physical sports or activities requiring muscular exertion. This is especially true with children. This transit intensifies the sex drive, resulting in serious sexual involvements.

If Mars is afflicted in the natal horoscope and makes adverse aspects while in this house, conflict could arise over sexual jealousy or frustration. There could be a lack of sensitivity and refinement in sexual pursuits. Under adverse transits natives are prone to act impulsively or rashly where investments are concerned. The probability of injuries or accidents through sports or other forms of physical activity increases under this affliction, an loud, uncouth horseplay during parties or at social affairs is not uncommon.

If Mars is well aspected, this could be a good period for initiating activities involving the education of children, especially in the area of physical education.

Mars Transit Through the Sixth House

Mars transits through the sixth house indicate much physical activity concerning work, service and health.

If Mars is afflicted in the natal horoscope and makes adverse transits while in this house, work an be disagreeable and conflict could arise with coworkers or employers. This transit is often related to strikes and labor disputes. Care should be taken to avoid occupational hazards during this transit, especially if the native uses tools, machinery or dangerous chemicals at work. Work-related stress can result in illness if Mars is afflicted. Many natives undergo surgery during this transit of an afflicted Mars, and medical problems can arise due to high fevers or accidents.

A well-aspected Mars while transiting this house will give the native the energy to be effective at work, accomplishing more than would ordinarily be the case. This is especially true if the work requires physical exertion or if it is related to engineering or manufacturing.

Mars Transit Through the Seventh House

Mars transits through the seventh house mark periods of great activity in the public sphere or corporate or professional partnerships. There is apt to be a close relationship with a dynamic, active person who will prod the native into action.

If Mars is afflicted in the natal horoscope and makes adverse contacts while transiting the seventh house, there can be conflict in partnership and marital relationships. The native could be overly aggressive toward others or they could be aggressive toward him or her. A likely result of this is conflict or disagreement which, in extreme cases, can bring about open enmity and even physical confrontation. A heavily afflicted Mars in this transit brings the danger of lawsuits, divorce and separation.

Mars Transit Through the Eighth House

This transit indicates dynamic activity in the sphere of business affairs. In some manner, the native is likely to be affected by death or the affairs of the dead. If Mars is afflicted in the natal horoscope and makes adverse aspects while transiting this house, there can be danger to life and limb or someone important to the native could pass on. The native could become acquainted with the occult. This isn't a favorable time to expose oneself to danger or situations of violence, especially if Mars is afflicted. The native could be involved in police investigations or in political or military strategy.

Under favorable aspects, this position could indicate inheritance, insurance, tax refunds, gifts, grants or investments.

Mars Transit Through the Ninth House

Mars transits through the ninth house emphasize a desire for travel, adventure and the aggressive pursuit of educational, philosophic or religious goals. During this transit the native could become a crusader for some favorite religious, educational, social or philosophic cause.

If Mars is afflicted while transiting this house, there is the danger of becoming a fanatic in the promotion of one's religious, educational or cultural convictions. There can also be danger while traveling due to accidents or conditions of unrest and strife in far away places. For those attending universities, there may be involvement in campus riots, political demonstrations or conflict with the college administration. The native could become involved in conflicts or arguments over religious beliefs.

Mars Transit Through the Tenth House

Mars transits through the tenth house produce aggressive ambition to further one's career. There can be active involvement in politics, corporate business or other activities designed to achieve greater status and personal authority.

If Mars is afflicted in the natal horoscope and makes adverse aspects while transiting this house, the native may become involved in professional or political power struggles. Authoritarian attitudes could result in conflict and difficulty in professional and political affairs.

If Mars is well aspected while transiting this house, the native can make important professional advances by initiating career activities and putting more energy into work. This can be a favorable transit for professions related to manufacturing, construction, police work, military service and large scale corporate enterprises.

Mars Transit Through the Eleventh House

Mars transits through this house indicate dynamic action in pursuit of personal goals and objectives connected with friends, groups and organizations. The native is apt to be motivated to take an active leadership role in group and organizational affairs. He or she will associate with friends who spur action or vice versa. There can be energetic and aggressive activity in support of scientific, humanitarian and political causes or reforms.

If Mars is afflicted in the natal horoscope and makes adverse aspects while transiting this house, there can be conflict or disagreement with friends or competition for leadership and control in groups and organizations. The native and his or her friends could encourage each other to become involved in risky or dangerous enterprises.

Mars Transit Through the Twelfth House

Mars transits through the twelfth house bring much behind the scenes activity in private affairs and psychological concerns. If Mars makes favorable aspects while transiting the twelfth house, the native can do constructive work in hospitals, religious institutions, prisons and other institutions. An interest in probing the subconscious mind might also surface, and investigations and activities may be carried on in secret so as to avoid confrontation and opposition.

If Mars is afflicted while transiting this house, the native could become implicated in secret intrigues or have secret enemies. This transit can stir up desires in the subconscious mind causing the native to act in peculiar or self-destructive ways through dishonesty, secret sexual involvements or concealed aggressive actions. If Mars is severely afflicted, this could bring about incarceration in a prison or institution or, at best, the native could be subject to maltreatment or persecution while in such circumstances.

Transit Mars Conjunctions

Transit Mars Conjunction Sun

This transit indicates an increase of energy and ambition. The native will seek to extend personal initiative and authority. He or she will demonstrate prowess in physical competitions and political ambitions and strive to succeed in professional and business affairs. If carried to extremes, the native can arouse opposition and resentment because of a tendency to disregard the autonomy and independence of others. In general, this aspect is a prime determining factor of personal action and initiative. During this transit, the native's competitiveness and ambition may lead to rash and impulsive actions where greater caution, deliberation and cooperation would better serve his or her purpose. Much depends on how Mars and the Sun are aspected in the natal horoscope, as well as other transit influences occurring at the same time. This is a powerful transit that can lead to constructive accomplishment if properly handled. The action involved often relates to some form of physical exertion which could be sports, outdoor activities, use of tools, or programs of physical exercise. This can be a favorable transit for natives who need to develop qualities of personal initiative, willpower and self-confidence. Natives who already have these qualities may attempt decisive actions which will further their ambitions and extend their sphere of personal influence.

If the conjunction is afflicted, the native should avoid becoming impatient or angry. Care should be taken to exercise diplomacy and consideration in dealing with people in positions of power and authority. The native could make aggressive advances in the romantic area to satisfy sexual and romantic desires. The native could develop an interest in the education of children, especially concerning their physical development and social adjustment.

Transit Mars Conjunction Moon

This transit indicates a period of possible upset for the native. If Mars and the Moon are well aspected natally, during this transit the native could become active in do-it-yourself home improvement projects or energetic family activities. If transiting Mars and natal Mars and Moon are afflicted, this transit often brings about emotional upsets, family quarrels and disruptive circumstances in the home, usually involving women. This is a good period to exercise extra caution in regard to domestic fire hazards and other dangers that could be the cause of accidents in the home. This is especially so where machinery, guns, knives, tools and sharp objects are concerned. The native often experiences indigestion caused by emotional upset or frustration. If Mars is afflicted, this transit frequently produces ulcers of the stomach. The native should avoid eating when emotionally upset. An afflicted Mars can cause quarrels and disagreements over domestic finances. Unpleasant emotional scenes can result from confrontations with women. In general there could be dynamic activities involving women. Women undergoing this transit can become aggressive in defense of their gender and personal emotional attitudes. If Mars is afflicted, men undergoing this transit can become aggravated with women and these confrontations often involve issues of family finances.

Mars Transit Conjunction Mercury

This transit indicates that the native will become intellectually ambitious and active. However, there is present the danger of making rash impulsive decisions and being prone to nervousness, irritability and argument. If the native can remain calm, he or she can accomplish much in the areas of writing, communication, media, scientific investigation, research, short-distance travel and business negotiations. This is a good transit for seeking knowledge and improving one's education and mental abilities. There is likely to be a great deal of communication and interaction with neighbors, brothers and sisters, or matters related to friends, work or health.

If this conjunction is afflicted by natal or other transiting aspects, there can be danger of automobile or other accidents. Caution is the word during this transit.

Mars Transit Conjunction Venus

This transit indicates an increased sex drive. During this transit the native is likely to become involved in romantic and sexual relationships. Unless other factors indicate a deeper level of understanding, these attractions may be of a physical nature. This transit marks a period when pregnancy is likely for women of child-bearing age and ability. The native will become more aggressive in seeking social activity and excitement. However, to obtain the greatest benefit, diplomacy and consideration should be used with the opposite sex. This can be a productive period for artistic and creative endeavors. It can also be a favorable time to conduct business affairs related to art, music and entertainment.

Mars Transit Conjunction Mars

This transit indicates the beginning of a new two-year cycle with respect to personal action, desire and ambition. The native will become more active and energetic in the affairs ruled by the sign and house that Mars is transiting and houses where Aries, Scorpio and Capricorn are found. These departments will be activated in some manner. Whether this action will be constructive or destructive will depend upon the combined influences of the aspects to Mars in the natal horoscope and the other effective transits to natal Mars. The native can obtain insight into the trend of this transit by turning his or her gaze back approximately two years to the previous transit conjunction of Mars to its own place and observing its effects. In general, this is a time when the native will become aggressively active in attempts to achieve personal desires and ambitions.

Transit Mars Conjunction Jupiter

This transit indicates expanded action in pursuit of travel, higher education, religion, philosophy and work involving churches and institutions of higher learning. The native will be aggressive in promoting personal religious, philosophic, educational and cultural beliefs.

If Mars and Jupiter are afflicted in the natal horoscope or by other transiting aspects, the native could become intolerant concerning other people's viewpoints regarding these matters. The hidden motive of self-seeking or ego gratification could be behind the native's outer show of concern for worthwhile causes.

On the positive side, the native will manifest a greater degree of self-confidence and a positive attitude with respect to his ambitions and endeavors. This will surface as enthusiasm that makes work seem lighter and easier. During this transit, the native is likely to put religious or ethical attitudes into action in a practical way.

Mars Transit Conjunction Saturn

This transit indicates a period in which the native will become more ambitious in the desire to achieve status and career advancement. The influence of Mars can help the native to overcome the fear and inertia of the negative side of Saturn. This is a good transit for work requiring discipline, determination, caution, precision and resourcefulness. The native can act in a well organized and methodical manner. Under this transit the native can become involved with machinery, industry, legal affairs, military matters and government.

The combination of adverse transits to Mars with afflictions in the natal horoscope and to Mars and Saturn could make the native hard, resentful, callous and selfish in attitude toward the affairs ruled by the sign and house where natal Saturn is found and the houses Saturn rules.

Transit Mars Conjunction Uranus

This transit can bring sudden dynamic and unexpected events into the native's life. The desire for independent action is intensified during this period. The individual undergoing this transit is likely to take drastic action designed to achieve independence and freedom. This is apt to put one into a revolutionary frame of mind that brooks no interference. The native can become interested in things related to machinery, electronics and technology. Changes can take place in friendships, group affiliations and corporate or professional affairs.

If Mars and Uranus are afflicted in the natal horoscope and Uranus receives adverse aspects from other transiting planets during this period, the native is apt to lose his or her temper, act rashly and sever friendships and group affiliations. There is the possibility that the native would be exposed to physical danger through impulsive, reckless acts.

On the positive side, the native can develop an interest in science, electronics, occult subjects, astrology, politics, economics or humanitarian reforms and organizations related to these things.

Transit Mars Conjunction Neptune

This transit indicates a time in which the subconscious psychological desires of the native will become actively apparent. If the conjunction is afflicted either natally or by other transits, bizarre psychological aberrations can make themselves apparent. There can be a strong desire for travel and adventure. The individual experiencing this transit may become active in pursuit or support of religious or mystical organizations and beliefs. During this transit, the native can have delusions of grandeur and may make unrealistic attempts to amass a fortune, promulgate some great spiritual reform or achieve power and high position. The native may even be carried away by an emotional impulse or a pie-in-the-sky proposition. Thus, during this period the native should strive to maintain a realistic outlook.

On the positive side, this is an excellent transit for spiritual healing and receiving important intuitive insights. The native can manifest greater faith and confidence. During this transit, one can become involved in such activities as dancing and artistic pursuits requiring physical exertion.

Transit Mars Conjunction Pluto

This transit emphasizes a period favorable to energetic physical action, with the provision that the native exercise common sense and caution. If this conjunction remains unafflicted, athletes experiencing this transit can achieve their highest level of performance. The native can become actively involved in corporate business affairs or other work requiring resourcefulness and ingenuity. The native could apply his or her will to some form of occult investigation or activity.

If the conjunction is natally afflicted or adversely aspected by other transits, someone of consequence to the native could pass away or there could be a threat to the native's life and limb. This is not a good period to expose oneself to situations of physical danger.

The native is likely to be motivated to adopt projects of self-improvement and professional advancement or to improve the affairs ruled by the houses where Mars, Pluto, Aries, Scorpio and Capricorn are found. In some way the native may have to deal with insurance, taxes, inheritance and the goods of the dead.

Transit Mars Sextiles

Transit Mars Sextile Sun

This transit indicates a time of great mental and physical exertion directed toward self-improvement, creative self-expression, business and professional advancement. The native may assume an active role of leadership in group and organizational activities or in the practical application of new ideas, and will manifest greater energy and self-confidence, thereby achieving greater personal success. This is a good period for undertaking work that requires energy, ingenuity and resourcefulness. Under this transit the native can become socially active in sports or other activities that involve friends. This is a good transit for handling mechanical jobs that require skill and know-how. The person experiencing this transit may become more bold in romantic advances. This could involve much short-distance travel in pursuit of romance and pleasure. The native is more enthusiastic about sharing activities and will have many new ideas or ways to educate and entertain them. The native may be more active in working with siblings and neighbors to bring about desired goals and projects.

Transit Mars Sextile Moon

This transit brings opportunities to make home improvements and advancements in business and financial affairs. At this time the home could be used as a place for business and professional activities. The native will activate or be activated by family members in the pursuit these projects. This is a period when one is apt to be more honest and straightforward regarding emotional feelings and reactions. This transit is the proverbial spring or fall house cleaning aspect. An interest could develop in gardening, farming, real estate, cooking, home and domestic products and services. These projects or business activities are likely to involve dealings with women.

Transit Mars Sextile Mercury

This transit indicates a time of increased intellectual acuteness and curiosity. This is a good time to pursue communication and negotiations in connection with business affairs, professional matters, the media, writing, teaching, lecturing and publishing. The native will have more energy to use in solving practical, scientific, business or mechanical problems. He or she can also use this transit to investigate and handle matters, should that be necessary. The native will be active and energetic with friends, groups and organizational affairs that have immediate goals and objectives. There is likely to be distance travel relating to business, study, work, health or scientific affairs and investigation.

Transit Mars Sextile Venus

This transit indicates a period when the native will generate ideas for action involving business, partnerships and social activities. He or she could develop greater skill and new techniques in artistic pursuits and activities. This would be especially true in areas requiring skill and craftsmanship. Under this transit, the native will act to extend social activities, friendship and group affiliations aimed toward the improvement of romantic prospects and business or social affairs. The native could become involved in psychological investigations and organizational or institutional social activities.

Transit Mars Sextile Mars

This transit indicates a time when the native can advance business and professional affairs through initiative and dynamic action. He or she will have more energy to devote toward accomplishing goals and objectives. This is a good transit under which to initiate programs of exercise or physical self-improvement. Many comings and goings are likely in affairs related to physical work and activity, building, construction or industrial affairs. The native could become involved in organizations of a military, industrial or political nature or could become associated with friends who are energetic, ambitious, hardworking and physically active. The native and friends could help each other achieve their goals and objectives through effective practical action. During his transit the native will have the opportunity to initiate a fresh course of action based on new ideas or communication.

Transit Mars Sextile Jupiter

This transit marks a period of potential expansion during which the native can make progress through intelligent and enterprising action in industry, professional matters, business, teaching, lecturing, travel, transportation, publishing and religious and educational activities. This is favorable time for the native to handle legal matters pertaining to religious, educational and charitable institutions. There is often involvement in group and organizational activities, or communication with friends and professional associates which enable one to realize goals and objectives. During this period the native will be inclined to put religious and philosophic ideas into action.

Transit Mars Sextile Saturn

This transit indicates a period when the native will apply greater discipline and ambition to work. It is especially favorable for work in the fields engineering and various types of skilled physical labor. The native can plan and carry out projects with greater efficiency, and is able to avoid wasted effort and make work safe and effective. Under this transit the native will be concerned with accomplishments of lasting practical value, and could work with friends, partners, brothers, sisters or neighbors to achieve these ends. A desire to protect the status quo will put the native in a politically conservative frame of mind. This could influence the native to enter into agreements or contractual arrangement that would further financial, professional or political goals. This is an especially good transit for working with machinery, tools and mechanical devices. It is also a favorable transit for seeing the dentist, particularly for work to be done on the upper jaw.

Transit Mars Sextile Uranus

This transit indicates a period of strong interest in electronic, mechanical and technological work and activities. It is favorable for work in business enterprises in these fields. The native will be more active in scientific, political, occult, industrial or community organizations. He or she could be interested in hobbies related to scientific, electronic or technical subjects, as this transit disposes one toward puttering with unusual gadgets. This is favorable transit for work and study in astrology. The native could be motivated to take steps toward self-improvement and self-protection during this transit. In general, the native will initiate unexpected action to achieve goals and objectives and meet unusual and dynamic friends who will present new opportunities. The native and friends will encourage each other to constructive action.

Transit Mars Sextile Neptune

This transit in a native's chart indicates a time of increased interest in psychological and occult faculties and abilities. It's a good transit for healing, psychic investigation or conducting work in secret or behind the scenes. The native can do constructive work in hospitals, schools and religious or charitable institutions, and initiate programs for helping those less fortunate. These efforts frequently involve brothers, sisters, neighbors, friends, groups and organizations. This transit can bring out intuitive abilities helpful to the native's career, business involvements, self-protection and self-expression. It is a favorable transit for artists (especially sculptors), dancers, musicians, actors, photographers or any occupation requiring imagination combined with skillful action. This is a favorable transit for seeking a physician's aid in curing a yet undiagnosed chronic illness. The native can become more interested in putting religious ideas and ideals into action.

Transit Mars Sextile Pluto

This transit indicates a favorable period for corporate business affairs, physical self-improvement, work requiring muscular exertion and scientific work related to advanced technology. The native could develop an intellectual interest in occult subjects, and intuition could be activated in the investigation of the superphysical forces of nature. This is a favorable transit for police investigation and military affairs. The native could work with friends and neighbors on political affairs, community projects, corporate business or programs of physical self-improvement. The native will act to improve the affairs ruled by the houses that Mars and Pluto occupy and rule in the natal horoscope.

Transit Mars Squares

Transit Mars Square Sun

Transit Mars square the Sun foreshadows an aggressive period when the native is apt to act impulsively. This can produce conflict with employers, police or others who are in positions of power and authority, which in turn can spark a period of rebellion by the native against authority figures of all types. Harshness in the native's own exercise of authority could arouse resentment and opposition in others. Aggressive action or impulsiveness can cause conflict in the affairs ruled by the signs and houses which transiting Mars and natal Sun occupy. Such discord may also affect affairs of the houses which Mars and Sun rule in the natal horoscope. During this transit the native should avoid arguments and physical confrontations. There can be the danger of physical strain through excessive work or exertion. In professional, political, family and domestic affairs, the native must consider the feelings and rights of others to avoid frustration and difficulty. The native should make a special effort to maintain a relaxed and considerate attitude in family and professional relationships. The native should cultivate moderation in pursuit of pleasure, and exercise consideration in romantic and sexual relationships.

Transit Mars Square Moon

This transit indicates a period when the native is prone to emotional excitability and displays of temper. Unconscious emotional patterns, often resulting from hereditary factors or early childhood experiences, are apt to be aggravated during this transit. This is not a favorable time for dealing with women. During this transit it is difficult to maintain harmony in family and domestic relationships. The native can become aggravated by petty daily annoyances and household affairs and this often results in family disagreements and emotional confrontations. If this transit is reinforced by other adverse aspects the native could be forced to leave the domestic scene or make an unwanted move. Emotional instability can result in difficulties at work or loss of job and there is the danger of being foolish or impulsive in financial expenditures. The native should be particularly careful with tools, machinery, guns or fire hazards in the home.

Transit Mars Square Mercury

This transit indicates a period during which the native is apt to be mentally irritable and argumentative. It is not a favorable time for communication or negotiation regarding professional or business affairs, nor is it a propitious period in which to conclude important contracts or sign legal documents. Arguments and disagreements can arise with brothers, sisters, neighbors, co-workers, employers or friends. Cautious driving habits should be exercised to avoid accidents, even arrest. This is not a favorable time for travel, short journeys, lecturing, mail or communication. Under this transit the native could suffer from or be the perpetrator of harmful gossip. Difficulties with health can arise from over-exertion, nervousness, infections or inflammation of various types. Care should be taken to avoid injury while working, particularly in the use of tools. An inclination to impulsive buying makes this an unfavorable time for extravagant purchases of clothing.

Transit Mars Square Venus

This transit indicates a period of impulsiveness in romantic and sexual advances on the part of the native. People undergoing this transit could attract men or women who display these characteristics. Impulsive spending on pleasure and a amusement can result in financial depletion. This is not a favorable transit for artistic creativity or social activity. During this period the native could display a lack of social grace and refinement which could have an adverse effect on the profession and social standing. There can be emotional confrontations in romantic and marital relationships and emotional problems can arise as a result of sexual frustration. If this transit square is combined with other indications, it could precipitate a divorce or breaking off of romantic relationships, especially if sexual jealousy is involved.

Transit Mars Square Mars

This transit indicates a period when the native is apt to be impulsive and highly aggressive. Obstacles and difficulties that block the path to success make this an unfavorable time to initiate new enterprises in business and professional affairs. It is wise during his transit to maintain the status quo and await a more favorable time to initiate new activities. Injuries could result from over-exertion or physical confrontations during this transit, and there is also danger of fevers and infections. This is not a good time for handling firearms, dangerous tools, knives or sharp objects. Sexual impulsiveness could get the native into trouble during this transit.

Transit Mars Square Jupiter

This transit can touch off a period when the native will be overly zealous in promoting personal, religious, philosophic, political and educational beliefs. There can be a tendency to overextend oneself in business or professional expansion, which could result in financial loss and damage to reputation. During this period the native should strive to cultivate an attitude of moderation. Caution should also be exercised in do-it-yourself home improvement projects. These could turn out to be dangerous, expensive and time consuming. It is better to wait for a more favorable transit for this kind of work. This is not a good period in which to embark on any long journey in search of adventure, for while on such a journey the native could be subject to injury, accident or loss. This is not a good time to initiate new moves regarding institutional, educational or political affairs.

Transit Mars Square Saturn

This transit indicates a period during which the native is prone to frustration and aggravation in work, business and professional affairs. It takes more than the usual effort to achieve the same result as that obtained during a more favorable transit. It is likely that the native will be subject to heavy work loads and responsibility imposed by an employer or others in positions of power and authority. The native should seek to maintain the status quo and await a more favorable time to initiate professional and business ventures and projects. To achieve even modest success under this transit, the native must apply an inordinate amount of effort and work in order to fulfill ambitions. Care and caution must be exercised to avoid accidents and injuries in the use of tools and machinery. This is especially true for those involved in industrial or building occupations. Skin inflammations, skin rashes, excessively dry skin or broken bones could occur during this transit.

Transit Mars Square Uranus

This transit indicates a time when the native is apt to be impulsive and aggressive. The native should be careful to prevent exposure to situations with a potential for violence or danger, and should be especially careful with firearms, tools, machinery, explosives and automobiles. Under this transit the temper is apt to be short, and the native will not tolerate interference with his or her freedom or self-determination. At the same time, friends or organizations may try to induce the native's cooperation in their personal enterprises without due consideration of the native's desires or the consequences entailed. This usually results in arguments or explosive situations. The native could even become a party to such tactics. In general, the native should exercise caution, patience and avoid precipitous action during this transit. Because of the double Scorpio/eighth house significance of this transit there could be the sudden death of a friend or family member. Under this transit, disagreement over joint finances or administrative affairs could become more pronounced.

Transit Mars Square Neptune

This transit indicates a period during which the native must adhere strictly to principle in professional and business affairs. The native must exercise caution in actions where family, professional and business affairs are involved because he or she is apt to be deceived as to their true import. During this transit it is easy to allow oneself to be controlled by subconscious emotional desires that tend to distort reason, good judgment and a realistic approach to matters. There can be strange psychological manifestations and in some cases abnormal sexual behavior. This, however, would only be the case if the natal horoscope indicates such tendencies. During his transit the native should avoid the temptation to undermine the positions of others, for there is the possibility that others will attempt to do the same. Such subversive activities could affect the native's business affairs, professional standing or psychological stability. Often the negative use of psychic powers can play an important role in this psychological demoralization. Care should be taken to avoid the excessive use of alcohol or drugs. Alcohol or drug abuse could lead to accidents or illness requiring hospitalization. Under the effects of this transit the native could be subject to cruel or abusive treatment while in a hospital or institution. Fevers or infection may affect the native's health, and both these and any existing maladies will be difficult to diagnose.

Transit Mars Square Pluto

This transit marks a period in which the native is prone to impulsive acts and overexertion. The native may selfishly attempt to coerce others or be subject such tactics. This is not a good period for handling important business affairs because conflict and power struggles are likely to arise concerning them. If the native is involved in police or military affairs, this transit indicates time when serious matters concerning life and death could arise. On the positive side, the native can initiate action toward self, business and professional improvement. If the native exercises caution, patience and good judgment, much can be accomplished and much that is superfluous and useless can be eliminated. The native should be careful while handling tools, firearms or machinery and should avoid being present in potentially violent situations.

Transit Mars Trines

Transit Mars Trine Sun

This transit indicates a time when the native can exercise personal creative initiative, and take the lead in professional, business, artistic and physical affairs. The expansive ninth-house significance of this trine gives the native the ability to draw on past experience in furthering his or her affairs. The native will be physically active, especially in sports, social life, travel and work, and is apt to be more aggressive, ardent and enthusiastic in affairs of the heart. This is an excellent transit for artistic expression through sculpture, dance or music that requires expenditure of energy. The native will have greater self-confidence and this composure may manifest through leadership in social, business or professional affairs. This is an especially good transit for working with children, particularly in matters concerning their physical education or training.

Transit Mars Trine Moon

This transit is favorable for home improvements fo the initiation of constructive family activities. The native will show more emotion, energy and enthusiasm for work and the handling of everyday practical, financial and domestic responsibilities. He or she may now be quite successful in business affairs dealing with real estate, farming, building construction, food, home and domestic products. There will be greater ease and facility in the pursuit and fulfillment of romantic, sexual and social activities. Benefits could arise through the native's engagement in constructive activities with women. Many natives will be involved in home improvement projects requiring the use of tools and physical force. This period will also swell the native's sense of patriotism, particularly when defending the nation from verbal or even physical attack.

Transit Mars Trine Mercury

This transit disposes the native toward rapid progress in intellectual, scientific and business affairs. It is a good transit for writing, teaching, lecturing, traveling, investigation and anything that involves the gathering or dissemination of information. Under this transit the native will display greater intellectual initiative and self-confidence in work and professional affairs. Corporate financial agreements and contracts can be favorably formulated, negotiated and concluded. Ideas that have been dormant in the native's mind will be reactivated and viably expressed. This is a good period for communication and cooperative efforts involving brothers, sisters, neighbors, coworkers, employers and those in positions of authority and leadership. There can be new intellectual or physical expression in cultural, educational or social activities. The effects of this transit can incline the native to work with young people and to devote considerable time to education, scientific research or police and military affairs.

Transit Mars Trine Venus

This transit indicates a period of progress in the native's artistic, social, romantic and business circles. This is a good transit for starting a business, Mars supplying the necessary initiative and Venus naturally ruling the second house of money. This is also a good period for public relations work in business affairs and professional matters. Mars, as ruler of Scorpio, deals with business, and its exaltation in Capricorn concerns the profession, while Venus, ruler of Libra, relates to public relations. Social and romantic matters are favored by this transit, and natives are apt to fall in love under this influence. Women who want children could become pregnant. Creative expression will come to the fore in sculpture, music, painting, crafts and the performing arts. This transit can also release an individual from situations of restriction or confinement.

Mars Trine Mars

This a period of increased physical activity. The native will be more ambitious in business and professional affairs. This is a good time to dispose of projects that require physical energy, action and enthusiasm. The native will have a strong sense of self-confidence and the capacity for personal leadership, and will be assertive and initiate action at the appropriate times. He or she could be active in sports, travel or physical education. Police work and military affairs can be successfully progressed or concluded. This is a good period for working with tools, machinery, metal and construction equipment.

Transit Mars Trine Jupiter

This transit indicates a period favorable to the expansion and promotion of educational, professional, corporate business, legal, political and religious affairs. The native can gain through travel and association with religious and educational institutions. He or she may be active in crusading for cultural, religious or educational causes and there will be a tendency to put these ideals into action. This transit can bring much activity in the home or an expansion of the family circle. In general, the native will be more optimistic, adventuresome and interested in expanding personal self-expression through action.

Transit Mars Trine Saturn

This transit indicates a period during which the native will become more organized and disciplined in work, business and professional matters. It is a good period for physical work involving the use of tools and machinery and the application of building and other manual skills to tasks requiring dexterity and precision. The native's managerial skills and practicality are enhanced during this transit. He or she could be involved in group or organizational work related to professional or political concerns. This period is excellent for reorganizing professional and business affairs. The native's approach to these matters will become more stern and serious and he or she is likely to accomplish much that has practical value. The native will be able to handle old business that demands attention to make further progress. This is also a favorable transit under which to handle police and military affairs. In general, this is a time of increased ambition, practicality and determination to succeed in professional and business affairs.

Transit Mars Trine Uranus

This transit is favorable for handling technological, scientific and occult matters. The native will be motivated toward physical and spiritual self-improvement, for this is the time to realize goals and ambitions through resourceful and dynamic action. He or she will be more outgoing and independent, establishing new friendships with interesting and energetic individuals. The native will effect concrete solutions to professional and business problems, and this may lead to a leadership role in a scientific, professional or humanitarian organization. Inventions, technological innovations and corporate business enterprises will progress rapidly toward completion during this period. During this transit the native can gain valuable insights into the occult laws governing the universe.

Transit Mars Trine Neptune

This transit will motivate the native to explore the creative possibilities of his or her imaginative and intuitive faculties. This activity will manifest itself in art, music, dancing, religion, healing, mysticism, photography or the unfoldment of intuitive faculties. The native may become active in the promotion of religious, educational, and philosophical beliefs because during this period the native can benefit in a special way through healing, meditation and religious practice. This is a particularly favorable period for using the home and family circle as a place of meditation and spiritual regeneration. This transit also favors the native's participation in business activities that require secrecy and a special strategic sense because the native can successfully conclude secret investigations of various types.

Transit Mars Trine Pluto

This transit promises a period of great energy and willpower for the native in programs of physical and spiritual self-improvement. Effects of this aspect will particularly aid athletes and those whose work involves strenuous physical exertion. Much headway can be made in business enterprises and their affairs. Research work in the technological field could reach fruition, or at least much progress can be made. This is a favorable period for handling the goods of the dead, tax matters, insurance, legacies, and joint finances, and the native may be adamant in the pursuit of occult knowledge and experience. In general, the native will be more energetic and competitive under this transit.

Transit Mars Oppositions

Transit Mars Opposition Sun

This transit marks a period during which the native is apt to be more aggressive and autocratic in relationships. For this reason, the native is likely to arouse resentment and in others. There is danger of rashness and impulsiveness that, when coupled with a short temper, could result in physical confrontations. The native should make an effort to be considerate and diplomatic in relationships because under the effects of this transit, he or she will constantly be made aware of other people's value, rights and needs for self-determination. The native should restrain selfish impulses in professional matters, joint finances and corporate business affairs. During this transit, impulsiveness and sexual aggressiveness can cause problems in romantic and marital affairs, and arguments and disagreements can arise over joint finances, inheritance and taxes. If Mars and the Sun are afflicted in the natal horoscope, the native must exercise extreme caution during this period to avoid personal injury. Such injury could result from carelessness with tools, firearms, knives, machinery, moving objects or fire. Situations of danger and potential violence should be strictly avoided. In general, this is a period when the native should exercise consideration and cooperation in dealing with others.

Transit Mars Opposition Moon

This transit indicates a period during there are apt to be disagreements with family members, those who share the same household, and lords or those with whom the native has business connections. Lack of patience and the aggravation of unpleasant subconscious memories often raise problems in family affairs that in extreme cases can cause separation or estrangement. Conflicts can arise over the handling of family finances or joint business ventures. Fire, accidents or carelessness in the use of tools and machinery could endanger both the native and his or her home. During this transit the emotions are aroused, and the native will be prone to excitability, emotional outbursts and loss of temper. Indigestion often results from such emotional upsets, and the native should avoid the ingestion of spicy foods for this reason. This is not a favorable transit for dealing with women or seeking their favor in professional or business affairs.

Transit Mars Opposition Mercury

This transit accents a period when the native is subject to mental irritation. Arguments and heated verbal encounters are apt to occur, and conflicts can arise with brothers, sisters, neighbors, coworkers and employers. This is not a favorable time for the initiation of professional or business negotiations, nor is it opportune for the conclusion of contracts or legal agreements, because the native is apt to be hasty and precipitous in reaching decisions; at best, it would be difficult to arrive at amicable agreements or settlements. Those involved in public life can receive unfavorable publicity during this transit. Women undergoing this transit are subject to unwanted pregnancies. Defensive driving practices should be exercised to avoid accidents. In general this is not a favorable time to reach decisions or to impress one's opinions on others. The native should think before speaking, avoid verbal battles and seek to cooperate wherever possible.

Transit Mars Opposition Venus

This transit is apt to bring difficulties in social, romantic, marital and business relationships. Sexual aggressiveness on the part of the native or the partner could cause difficulty in the relationship. There will be a tendency for the native to ignore the feelings of others in pursuit of his or her own desires and this could cause a breakdown in relationships with consequent emotional antagonism.

Transit Mars Opposition Mars

This transit is apt to stress overt aggressiveness in the native's pursuit of personal gratification. Arguments and difficulties are likely in sexual, professional, financial, business and corporate relationships. Conflicts could arise over joint finances, corporate money, insurance, taxes, alimony or inheritance. In extreme cases this could result in physical confrontations. Carelessness and impulsiveness in actions could result in physical injury. For this reason caution should be exercised in the use of fire, firearms, machinery, knives, sharp tools and automobiles. This is not a good time to seek the favor of those in positions of power and authority. In general the native should avoid aggressive, inconsiderate actions lest others respond in the same manner.

Mars Transit Opposition Jupiter

This transit marks a period of possible embroilment in controversy or conflict over educational, philosophic and religious beliefs. Often the native is approached by representatives of an aggressive religious organization or cult whose purpose it is to convert the native. Then, again, the native could become overly aggressive in the promotion of personal beliefs and arouse resentment and opposition in others. Disagreements could arise within the family over cultural, religious and social viewpoints. In some cases this could lead to separation or estrangement. This transit is not favorable for dealing with hospitals, institutions, legal affairs or medical matters; nor is it conducive to long journeys or adventures. Difficulties could arise in distant places or in foreign countries. Extravagance and overexpansion in business endeavors could bring financial losses or possible disaster. In general the native should avoid a might-makes-right attitude, and should be careful not to promise more than can be delivered.

Transit Mars Opposition Saturn

This transit indicates a time of difficulty in the native's relations to established authorities and organizations. Disagreement and conflicts could arise with employers, government, police or financial institutions. The native is apt to feel frustrated by established authority figures who block personal progress and the fulfillment of desires. Conflict and legal battles can arise in marriage and business partnerships. In some cases, where the native is personally identified with the Saturn principle, he or she is apt to feel animosity toward upstart competitors who pose a threat to his or her security and established routine. During this period the native should seek to maintain the status quo and await a more favorable time to approach those in power and authority. Under this transit the native should be careful to avoid excessive physical strain or muscular exertion. The danger of accidents with tools, weapons, machinery and automobiles becomes more pronounced, and fevers, broken bones, and skin and teeth problems frequently appear during this period. If the native should be ill, he or she may experience fever and chills. In general the native should curb impulsiveness and avoid situations of potential danger and violence.

Transit Mars Opposition Uranus

This transit marks a period in which the native may experience difficulties getting along with friends, organizations and business and professional associates. The native is apt to act rashly and impulsively, quite often losing his or her temper. There can be separation or estrangement from friends or organizations in which the native has had real interest. The native should exercise caution in the use of tools, electricity, explosives, machinery, automobiles and firearms. Extreme care is necessary if one is engaged in military, police or dangerous scientific or industrial work in order to avoid the danger of real physical damage. Conflict can arise over corporate business matters, inheritance, alimony, joint finances or the financial affairs of groups and organizations. This is not the time to initiate new projects, group activities or technological innovations.

Transit Mars Opposition Neptune

Under the effects of this transit the native may be involved in secret schemes and plots that could bring about his or her undoing. The native may be either the perpetrator or the victim of such activities. This is not a favorable time for the native to enter into business, marital or professional partnerships. The native's secret enemies will be a constant source of bewilderment, and there is danger of fraud in joint finances, taxes, insurance, inheritance, professional affairs, hospitals, and religious or spiritual institutions. The native must be extremely wary and not permit the luxury of any such costly illusions. In general this is not a favorable time for important business dealings or disturbing the status quo of professional affairs. Instead, this period calls for realism, patience and a practical outlook. Illnesses, often psychosomatic or brought on by emotional imbalance, will be difficult to diagnose and cure. Institutionalization or hospitalization of the native during this period may subject him or her to ill treatment or improper medication. The use of alcohol or drugs should also be avoided. It is best to stay clear of occult activities of dubious value for there may be the danger of negative psychic influences during this transit. Finally, a note of warning: Mars' rulership of the eighth house and Neptune's astrological association with bacteria may place the native in danger of contracting a social disease from a sexual partner under this transit. This danger is especially pronounced in the fifth house or if the natal ruler of the fifth house is involved.

Transit Mars Opposition Pluto

This transit indicates a period when the native's attitudes are apt to become overly aggressive and autocratic. Difficulties can arise in professional, business and personal affairs. During this transit the native may encounter others with equally aggressive, stubborn attitudes. The native and his or her associates are apt to try to change each other's views, causing resentment, arguments and, in extreme cases, physical confrontations. Arguments and disputes can also emerge over money, insurance, taxes, inheritance, alimony and the goods of the dead. The native should be careful when in the presence of weapons, firearms, radioactivity, crowds, machinery, dangerous chemicals and other sources of physical danger. In situations of war or revolution or in police affairs, there can be a serious threat to the native's well-being. The native could be the target of criminal activities or, if Mars and Pluto are afflicted in the natal horoscope, the native may even become party to them. This is a period when dubious occult practices should be strictly avoided. The native could even become the victim of such forces.

VI

Transits of Jupiter

Transits of Jupiter Through the Houses

In whatever house Jupiter is found, there is sustained optimism and a generous attitude that stimulates a sincere concern for the welfare of others. Jupiter brings the native much benefit through the affairs ruled by the house that Jupiter is transiting. These affairs will proceed smoothly and easily, and thus a sense of abundance is created.

If Jupiter makes favorable transits while in a particular house, the native will be inclined to share his or her blessings with others; this promotes an even greater sense of good will and in turn leads the way to additional blessings.

If Jupiter makes unfavorable aspects while transiting a particular house, there may be a tendency for the native to take too much for granted or a tendency to embrace hypocritical attitudes relating to the affairs of the house that Jupiter is transiting. There is the possibility that these false attitudes may inevitably lay the groundwork for a future fall from grace. In general, however, the native should anticipate benefits from the house which is visited by transiting Jupiter.

Transit Jupiter Through the First House

Jupiter's transit through the first house usually heralds a time when the native is able to develop a more positive self-image. While under this transit the native expresses greater optimism and self-confidence, and often acquires a sense of spiritual renewal and a greater concern with leading a spiritual way of life. If natal Jupiter is well aspected in the horoscope and transiting Jupiter makes favorable aspects while in the first house, there can be ethical self-reform and greater personal interest in following a constructive way of life leading to further reform and moral growth. Since the influence of Jupiter is expansion, growth and increase, and since the first house rules the physical body, one has a tendency to put on weight during Jupiter's transit of this house. However, the principle of expansion can also bring opportunities called good luck.

If Jupiter is afflicted in the natal chart or makes many adverse aspects while transiting this house, the native may be extravagant, conceited, over-confident or wear an air of false bravado.

Transit Jupiter Through the Second House

Jupiter's transit through the second house is usually one of the most welcome of all transits since it brings an improved financial fortune. The native finds it easier to make money and has a more optimistic attitude toward personal business affairs. This greater financial optimism and prosperity can help the native to be more generous with money and to acquire a more honest, ethical attitude in business dealings. Funds may become available for higher education or travel. Travel can in turn lead to improved business and financial prospects. The native can be inclined to make contributions to religious, charitable or educational causes, and can use an increased understanding of large-scale business and sociological trends to improve the marketing appeal of products and services. The native may become involved in business activities related to education, publishing, teaching, lecturing, religion, travel or law. Financial blessings will be permanent if the native shares them with others while Jupiter is transiting the second house.

If Jupiter is badly afflicted in the natal horoscope and transiting Jupiter makes adverse transits while in the second house, the native may squander money and material resources or may over-extend financial commitments, inviting future financial loss and indebtedness. A tendency to take too much for granted can be dangerous.

Transit Jupiter Through the Third House

Jupiter's transit through the third house usually brings about a more philosophical mental focus and the native is likely to develop an increased interest in education, religion, philosophy or social sciences. This interest can take the form of study, writing or formal programs of education, teaching or travel. There is likely to be increased communication and much traveling about. This is a favorable transit for communication in general. If Jupiter is afflicted in the natal horoscope and makes adverse aspects while in the third house, the native can be prone to intellectual pride and arrogance. There can be an active involvement with brothers, sisters, neighbors and neighborhood or community affairs, particularly those concerning church and social activities. This is a favorable time for writing and publishing unless Jupiter is badly afflicted in the natal horoscope and makes adverse transiting aspects.

In the in the third, Jupiter is in the house of its accidental detriment and so there can be a tendency to think too much in generalities. As natural ruler of Sagittarius and the ninth house, Jupiter is concerned with values, while Mercury, Gemini and the third house are concerned with impersonal facts. Thus, Jupiter's transit of the third house can induce the native can induce the native to use facts with a spiritual and ethical purpose.

The native's social, religious, and moral prejudices may cause him or her to ignore some facts and to overemphasize others, distorting the perception of reality if the energy of Jupiter in the third house is used unwisely. The native should seek to pursue altruistic ideals in a realistic, practical manner. The native must test facts for their correspondence to truth. It is essential that the native see reality as it is while making a special effort to avoid overly optimistic thinking.

Transit Jupiter Through the Fourth House

Jupiter's transit through the fourth house usually indicates a time of benefit to the native's family and financial affairs. At this time the native may live in a large house or in an institution with many other people. This transit tends to make the native more conscious of religious and spiritual values as they relate to family life. This increases harmony in the home and has a beneficial social effect on both parents and children. The home is likely to be a center for religious, social, and educational activities. This sharing in the home creates an atmosphere of congeniality and friendliness. While Jupiter transits the fourth house the home is likely to be used as a place of spiritual retreat and meditation. This is especially true if Jupiter makes favorable transits to other planets while it is transiting the fourth house.

Because this is the house of Jupiter's accidental exaltation, many important benefits can be derived from its visit here. This is a favorable transit for business concerns related to real estate, food, farming, building, home improvements and domestic products and services. This is a favorable time to establish a home, buy property or make home improvements. Relationships with parents and other family members can be improved during this period.

If Jupiter is heavily afflicted in the natal horoscope and makes adverse transits while in the fourth house, the native may become hypercritical toward family members or others with whom he or she lives. There can be a tendency to be ostentatious in the home by placing too much value on physical beauty and opulence.

Transit Jupiter Through the Fifth House

A favorable period for romance, creative expression, work with children and children's educational and financial matters is indicated by Jupiter's transit through the fifth house. Much depends upon how Jupiter is aspected in the natal horoscope and what kind of transiting aspects Jupiter makes while in the fifth house.

Since the fifth house rules pleasure, if Jupiter is afflicted, the native can pursue excessive or unwise pleasures such as gambling, meaningless socializing and sexual encounters, drinking or unwise stock market speculation. Wasted energy and resources is the result. It should not be forgotten that Jupiter also rules Pisces and the twelfth house, so self-undoing is possible with this transit.

On the positive side, Jupiter in the fifth house can bring about a romantic relationship with deep spiritual, philosophic and cultural meaning, a relationship that goes beyond the physical, sexual level. The native can develop a love of children and be genuinely concerned about their ethical and spiritual development. This is a favorable transit for creative and performing artists. Often the native's artistic creations will express a deep spiritual and philosophic message or significance. Art may be used as a vehicle for social commentary. This is a favorable time for reasonable financial investments and speculations, provided Jupiter makes favorable transiting aspects and there are no unfavorable indications involving the fifth house and its rulers. Religious teachers and those involved with primary level education or those studying to become teachers should find Jupiter's transit through the natal fifth house especially favorable.

Transit Jupiter Through the Sixth House

Jupiter's transit through the sixth house indicates a time of increased opportunity with respect to work and employment. Unless Jupiter is very afflicted in the natal horoscope and makes adverse aspects to planets in the natal horoscope while in the sixth house, the native will enjoy better health and find it easier to get employment. There will be improved working conditions and better relationships with coworkers and employees. The native's work may involve publishing, teaching, religion, travel or efforts concerning educational or medical institutions. The native may do volunteer work for religious, educational or charitable institutions. Some natives will develop an interest in faith healing or spiritual healing of various kinds. In general the native will have a greater consciousness of the need to put religious and philosophical concepts into some kind of practical, constructive expression through work and service.

If Jupiter is badly afflicted in the natal horoscope and makes adverse transits while in the sixth house, there can be a tendency to be lazy, inattentive and unreliable on the job and to abuse the health through excessive eating, alcohol, improper diet or drugs.

Transit Jupiter Through the Seventh House

Jupiter's transit through the seventh house of the horoscope usually indicates a time of improved human relations for the native, especially in important partnerships and close friendships. If the native is not married, this period may bring an opportunity for marriage. The native becomes more friendly, cooperative and outgoing and this naturally elicits a similar response from others. This is a good transit for people who work with the public, arbitrators, lawyers, judges, counselors, public relations people, politicians, performing artists, lecturers, teachers, ministers and psychologists. If the native is at all spiritually awake, he or she will develop a genuine concern for the welfare and happiness of others. To varying extents the native will try to apply the rule, "Do unto others as you would have them do unto you." This is a good time to establish partnerships or enter into cooperative endeavors of all kinds. The native is more inclined to look at the positive side of relationships and will meet other people half-way. This is generally a good time to handle pending court appearances, lawsuits or legal proceedings unless Jupiter makes adverse aspects to natal planets. Disputes can often be settled amicably out of court.

If Jupiter is badly afflicted in the natal horoscope and makes adverse transits while in the seventh house, there can be a danger of taking too much for granted in relationships, of being overly critical and of using other people for one's own ends.

Transit Jupiter Through the Eighth House

This is a time when the native can benefit through business or financial endeavors, insurance and inheritance. The native's spouse or partner may also enjoy prosperity and this will benefit the native. All financial concerns related to the eighth house such as insurance, taxes, wills, inheritance, goods of the deceased, alimony and business funds can be handled with ease and benefit to the native. Jupiter transiting this house can cause religious or philosophic interest in occult studies and such matters as reincarnation and life after death. If the natal horoscope reveals a capacity for clairvoyance and makes transits to Uranus, Neptune or Pluto while in the eighth house, the native may have psychic experiences which could be of religious significance. The native may be involved in business affairs connected with fund-raising for religious, educational or charitable institutions or in the fields of travel, real estate, education, publishing and law. It is especially likely that corporate law and law related to insurance, inheritance, alimony, divorce settlements, taxes and property will have some appeal or significance at this time.

If Jupiter is badly afflicted in the natal horoscope and makes adverse transits while in the eighth house, the native may be over confident, dishonest or negligent with regard to these affairs and consequently suffer losses.

Transit Jupiter Through the Ninth House

Jupiter's transit through the ninth house usually indicates a time of increased interest in education, religion, philosophy, spiritual pursuits and/or travel. The native is motivated to find some religious or philosophical system by which to regulate the affairs of his or her life. Consequently, the native will often embrace some kind of ideology that appeals to his or her level of mental, cultural and spiritual awareness. The native is likely to crusade or proselytize for pet beliefs at this time and often join an organization with which he or she feels both a sense of mission and acceptance. This can have an elevating effect on ethical behavior and spiritual awareness.

If Jupiter is afflicted in the natal horoscope or makes adverse transits while in the ninth house, the native sometimes becomes narrow minded, sectarian and fanatical. The native can display an aggressive, one-sided zeal that becomes an annoyance to others.

For others who are intelligent and have a reasonably high degree of cultural awareness, this is a favorable transit for pursuing higher education or university studies. Jupiter's transit through the ninth house favors travel, teaching, lecturing, publishing and working with or for religious and educational institutions. In general the native experiences an increased and beneficial spiritual and cultural awareness.

Transit Jupiter Through the Tenth House

This is a time of professional advancement and greater public recognition usually results. The extent to which the native benefits will of course depend upon education, work and experience. There will be opportunities for better jobs and greater social prestige. This is a favorable transit for lawyers, politicians, educators, lecturers and those in professions that depend upon public recognition. The native is likely to take more active interest in community affairs, politics and career advancement, and can develop a greater social conscience and sense of cultural responsibility. He or she will be more conscious of ethics in professional, political, community and business, and may be involved in professional and business concerns related to travel, religion, education, lecturing, publishing, law, real estate, building or domestic products. In general the native is likely to place greater emphasis on business and professional affairs and will be more ambitious to achieve advances that will bring prestige and social recognition.

If Jupiter is badly afflicted in the natal horoscope or makes adverse transits to natal planets while in the tenth house, selfish personal ambition for wealth and status may cause the native to misuse a privileged position of wealth, public responsibility and trust for the sake of personal self-aggrandizement. This will even usually lead to disgrace and reversal of fortune.

Transit Jupiter Through the Eleventh House

Jupiter's transit through the eleventh house usually indicates a time of increased benefit through friendships and group associations. The native acquires a more outgoing and humanitarian attitude which increases social awareness and expands the circle of friends, and is more genuinely concerned about the happiness and well-being of others. Groups and organizational activities that have a cultural, religious, philosophical, educational or humanitarian purpose take on added appeal and significance. There is a strong tendency to exchange life experience and awareness with others. The native stands a better chance of realizing goals and objectives during this transit, and is likely to establish friendships with those who can contribute to cultural, spiritual and philosophic knowledge and awareness or with those the native can teach. He or she may go on long trips or tours with friends. Because of Jupiter's exaltation in Cancer, the home is often used as a place for social gatherings. A club or other place of social gathering may become a second home for the native at this time or the native may find a religious retreat to be a suitable environment for social contacts.

If Jupiter is badly afflicted in the natal horoscope or makes adverse transits while in the eleventh house, the native may be led astray by friends, or the native and or friends may have ulterior motives in their association. Usually this merely takes the form of some unwise self-indulgences, aided and abetted by others who are also seeking unwise, short-sighted, hedonistic self-gratification. It is possible that the native and his or her friends may be well meaning but misguided in their advice to each other when Jupiter is thus afflicted.

The wise astrologer should examine the natal horoscope to determine the native's innate capacity for self-discipline and discrimination when assessing these potential dangers. In general this is a favorable period that increases the native's happiness through a greater sense of social belonging.

Transit Jupiter Through the Twelfth House

A time of increased introspective activities and an inner spiritual search is usually signified by Jupiter's transit through the twelfth house of the horoscope. The native may be involved with a hospital, retreat, monastery, charitable institution, asylum, church or educational institution. The rest of the horoscope will indicate whether this involvement will be that of helping or being helped. The home may be used as a place of inner spiritual search. Because Jupiter is accidently dignified in this house, much can be gained in terms of intuitive insight and the native can gain a greater sense of compassion toward those less fortunate.

If Jupiter is afflicted in the natal horoscope and makes adverse transits while in the twelfth house, the native may become prone to self-pity or useless fantasies. The native may lack discrimination in bestowing help and sympathy, and may become a ward of some charitable or religious institution or in some way live off the work of others. There could be a neurotic possessive attachment to family members or to close friends. In extreme cases the native could be institutionalized in a psychiatric facility, nursing home or another place for those unwilling or unable to cope with daily life.

On the positive side, this transit can confer a deep spiritual, intuitive insight into the past and future. There can be an appreciation of beauty and the deeper meaning of life. Religion, art and music can have special appeal at this time.

Transit Jupiter Conjunctions

The conjunction of transiting Jupiter to a natal planet generally indicates a time of increased self-confidence and constructive action with respect to the affairs ruled by the planet being aspected. The native will acquire a more generous, philosophical and spiritual attitude toward these affairs. Because the native is considering the welfare of others, he or she will be a able to gain their cooperation and support in activities and goals. The native may assume a role of social leadership with regard to the affairs ruled by Jupiter and the planet being aspected in the natal horoscope. This is likely because of the Aries or first house influence of the conjunction aspect.

Transit Jupiter Conjunction Sun

A time of increased good fortune, greater personal optimism and constructive self-confidence is brought about by this transit. The native finds it easier to gain the acceptance and cooperation of religious, educational, legal, business and social organizations of importance to the individual. This is a good time te seek the recognition and favor of people in positions of power and status. The native is interested in self-betterment and may experience a renewed interest in education, spiritual pursuits or ethical reform. This transit favors reasonable financial investments, social activities, romance, trave, sports, work with children and artistic expression, especially in the performing arts. The native gains social acceptance and prestige more easily, largely because he or she is more likely to take a genuine interest in the happiness and well-being of others, and to look more on the positive side of life as a basis for self-expression and action. This aspect can result in improvement in the native's energy, vitality and general level of health. Many natives will take an interest in helping those less fortunate than themselves. Often this will involve working through some religious or charitable organization. Women with this transit will find it easier to understand and gain rapport with men. Many natives will become interested in religion or some form of spiritual philosophy and practice that will improve their way of life and lead to greater personal happiness. This transit is generally considered to be one of the most fortunate of all transits.

Transit Jupiter Conjunction Moon

Under this transit definite improvement is realized in the native's family, financial and domestic affairs. The native will become more generous, cooperative and benevolent toward other family members, and is likely to make a genuine effort to apply religious, ethical and spiritual principles in practical, everyday affairs and family relationships. Because this transit has a double Cancer significance, the native will have a more serene and happy emotional outlook and consequently will be liked and accepted. Men with this transit will find it easier to empathize with, understand and get along with women. This transit presents an auspicious time for improving parental relationships. Because of the Moon's exaltation in Taurus, this is an excellent time for business and financial activities, especially those related to real estate, building, domestic products and food. The native may be interested in using his or her home as a place of religious or educational activity, and in any event the home will be a place of warmth and social conviviality. There is likely to be a chance to make home improvements, expand the home or move to a more satisfactory house. Sometimes, this means the return of family members to the home or the inclusion of friends in the family circle. The native is likely to be more interested in food and cooking, which can improve health, provided it does not lead to overeating or excessive indulgence in food. In general the native is likely to remember the good things from the past and be willing to overlook the bad. This improved emotional outlook will lead to greater generosity toward others and improved harmony in social relationships. The native may become interested in serving religious and charitable causes.

Transit Jupiter Conjunction Mercury

The native will have a more optimistic and positive mental outlook as a result of this transit. Study and educational endeavors are favored. The impetus of this transit is excellent for teachers, writers, lecturers, lawyers, ministers, those in communication and media fields and anyone who requires ease and skill in writing and speaking. Inspiration in writing and an easy flow of words are stimulated by this transit. The native will have greater self-confidence in expressing ideas. This time is especially favorable for beginning higher education or seeking publication of books and articles. It is one of the most favorable of all transits for both long- and short-distance travel. During Jupiter's transit over natal Mercury, the native can gain profound insight into historical, current and future trends of social and political significance. Study of religion, philosophy, law, history and foreign cultures is especially favored by this transit. It is, a propitious time to establish new friendships, participate in group activities and improve relationships with brothers, sisters, neighbors and family members. It is favorable for signing contracts, formulating agreements and handling other legal affairs. Matters can be expedited with a minimum of difficulty and in a way that is fair to all parties concerned. The native is likely to be more ethical and constructive in speech and communication at this time; this will lead to greater harmony and friendliness in relationships.

Transit Jupiter Conjunction Venus

For success and harmony in all social, romantic and artistic affairs, this is one of the most favorable transits. The native is more likely to have a happy, joyous and friendly attitude toward others that will lead to greater popularity and increased opportunities for attracting a romantic partner. In many cases this transit indicates an opportunity for marriage if there are no factors to the contrary. Artistic forms of self-expression such as music, painting, crafts and acting are favored. The native may be drawn to artistic motifs of a religious or philosophic nature, or use art and music as a means of conveying religious or philosophic ideas. This often takes place m the context of social gatherings. During this transit the native may organize social activities and festivities associated with church, family, school or private gatherings, or merely participate in such activities. However, by organizing such activities the native can bring much joy and happiness to others, thus increasing his or her popularity. This is a good transit for planning parties. Benefit performances and parties are likely to be highly successful in raising money for religious, educational or charitable causes, and the native can accomplish much good by helping to organize or by initiating such activities.

Since this transit can make people happier and more outgoing, this is an excellent transit for people who are normally shy, introverted or emotionally depressed. However, for those who are already hedonistically oriented, transiting Jupiter's conjunction to natal Venus may impel too much of a good thing. It could lead to idleness and overindulgence in sex, food, alcohol or other dissipating activities. For people undergoing hardships, this transit can be a potent antidote leading to a more spiritually joyous outlook. Some natives will incur good karma by helping to bring joy into the lives of those less fortunate. The double Pisces connotation of this transit underlies this impetus. Success in business, especially those businesses related to art, decorations, music and luxury items, is favored by this transit. It is also an excellent time for partnerships, establishing new friendships, seeking the favor of the opposite sex and engaging in public relations activities.

Transit Jupiter Conjunction Mars

Personal action of a constructive nature is highly favored by this transit. The native experiences more energy and self-confidence, and worthwhile accomplishments often result. This is a favorable time for seeking employment or undertaking career training. It is a favorable time for sports, travel and adventure. The native will generally put more energy into business and professional affairs, and these ambitions will result in greater financial and professional advancement and in improved status. This transit is especially favorable for business and professional activities related to building, engineering, politics, law, religion, medicine, education and real estate as well as police and military affairs.

The native should avoid taking too much for granted or having a cocky attitude. He or she may become a crusader for a favorite religious, philosophical, political, educational or charitable causes and can accomplish much good, provided the native does not assume an intolerant, sectarian attitude. This transit is helpful to coaches add those involved with physical education and sports. There will be a sense of personal honor and fair play according to the best of the native's understanding. Because of the Mars rulership of the natural eighth house, this transit is favorable for business related to affairs of the dead, tax accounting, insurance and legal affairs related to inheritance and corporate finance.

Transit Jupiter Conjunction Jupiter

This transit brings a period of renewed personal optimism and of increased interest in constructive activity related to the affairs ruled by the house where Jupiter is placed and the houses where Sagittarius, Pisces and Cancer are found. The native will generally become more interested in religion, philosophy, travel, education, charitable work and in improving family and domestic affairs. The native will be begin a new cycle with respect to philosophic and ethical development and will become more seriously concerned about the ultimate long-range values and issues of life. This can lead to spiritual renewal and pursuits of a happier, more meaningful way of life. The native will show an increased interest in sociological and cultural matters and activities, especially as expressed through the affairs ruled by the sign and house that Jupiter occupies. The native may develop a strong interest in foreign cultures and countries that could be an inducement to travel.

Transit Jupiter Conjunction Saturn

This transit introduces a time of serious hard work and slow, steady progress in professional affairs and educational, philosophical and spiritual pursuits. It is a fine aspect for pursuing programs of higher education for the purpose of career advancement. This aspect marks a critical period for politicians, business executives, lawyers, administrators and anyone who must maintain high public esteem. If the native is to be successful during Jupiter's transit over natal Saturn, he or she must scrupulously adhere to the highest ethical level. Decisions made and actions taken at this time can have far reaching consequences for the native's future career progress, status and reputation.

This is a favorable transit for work in fields such as law, politics, education, public relations, publishing and administration. It is an important transit for handling financial affairs and all types of business matters. The native may be responsible for handling the administration and business affairs of groups, organizations, schools, churches or other institutions. In any event, this is a time when the native must handle serious responsibilities and should try to make the practical affairs of life conform as possible to his or her philosophical deal.

Transit Jupiter Conjunction Uranus

Sudden and unexpected good fortune can result from this transit. The time is opportune for embarking upon experiments in group activities, religion, philosophy, education and travel. The native is likely to be exposed to advanced ideas in spiritual philosophy, sociology, and group cooperation, perhaps for the first time. Many new friends and organizational contacts come into the native's life, stimulating the imagination and thinking. The native can have unexpected, exciting and unusual opportunities for education and travel.

This is an excellent time for a scientific approach to the study of mystical or occult phenomena. The native may have some unusual, startling and inspiring clairvoyant or intuitive experiences. This is one of the best transits for the study and practice of astrology. The native may be drawn to participation in humanitarian, education and spiritual activities which can have an uplifting effect upon the larger society and make valuable contributions to the progress of civilization. There will be an interest in reincarnation, life after death, out of the body experiences and other occult phenomena that fall under twelfth house jurisdiction. The native will he more open-minded than usual to new ideas and universal, non-sectarian spiritual concepts. He or she is less likely to accept blindly any system of belief that cannot be directly experienced and proven. In general the native will be more humane and generous toward others and will take a fresh, unbiased view of all aspects of life. The extent to which these potentials will be realized will be realized will naturally depend upon the indications of the natal horoscope, other transits and progressions. If Uranus and Jupiter are inharmoniously aspected in the natal horoscope and there are other unfavorable transiting aspects made to this conjunction, there is danger of extravagance, recklessness, or idealism that lacks practicality and the test of experience.

Transit Jupiter Conjunction Neptune

A strong mystical, emotional religious tendency within the native often comes to the fore under this transit. Feelings of universal love and benevolence or a strong sense of devotion to some spiritual ideal, guru or spiritual teacher results. Whether these feelings are translated into practical service and action will of course, depend upon the natal horoscope and other predictive factors. For some natives this transit can mark a turning point away from agnosticism, atheism or perhaps just a negative emotional outlook toward a full, rich, recognition of the reality of God and an all-pervasive, divine love. This transit often brings about worthwhile service by causing such an inner attitudinal change. As a result of this increased spiritual awareness, the native may become more compassionate and generous toward those less fortunate and will manifest greater joy, radiance and generosity of spirit in relationships. Such a positive attitude is infectious and can do much to make the world happier. The native's imagination can be stimulated, resulting in creative work in art, philosophy, music, poetry and forms of religious expression. The native becomes fond of singing, religious activities and rituals of a spiritually uplifting nature.

This transit primarily affects the emotions and increases the devotional aspect of the native's expression. The native's attitudes toward family and the domestic circle may improve. There is often an inclination to join a religious or spiritual community. The home is used as a place of service as well as spiritual meditation and activity. The native may want to take in friends, even strangers, and try to "mother the world." This same attitude is extended toward the native's own family with consequent improvement in domestic relationships.

Transit Jupiter Conjunction Pluto

Although it is subject to modification by the potentials of the natal horoscope and other predictive factors operative at the time, this transit can bring a strong impetus to self-improvement and spiritual regeneration. The native finds it easier to see through the veil of illusion and perceive that everything in existence as a result of the vibration of cosmic energy or an all-pervasive divine reality. To the extent that this truth is sensed, the native is inspired to regenerate and improve the personal life to a point where he or she can share more fully and consciously in this fundamental evolutionary power of life.

The native may acquire recognition of reincarnation and life after death, as well as many other clairvoyant, spiritual experiences. He or she can begin to realize that all space and time is filled with divine intelligence that is unceasingly guiding all evolving life forms toward ever higher and more conscious goals. Under this transit the native may experience higher states of consciousness whereby this truth becomes a personal reality rather than a mere intellectual belief. Such realization will give the native greater determination to contribute something worthwhile and lasting to man's upward evolution.

On a more mundane level this transit is generally favorable for corporate enterprises, educational endeavors, and religious and charitable activities. The native may benefit through gifts, inheritance, insurance payments and corporate investments. It is an especially favorable transit for leadership in and cooperation with educational, religious and charitable organizations designed to improve existing social and economic conditions. The native should avoid embarking on a personal power trip and should endeavor to have a humble, reverent attitude in work and service.

Transit Jupiter Sextiles

Usually the sextiles of transiting Jupiter to natal planets indicate opportunities for growth with respect to the affairs ruled by the natal planet receiving the sextile. This usually takes the form of expanded intellectual awareness, increased openness to communication and contacts made through friendship and group associations. The native is more mentally awake and optimistic and recognizes more possibilities for constructive action. Communication with brothers, sisters friends and neighbors reveals new and sometimes unexpected opportunities for growth and development. The native realizes that a positive mental outlook is the key to progress regarding the affairs ruled by the planet that Jupiter is sextile.

Transit Jupiter Sextile Sun

Opportunities for personal creative expression and leadership arise with this transit aspect. The native acquires more self-confidence and uses his or her abilities for the benefit of the larger social milieu. Consequently, the native will be encouraged, admired and respected. He or she may take an active interest in religious, philosophical, sociological or political issues. This is a favorable transit for creative work in art, philosophy, writing, teaching, publishing and lecturing. The native usually finds it easier at this time to gain the support and acceptance of existing social, religious, educational and governmental institutions for ideas, projects, ambitions and further education. This is a favorable transit for vacation and travel.

Transit Jupiter Sextile Moon

This transit brings opportunities for improved communication and cooperation with family members and with friends who are part of the domestic scene. This is a favorable time for business activities related to real estate, building, home improvements, food and domestic products. The native tends to remember the positive aspects from the past and assumes a happier, more optimistic emotional outlook. The native may have ideas for home improvement and the home may be used as a gathering place for social, religious or cultural groups. In any event the native will become interested in making matters a part of the home life. This transit usually brings a period of greater financial prosperity and security, unless there are strong indicators to the contrary. Such increased security also contributes to a happier outlook on life.

Transit Jupiter Sextile Mercury

This transit acts as a definite mental stimulus. The native is inclined to positive thinking. Increased positive communication with brothers, sisters, neighbors and friends leads to new ideas and a realization of many new ways for attaining personal goals. The native can receive real education through these contacts and acquire valuable information for future use. Golden opportunities for further education and general philosophic and cultural enrichment can arise. It is a favorable time for beginning formal university programs of education and for gaining admittance to these institutions. This is an excellent period for writers, teachers, lecturers and all whose work requires creative thinking. This transit is favorable for those working in advertising or the promotion of some idea, philosophy or cause. The native will have opportunities for travel and study of foreign culture, religion or history. This is a favorable time for signing documents and formulating legal agreements.

Transit Jupiter Sextile Venus

The influence of this transit can be seen in increased social activity and artistic expression. The native has opportunities for romance and, if other predictive factors affecting the horoscope bear it out, perhaps even marriage. This is an excellent transit for those who normally have a depressed, gloomy outlook; such individuals are now more likely to smile and realize that life is much easier when one appreciates the beautiful and cultivates a happy outlook. Artists, musicians an performing artists will feel greater inspiration and a keener sensitivity to beauty. Artists experiencing this transit may find themselves attracted to religious forms of art, or art that conveys a spiritual or philosophic message. This is a favorable transit for organizing parties, festivals, dances and fund-raising activities sponsored by churches, schools or other clubs and organizations. This transit can indicate a time of increased financial prosperity for the native, especially for artists or those engaged in businesses related to art, music and luxury items.

Transit Jupiter Sextile Mars

This transit indicates a time of opportunity for constructive ideas to be put into action. Usually this takes the form of the native working to further professional and business ambitions. This is a favorable transit for those engaged in business or professions related to engineering, building, insurance, accounting, law, politics and corporate finance. The native may become a moving force in a religious, cultural or organizational activity. He or she may become a crusader for a worthy cause and because of this energy and enthusiasm can inspire others to action. thereby accomplishing much that is worthwhile. The native undergoing this transit may take an interest in sports, hiking, camping and other outdoor activities. He or she may travel or engage in strenuous physical activity as a means of seeking adventure.

Transit Jupiter Sextile Jupiter

This transit indicates increased opportunities for the native to pursue philosophic, cultural, religious and educational activities. The native may become involved with some kind altruistic work or service, often related to churches, schools, hospitals or charitable institutions. The native may make financial contributions to such institutions, and can develop a stronger sense of cultural, ethical and spiritual awareness and thus gain an expanded understanding of life and potential for personal growth. He or she will also become more positive and constructive in family relationships and domestic affairs, and is likely to travel or seek higher education at this time.

Transit Jupiter Sextile Saturn

With this transit come opportunities for education, business, and career. The native acquires a more serious, purposeful attitude toward attaining long range, personal goals that will bring professional advancement, money and enhanced status in the community. This is a favorable time for the native to seek the recognition and support of those in established positions of authority or to gain the support and cooperation of religious, educational and governmental institutions. The native may work in business, professional, educational or cultural groups and organizations that have, some far-reaching purpose. This is a favorable transit for active involvement in politics, although the native may tend toward a conservative viewpoint at this time. It is favorable also for business people, lawyers, judges, politicians, public relations personnel, school and church administrators and government officials. In general the native will have a more practical, realistic and businesslike approach to growth and progress in areas of importance.

Transit Jupiter Sextile Uranus

The native's intellectual and philosophical horizons expand rapidly under the stimulus of this transit. He or she can be introduced to many new spiritual and metaphysical concepts at this time, and is likely to establish many new friendships that will bring exposure to exciting new ideas. This is an excellent time for the study and practice of astrology and other parapsychology, occult, or metaphysical pursuits. The native may have some startling personal, intuitive or clairvoyant experiences if the natal horoscope indicates a capacity for this. He or she is likely to engage in group activities of a spiritual, educational, religious, scientific or humanitarian nature. Regarding these fields, the native becomes more broad-minded and open to new concepts. A new level understanding can lead to a more positive, constructive, optimistic outlook on life. There can be can interest in making spiritual concepts more scientific and vice versa. This is an excellent transit for all kinds of consciousness expansion and spiritual healing pursuits. The native may have unexpected opportunities for pursuit of higher knowledge or for travel. Many unlooked-for and exciting experiences, adventures and new friendships can materialize while traveling.

Transit Jupiter Sextile Neptune

This transit brings a time for greater faith and spiritual uplift. Whatever intuitive and mystical tendencies the native may have are likely to be increased. The native will generally be more devotional in his or her approach to spirituality. This can come about through exposure to some kind of religious philosophy, cult, system of belief or the influence of friends and acquaintances. The native can become more generous and humanitarian toward those less fortunate, and may be involved with religious organizations of a charitable or evangelical nature. He or she may go on a long journey in search of a spiritual teacher or to go on some kind of religious pilgrimage. There can be an exalted spiritual joy and sense of mystical contact with the infinite at this time. How strongly this will manifest will depend upon the tenor of the natal horoscope. Some natives will seek seclusion in religious retreats as a means of pursuing an inner meditative spiritual search. The home may also be a place of quiet meditation and retreat.

Transit Jupiter Sextile Pluto

This transit can bring about a period of spiritual regeneration and rebirth based upon new exposure to and understanding of a more advanced form of spiritual philosophy. Natives whose natal horoscope reveals a capacity for clairvoyance can have most interesting inner experiences at this time. The native can play an active role in improving and expanding existing social, educational, religious or cultural institutions, and is also likely to develop an interest in reincarnation, life after death and other occult phenomena. He or she can assume a role of leadership in spreading scientific, occult, philosophical, metaphysical or religious knowledge. This aspect can be auspicious for corporate business, inheritance and insurance, as well as large-scale scientific and business projects, endeavors and research.

Transit Jupiter Squares

Transit Jupiter Square Sun

This transit can indicate a time of false optimism and overexpansion in the affairs of life ruled by the houses in which Jupiter and the Sun are natally placed and the houses which they rule, as well as the house through which Jupiter is transiting. The native is likely to go to excesses and extremes of some kind that lack economy, practicality and realism. There may be generous motives but a lack of discrimination. This transit can also indicate self-indulgence in pursuit of pleasure or unwise financial speculation with a willingness to gamble or take risks. Because of the Sun's rulership of the fifth house there can be a general tendency to laziness and indifference.

The native can be attracted to some form of religious or philosophic pursuit but fails to apply it effectively to everyday life. There is also danger of developing spiritual pride, conceit and hypocrisy. Cultural and family conditioning may stand in the way of real progress and unbiased understanding. Seemingly generous gestures or grandiose attempts at self-expression can be performed out of a sense of personal pride and social ambition. A need for personal recognition and adulation may be the real reason behind the native's activities at this time. Much depends on how much practicality, discipline, mental impartiality and common sense the natal horoscope shows, as well as other concurrent transits. This transit can be a counter irritant to oppressive Saturn aspects in the natal horoscope or to those formed by transiting Saturn, in as much as it could increase optimism and self-confidence.

Transit Jupiter Square Moon

This is a transit of emotional excess and sometimes maudlin sentimentality. The native often makes extravagant expenditures of money and emotional energy on the home and family members without having a clear understanding of what is really needed. Display of family love and affection may arise more out of a need for emotional security than a real understanding of and concern for others. The native's emotional attachment may even be an annoyance and embarrassment to other people, family members in particular. Because of the tendency to extravagance and unwise financial expenditures and business investments, this is not a good time to deal in real estate, building, home improvements and domestic products. Many natives will have a tendency to overeat and put on weight under this transit. The native should avoid alcohol and fattening foods. Religious, philosophic, cultural and educational outlooks may be biased at this time by hereditary and cultural prejudices and inadequacies of the native's family and childhood social environment. The native can be influenced by national and class gender or lifestyle discrimination. In many cases this transit will produce many noble sentiments but with a lack of discipline, practicality and real understanding necessary to put them into practice. Often the result is inertia.

Transit Jupiter Square Mercury

This transit can indicate a time of mental confusion and lack of practicality. The native is apt to confuse attitudes with facts and let religious, social or philosophic prejudices and viewpoints interfere with a balanced perception of factual reality. Conversely, there can be a lack of spiritual awareness of the proper use of practical knowledge and factual information. The native does not understand that his or her duty is to work at perceiving reality exactly the way it is, as far as is within his or her power to do so, and then ethically determine how this factual understanding is to be used. There may be inattentiveness and lack of focus and discipline in studies or other intellectual pursuits. The native may be subject to prejudiced viewpoints. This is not a good time tor travel, higher education, legal affairs, contracts, lecturing or teaching. The native may tend to verbosity in speech and writing without really getting the point across. Communication can be confused and ambiguous. There is a tendency for the native to be inattentive and lazy in work or to use hypochondria or other excuses as a means of avoiding responsibility. The native is likely to arrive late for work or other important meetings or get appointments confused. During this transit the native should be especially attentive while driving.

Transit Jupiter Square Venus

This transit is apt to produce a time of overindulgence in luxury, expenditures and social activities that can be dissipate finances and vitality. The native should avoid excessive alcohol, food and sex. Marriages and partnerships entered into at this time can lack a basis in mutually shared practical experience and responsibility and are likely to fall apart eventually. Ambition for luxury, material wealth and status may assume undue importance for the native during this transit. This transit can be a good influence for someone who is usually too gloomy, introverted, depressed or burdened with responsibility. For those who lack discipline and purpose, however, it is definitely an adverse influence. The native may show an interest in art and music but without taste and real sensitivity. The main difficulty of this transit is laziness and lack of moderation.

Transit Jupiter Square Mars

This transit can lead to misguided and excessive ambition for personal glory, leadership and status. The native may be prey to a might-makes-right attitude. There is danger of hypocrisy and unjust ulterior motives in business dealings and professional and legal affairs. As with all transits, these influences will not be pronounced unless they stimulate a similar potential in the natal horoscope. The native can become hasty, impatient, reckless and careless. There is a tendency to plunge into an activity or endeavor without adequate examination and knowledge of what is involved in time, money, effort and future obligation. The native may take dangerous and unnecessary risks in sports, travel or driving or with tools, machinery and firearms, This is not a favorable time to start a new project, seek employment, change jobs or handle legal affairs or to be involved in financial and insurance matters or taxes and legacies. Some natives may become aggressive in crusading for their religion, philosophy or social or political ideology to the point of annoying and exasperating others They may attempt to accomplish some noble or even charitable endeavor without a practical or well-grounded approach. There is often considerable personal competition, and major projects require an attitude of and humility to be successful. In extreme cases the native may seek to profit through business dealings in weapons and sales, the black market, smuggling or other businesses of negative or questionable social value. There can be a crass let-the-public-be-damned attitude. However, similar indications in the natal horoscope must confirm this.

Transit Jupiter Square Jupiter

Under this transit the native is prone to various kinds of extremism and excess. These can take the form of one-sided religious, philosophical, social and cultural attitudes or of overindulgence in food and drink. The native is prone to unwise, extravagant financial expenditures. There is also a tendency toward laziness, self-indulgence, daydreaming and impracticality. This is not a favorable time for handling legal matters or making important decisions regarding education, domestic or private affairs because the native is apt to be swayed by sentiment and can lack a realistic approach. The native can also pursue aimless nonproductive travel.

Transit Jupiter Square Saturn

This is not a favorable time to make major moves or decisions regarding career, higher education, employment, business or legal matters. Sometimes natives suffer financial difficulties, lack of business or lack of employment. There is often bad timing and the native acts too early or too late to gain the benefit he or she hopes to achieve. The native's effort may suffer from a lack of adequate planning and organization. It is a good idea to maintain the status quo in important affairs of life until this transit passes. Lawsuits should be avoided, as should buying or selling property. The native can become painfully aware of the dichotomy between goals and ideals and what can actually be attained under existing circumstances. This is a time that requires patience and moderation. Psychologically there is a tendency to vacillate between extremes of optimism and pessimism. The native's ambition add creative insights may be blocked by the rigid policies and inertia of established business or educational or governmental institutions. Under these circumstances it is difficult for the native to sustain energy and enthusiasm.

The native can develop overly conservative religious, philosophical, cultural, educational and political viewpoints. Career responsibilities can stand in the way of educational and spiritual goals or vice-versa. Sometimes the native is burdened with more responsibility than can be handled. There can be a conflict between professional and family responsibilities during this transit. However, this transit can increase the native's ambition, seriousness and sense of purpose with respect to job or profession.

Transit Jupiter Square Uranus

In general the native under this transit will tend to lack discipline, organization and common sense. The native is inclined to jump to conclusions, take too much for granted and listen to the advice of misguided, unreliable people. There can be laziness and a desire for freedom without self-discipline. This transit often indicates impatience, foolishness and unrealistic optimism with respect to philosophic, business, financial and social affairs. Som natives fall prey to get-rich-quick schemes and suffer grave, sometimes disastrous, financial losses. There is a tendency to become involved in eccentric religious cults and group activities of questionable value. If the eighth house is involved, unexpected demise of a friend or acquaintance is possible. This is not a good transit for steadiness in pursuit of higher education. The native may have to deal with people of eccentric and unreliable habits. There can also be daydreaming and the desire to take off on a strange adventure of questionable value that will affect the stability of the native's practical affairs. This is not a good transit for psychic experimentation, travel or espousing new religious, philosophic and educational beliefs even though the native is apt to be attracted to all of these.

Transit Jupiter Square Neptune

The influence of this transit is highly illusory. The native is apt to get lost in daydreams and often there are strong, misguided, mystical and religious sentiments. Under this transit natives can become ensnared in the delusion that they are the chosen instrument of some divine revelation or the special disciple of a great spiritual master or being. If the natal horoscope shows strong tendencies toward common sense and practicality, the more extreme tendencies of this transit are not likely to manifest. For people prone to self-deception it is one of the most dangerous transits for real spiritual maturity. There can be strong escapist tendencies whereby the native seeks to avoid the practical responsibilities of life through fantasy, indulgence in alcohol or drugs or impractical, mystical cults and practices. The native is inclined to flowery spiritual sentiments with little practical service and discipline to back them up. Sometimes the native is inclined to be simply lazy. In general this transit is prone to a lack of discipline, common sense and practicality.

Transit Jupiter Square Pluto

This transit can result in extremist tendencies and ambition for personal power and social, political, cultural and religious influence. The native can display a desire to spiritually reform others while ignoring his or her own deficiencies. Sometimes this transit brings about disturbing psychic experiences. Dabbling in magical practices is ill-advised at this time. There can also be a tendency to become involved in extreme religious or spiritual viewpoints. The native can experience difficulties through legal affairs regarding taxes, insurance, legacies, inheritance, business finances and alimony settlements. Dubious cults and religious practices should be carefully examined before they are blindly accepted. All that glitters is not gold. The native should be careful to maintain strict honesty and integrity in business and professional dealings and should only be involved with people of like character. Impatience, pride, arrogance and attempting anything grandiose without having mastered the small things should be avoided.

Transit Jupiter Trines

Transit Jupiter Trine Sun

This transit brings a period of rapid personal advancement and fulfillment. The native has opportunities for higher education and for self-expression through the arts, theater or other creative enterprises. This is an excellent time for travel and pursuit of higher education and personal spiritual growth. The native becomes more generous and optimistic in his or her attitude toward others. This is a good aspect for speculative investments, provided they are made with a reasonable amount of common sense. This transit can also bring romantic opportunities, especially in the case of a departing fifth house trine of Jupiter to the natal Sun.

The native is generally more philosophically inclined and generous toward others and this gives the benefits that attend greater popularitly. The native can never be completely down and out while under the influence of this transit despite any other in indications to the contrary. There will always be a saving grace in his or her situation. If circumstances in other respects are favorable, this period may well be looked upon as one of the happiest and most successful in the native's life. This is good time to see favor and recognition from people in positions of power and authority. Artists, playwrights, actors, musicians and other performing artists can have their big break during this transit when they are given the opportunity to display their talent to a significant audience. This is an excellent time to seek admission to an institution of higher education. The native usually enjoys increased financial prosperity during this period or at least receives benefits and advantages that can ultimately mean greater earning ability.

Some natives will take a greater interest in spiritual pursuits or a contemplative way of life. Sometimes the native undergoes a spiritual or ethical reawakening and applies self-will constructively to reform his or her way of life. The native often develops a more positive self-image and develops greater self-confidence that leads in turn to a more positive and actively constructive way of life. The native often develops an interest in foreign countries and other cultures and sometimes in their religions. On a general level natives under the influence of this transit expand their cultural horizons and become interested in social progress trends and activities. They are apt to take a greater interest in children and their education during this transit. It is an excellent time for those in the teaching profession. It is easier for women to relate to men during this transit. Under transiting Jupiter trine natal Sun the native may assume a role of leadership in humanitarian, religious, educational, legal or charitable activities. He or she is more inclined at this time to help those less fortunate. This is the time when the native is apt to reap the rewards of previous good deeds.

Transit Jupiter Trine Moon

This transit indicates a time of increased prosperity and emotional well-being. It ushers in a favorable time for improving domestic affairs and establishing more constructive relationships with family members. It is generally easier for the native to relate to women at this time because the native is likely to have more emotional sympathy and sensitivity. This is a good transit for business activities, especially those related to real estate, building, farming, food, home and domestic products. The native will remember the good things of past family life and parental up-bringing and will seek to express these things in present family affairs. During this transit the home is often used as a gathering place for social, religious, cultural or educational activities. The native may also befriend those less fortunate, and welcome visitors into the home. This is a good transit for women who are pregnant or who are undergoing childbirth since it tends to as-sure a speedy and safe delivery. This transit, along with transiting Jupiter trine Sun, is excellent transit for working with children and caring for babies. In general the native will become more peaceful emotionally and more sympathetic and kind in his or her attitude and will consequently attract a favorable response from others. Good fortune will come through the affairs ruled by the houses that the Moon and Jupiter occupy and rule in the natal horoscope.

Transit Jupiter Trine Mercury

This transit indicates a period of rapid intellectual progress. The native becomes mentally posi-tive and optimistic. This is an excellent time to seek admission to a university or institution of higher learning or to travel, lecture, teach, publish or work with communications media. This is the best time to plan a journey if it can possibly be arranged. The native has many worthwhile constructive new ideas which can lead to advancement in work, education and friendships. The native's improved ability to communicate leads to the formation of worthwhile new friendships and group activities as well as improvement of established friendships. There is often improved efficiency and better relationships at work that can lead to advancement and promotion. Study and education also greatly enhance the native's value on the job. A more positive mental out-look makes the native less nervous land more relaxed, bringing about better health, the native is apt to be more conscious of correct diet and personal hygiene. Relationships with brothers, sis-ters, neighbors improve and the native becomes a more careful and considerate driver. There is usually better communication in domestic and family relationships, with a more harmonious family life. The native will be more inclined to send mail and stay in communication with friends and relatives, and will also come up with good ideas as to how to improve the effective-ness of charitable activities designed to help those in need. Often these ideas relate to how to publicize or promote such work as well as fund-raising efforts. In general this is an excellent transit for students and teachers and all people engaged in intellectual work or some kind of communication.

Transit Jupiter Trine Venus

This transit brings about a happy and fulfilling time in terms of romance and social relation-ships. The native will be invited to many social affairs. This is also an excellent time to plan or host a party. Social gatherings can also be used as fund-raising activities by those working with churches, charitable institutions or schools. Such activities can include art shows, benefits, mu-sicals or stage performances. This is an excellent transit for musicians and creative artists of all kinds. Artists can make money and gain recognition from people and institutions of wealth and prominence. This is also a good transit for vacation trips and pleasure travel. Natives may have opportunities for marriage if other factors concur. It is a good time to plan a marriage and honey-moon trip. The native is likely to become interested in serious music and religious art forms, and also may seek to help and understand those who are less fortunate. In general there is more kindness and sensitivity toward others. This is an excellent transit for people who are normally overly shy and introverted. It is also good for business, especially those related to music, art, psychology and luxury items. The native may gain special insights into how to make a product or service appeal to the public.

In the case of those who lack discipline and sense of purpose and who have been spoiled by having everything given to them, this transit can be too much of a good thing and can lead to self-undoing through dissipation. However, this transit can do a great deal to brighten and make more happy an otherwise difficult period in the native's life.

Transit Jupiter Trine Mars

This transit gives natives increased self-confidence and constructive ambition. The native will take positive action in business, profession, self-improvement and personal expression. There can also be increased interest in outdoor sports, physical exercise, hiking, travel and camping. This is a good transit for business related to law, finance, engineering, machinery, construction, real estate, building, insurance, tax accounting and fund-raising, The native may also take action in behalf of community organizations, churches, charitable institutions, universities or other worthwhile cultural activities and organizations. This is a good transit for political work. The native often is inspired to take the role of personal leadership in some worthwhile project or endeavor. There can also be active efforts at self-improvement or personal reform on some level. This will manifest as action taken through the affairs ruled by the houses which Mars and Jupiter natally occupy and rule and the house through which Jupiter is transiting. This is a good time for active, practical work related to university studies or programs of higher education. The native may also offer his or her personal work and service to a worthwhile activity or organization designed to help people. In general the native is likely to make a practical attempt to put religious, philosophical, ethical and social convictions into action. This is a good transit for coaches and people who work in the field of sports and physical education. The native will be more conscious of personal honor and fair play.

Transit Jupiter Trine Jupiter

This transit indicates a time of increased optimism and cultural and spiritual awareness. It is a favorable time for travel and pursuit of higher education, philosophy and spiritual knowledge. The native generally becomes more generous and interested in the well-being of others, and may help those in need and be involved in charitable work. Family and domestic affairs can also be improved under this transit. It is a good aspect for buying and selling real estate.

Transit Jupiter Trine Saturn

This is a favorable transit for professional and business affairs. It is a good time to enter into serious contracts and agreements and to handle legal affairs and matters relating to the government. This transit provides a good time to begin programs of higher education for the purpose of career advancement. The native generally becomes more serious-minded and assumes a more responsible attitude toward important long-range goals and responsibilities. Friendships and organizational associations are established with mature individuals and groups that are formed for the accomplishment of a serious professional, scientific, social or humanitarian purpose. The native may also assume a more constructive sense of responsibility with respect to family and domestic affairs. This is a good time to seek permanent employment and further one's career ambitions. The individual will develop a more patient attitude and will be neither too optimistic or pessimistic, and is apt to travel for business or professional reasons. In general the native is more inclined to be ethically responsible during this transit and concerned about maintaining a high degree of personal integrity. he native will attempt to apply religious, ethical, cultural, and philosophic ideas and standards to the practical affairs of life.

Transit Jupiter Trine Uranus

This transit can bring exciting, unexpected and uplifting events into the native's life. There can be sudden opportunities for higher education and travel. The native makes many exciting and inspiring new friends who often have unusual talents and spiritual insights, and may join occult, fraternal or humanitarian groups and organizations. Natives generally become more broad-minded and inspirationally intuitive in their philosophic and spiritual outlook. This is an excellent transit for the study and practice of astrology and all other constructive intuitive occult pursuits. Some natives may have unusual psychic or clairvoyant experiences and visions. The native becomes more generous, outgoing, friendly and optimistic in attitude toward other people which attracts friendship and leads to unexpected and interesting experiences. He or she may also carry on unusual activities in the home or use the home as a meeting place for spiritual work, organizational meetings or merely as a gathering place for friends. Many natives will introduce scientific, occult or mystical concepts into their religious and philosophical beliefs. This often comes about as a result of some insightful personal experience. This transit can bring the opportunity to do something new and exciting or original.

Transit Jupiter Trine Neptune

This transit brings about a time of emotional and spiritual uplift. The native becomes more devotional and mystical in the attitude toward life. Many will benefit through the practice of meditation and yoga. Some natives go on long journeys or religious pilgrimages or seek out the instruction of a spiritual teacher. Natives generally show more compassion than is usually their habit and will sometimes go out of their way to help those in need. Some people have strong clairvoyant, mystical experiences that may change their basic philosophy of life or remind them of the importance of spiritual principles they once upheld or believed in. Some may go on spiritual retreats or use their homes as places of meditative introspection or as a means of helping and serving others. This transit greatly increases the imaginative faculty and may bring out musical or artistic talents. These talents could be used to express intuitive feelings or spiritual ideas and philosophies. Natives can manifest greater empathy, understanding and intuitive rapport with those around them. In general the native is more kind and spiritually aware under the influence of this transit.

Transit Jupiter Trine Pluto

This transit can bring about spiritual regeneration in the lives of those who experience it. Natives become interested in the deeper underlying spiritual forces of life, often as a result of a personal, intuitive or clairvoyant experience. There can also be an interest in social reform and helping others live a more spiritually vibrant and constructive life. The experience of this transit can greatly enhance the native's faith in and understanding of universal spiritual laws and principles such as karma, reincarnation, intuitive guidance and the existence of a beneficent universal power. This faith gives the native greater courage and confidence to regenerate the affairs of his or her life, especially with respect to the. affairs ruled by the houses that Jupiter and Pluto natally occupy and rule and through which Jupiter is transiting. Natives sometimes benefit through insurance, inheritance, gifts and legacies under this transit. This transit greatly enhances the positive development of clairvoyant intuitive faculties and favors the study of the occult. This is also a good transit for people engaged in large scale business enterprises or those who work for the growth and improvement of religious, educational, cultural and charitable institutions. This is also a good time for home improvements and improving family and domestic affairs.

Transit Jupiter Oppositions

Transit Jupiter Opposition Sun

This transit indicates a time when the native can have unrealistic expectations regarding social relationships. This is not good time for financial speculation or investments made on ungrounded over-optimistic expectations. The native can tend to take too much for granted at this time with respect to romantic relationships or other social relationships. Some natives develop an egotistical attitude that becomes an annoyance to others. This often takes the form of moral sermonizing or religious proselytizing of whatever sect or belief the native subscribes to. In other cases natives can become lazy. If the native is a humble and conscientious person by basic character he or she may be eager to please others during this transit, even to the point of unnecessary self-sacrifice. There can be social difficulty created by generosity without discrimination whereby the native embarrasses other people by doing too much or unnecessary things for them, creating an unwanted sense of obligation. The native may have ulterior motives behind his or her generosity in which case these feelings on the part of others may not be entirely unfounded.

Transit Jupiter Opposition Moon

This transit indicates a time when the native is prone to emotional and financial extravagance. The native may take too much for granted with respect to family and domestic relationships. Financial extravagance can lead to bad relationships with creditors. Some natives will show excessive sentimentality and emotionalism. The native is prone to overindulgence in food and drink in social gatherings. People with this transit can become overly solicitous and protective toward their families and offspring. Social activities can lead to laziness and inattentiveness in work and study. The native's philosophic and religious outlook can be influenced by family and cultural prejudices at this time. Natives sometimes acquire an attitude of smug self-righteous-ness. In many cases the result will simply be laziness and inattentiveness to work. This is not a good time for business affairs related to real estate, food, building, farming and domestic products. In an effort to please others, natives may promise more than they can deliver and consequently suffer. Emotional memories and past sentimental attachments, often those related to the family and the native's early environment, can prevent the native from making the best use of present relationships or can distort his or her attitude toward such relationships.

Transit Jupiter Opposition Mercury

This transit usually indicates a time of mental confusion and of taking too much for granted in interpersonal communication. The native may profess to know more than he or she does or socially indulge in long-winded philosophical generalities of little practical meaning and value. Some natives may be gullible and subject to fraud and deception. The native may become lazy and inattentive to study and work. A tendency to engage in idle talk and socializing with co-workers and other employees can cause inefficiency on the job. Carelessness while driving and traveling can also be a danger. The native may be taken in by people who promise more than they deliver, and the native may also be prone to such behavior. This is not a good time to sign documents, make agreements or handle legal affairs. The native's philosophical and religious values can become vague, impractical, fanatical or one-sided. Generally, the native does not pay enough attention to detail and the practical application of ideas. A tendency to ramble on verbally can be an annoyance to family and friends.

Transit Jupiter Opposition Venus

This transit indicates a time when the native can be swept up in social gatherings and relationships to the point where money, time, energy and health are dissipated. There is also a tendency to financial extravagance on luxuries and entertainment. Some natives will be overindulgent toward others without discrimination. There is also the danger of entering into marriage and romantic relationships without the practical experience of getting along with the other person under conditions of work, responsibility, stress and difficulty. (Pre-commitment relationships developed only at parties and on dates may lead to a ride awakening.) For people who are accustomed to a lot of discipline and struggle in life or who are too shy and introverted, this transit can be good. It will help them to relax and enter into relationships which are more fun and will encourage them to unwind and come out of their shell. Over-expansion in business matters may lead to difficulty and indebtedness. This is not a favorable time for formulating business partnerships. Sensuality and self-indulgence should be avoided.

Transit Jupiter Opposition Mars

This transit can create a mood of overconfidence and aggressiveness in the native. He or she may encounter people who try to force their political, philosophical, religious or social ideologies on the native, or the native may treat other people in a similar way. This transit can also bring legal disputes over finances, inheritances, insurance, taxes, alimony or business dealings. Some natives may indulge in sexist or militaristic attitudes or become subject to racial, political, family, religious or social biases and prejudices. There can be conceit or overestimation of one's ability and worth. Some natives will tend to be overly ambitious and self-confident in business and career projects, leading to later disgrace, indebtedness, failure or self-undoing if these tendencies are carried too far. This is a time when the native is prone to wastefulness, extravagance and excessive self-indulgence. There can be the temptation to use unfair

means in sports and other competitive activities. A know-it-all attitude can generally make it difficult for the native to cooperate with others, and the native may have to deal with people who have such an attitude. Generally there can be insufficient regard for the rights and feelings of others.

Transit Jupiter Opposition Jupiter

Under this transit the native can be overly optimistic with respect to personal relationships and social interactions. The tendency to take too much for granted can lead to difficulty with respect to religious, legal, educational, domestic and social interpersonal affairs. There can be the tendency to proselytize for one's own religious, social, philosophical and political views to the point of annoying others. In general this aspect tends toward foolish optimism and gullibility on the native's part. If the native is naturally level-headed it may not have too much effect. Over-extension can create difficulties through affairs ruled by the houses that Jupiter rules and occupies in the natal horoscope and through which Jupiter is transiting.

Transit Jupiter Opposition Saturn

This is a transit that can bring about financial and legal difficulties through partnerships, marriage, legal affairs, organizational endeavors and dealings with religious and educational institutions. The native may experience bad timing, rebuff and discouragement in dealing with others or in gaining their support in organizational and professional endeavors He or she may be too conservative in attitude or encounters with people. There can be the temptation to use unfair or dishonest tactics to further one's own financial interests, professional advancement or status. The native and/or others are apt to have ulterior motives of money, status and professional advancement in interpersonal dealings, friendship and partnership, and social, legal, religious and organizational affairs. There can also be kind of dog-eat-dog business and professional competition which wears on the native's nerves and psychological and spiritual well-being. Professional and status interests can lead to religious and philosophical hypocrisy. The native may also encounter red tape and legal obstacles to plans for growth and expansion.

This is not a good period for political, legal, business, professional and educational endeavors. The native runs into financial difficulties or encounters inertia and the inability to change existing educational, religious, business or governmental institutions. The native should try to maintain the status quo in professional, educational, cultural, domestic and financial affairs until this aspect passes. There could be conflict between professional and family responsibilities.

Transit Jupiter Opposition Uranus

This transit is likely to bring unusual but not stable friendships, acquaintances and ideas. These ideas are apt to be lacking in balance and practicality. Natives should be alert to con artists and their get-rich-quick schemes. The native is not apt to sustain enthusiasm for one ideology and instead will skip from group to group with little to show for the effort. In general there tends to be a lack of discipline and common sense at this time. Business affairs are apt to be unstable and the native is prone to unwise and extravagant investment in projects of unreliable and dubious value. Many natives tend to get wanderlust at this time and to travel for adventure, often leaving practical affairs in shambles. The odd friendships established at this time are not apt to prove lasting or reliable. This is not a good time for stability in business and some natives become involved in financial lawsuits or other difficulties There can also be problems over joint finances, taxes, insurance, inheritance, alimony and credit.

Transit Jupiter Opposition Neptune

This transit tends towards eccentric religious involvements. The native is likely to profess much sympathy, spirituality and religious sentiment but lacks practical application and discrimination. This transit also inclines natives to aimless wanderings in search of some vague mystical goal, or simply new acquaintances and experiences. This transit can also produce bizarre dreams, visions and psychic experiences, usually strongly colored by the native's own unconscious mind. The imagination can run wild and lead to useless fantasies and daydreaming. Natives can also be prone to maudlin sentimentality and useless emotional outpourings with respect to family, close relationships and objects of religious devotion. Some natives lose contact with their environment and the people in it. Indulgence in alcohol and drugs is ill-advised at this time. Natives who have a strong practical orientation and well-developed capability for self-discipline may not be too strongly affected by this transit, but they may have to deal with people who display the above-mentioned characteristics. This transit can intensify any neurotic or psychotic tendencies a native may already have. Some natives will try to use their philosophy or religion as a crutch or as an escape from work and responsibility.

Transit Jupiter Opposition Pluto

This transit can bring out autocratic tendencies in the native. Natives may try to reform those around them while neglecting their own development. In extreme cases some natives adopt fanatical or one-sided religious and philosophical viewpoints and attitudes and try to force them on others. This naturally causes resentment and conflict. This transit tends to increase whatever latent delusions of grandeur the native may have and in extreme cases can lead to a messianic complex. This is not a good transit for handling lawsuits, legal matters, business, taxes, inheritance, insurance and other business dealings related to partnerships or governmental, political, educational or religious institutions. The native should generally strive to maintain an attitude of balance and humility and to avoid excessive or extreme measures.

VII

Transits of Saturn

Transit Saturn Through the Houses

Saturn's transit through the houses of the horoscope indicates the department of life through which the native will experience an increased sense of responsibility and seriousness. There will be difficulties, delays and obstacles relating to the affairs of the house that Saturn is transiting. Often the native has the feeling that he or she is working harder than ever to achieve the desired result. The affairs of the house Saturn is transiting somehow may be linked to professional, governmental, legal, partnership, group or organizational responsibilities. Saturn's transit through a house brings serious and meaningful lessons of work and responsibility in the affairs of the house that Saturn transits, thus building structure into the life as the native climbs one more hill toward self-unfoldment and self-mastery.

Transit Saturn Through the First House

Saturn transiting over the Ascendant and through the first house usually brings about increased reserve, while making one austere and serious in expression, personal appearance and mannerisms. If Saturn makes favorable aspects while transiting the first house, the native may apply constructive self-discipline, resulting in increased work and personal accomplishment, giving the native a deeper understanding of life's intricacies. If Saturn is afflicted in the natal horoscope and makes adverse contacts while in the first house, the native may experience a lack of confidence, a worrisome attitude and ill health. A negative attitude during this transit may alienate the native from others.

The personal ambitions of the native may cause him or her to run into difficulties and obstacles which could somehow be linked to governmental, legal, partnership, marital or group restraint. The native could also be thwarted because of difficulties in obtaining the cooperation of others who feel they don't want to become involved or believe that there is nothing of value in the situation for them. Any selfish motivations and ambitions on the native's part will be blocked as

Saturn transits the first house, thereby forcing the native to learn concern for the needs and rights of others. Saturn is exalted in Libra, which is the seventh house sign of the partner. Saturn transiting this first house of self-hood usually teaches the native a greater sense of personal responsibility, self-reliance and responsibility relating to the rights of others.

As Saturn transits the first house, digestive problems caused by the restriction of gastric juices may occur. During this transit it is wise to follow a sensible diet. Saturn is accidentally in its fall while transiting this house, and one is therefore likely to feel occasionally tired during this period or even generally debilitated. Regular periods of rest will help overcome the weariness of the bones. Relaxation is recommended.

Transit Saturn Through the Second House

Saturn transiting the second house usually relates to a time of increased financial and business responsibility. The native is forced to become more prudent, economical and efficient in the use of personal resources. Under this transit, the native must take full responsibility for his or her own financial security, and is thus forced to work hard for a living.

If Saturn is natally well-aspected and makes favorable contacts while in the second house, the native develops business insights and skills. Under this transit one may acquire wealth through hard work, good organization, resourcefulness and the steady application of abilities. The affairs ruled by the houses in which Capricorn, Libra and Aquarius are found may present business opportunities. In general the native will become more frugal and conscious of material values. However, if this is carried to extremes, it could result in a materialistic attitude or an outlook on financial responsibility that could eventually lead to excessive worry and tension.

If Saturn is afflicted while transiting this house there can be financial loss and limitation; delays in business affairs, legal, governmental and partnership difficulties may occur. Obstacles that impede the native's financial well-being may arise through the affairs ruled by the houses in which Capricorn, Libra and Aquarius are found.

For the native whose natal horoscope indicates a need for more practicality, economy and self-sufficiency, this transit of Saturn can be an especially valuable, evolutionary experience. It is characteristic of this transit that the native is not given any material or financial support that is not earned through work. If Saturn is well-aspected while transiting the second house, one ends up with a substantial sense of value regarding materialistic matters, and finances are put on a more stable basis.

Transit Saturn Through the Third House

Saturn transiting the third house indicates a time of increased seriousness and discipline in the native's intellectual outlook. He or she is apt to become more cautious and reserved in speech and writing. The native may become interested in structured intellectual studies such as mathematics, science and philosophy.

If Saturn is natally well-aspected and makes favorable contacts while transiting this house, it is an auspicious time to undertake formal educational programs, especially in order to increase career potential or general cultural enrichment. The powers of mental concentration are enhanced, and the mind becomes more methodical and systematic. This transit by itself does not give mental originality, but it does impart good organization and mental focus. During this transit the native's professional responsibilities, group associations and partnerships may become involved in some manner with communication, writing, education, news media or scientific and intellectual pursuits.

If Saturn is afflicted in the natal horoscope and makes adverse contacts while transiting this house, the native may be prone to negative thinking, pessimism and worry. Difficulties with transportation and delays in communication may occur. There may be unpleasant or cold relationships with brothers, sisters and neighbors. The native should exercise great caution while signing contracts and written agreements.

Transit Saturn Through the Fourth House

Saturn crossing the Nadir and transiting the fourth house usually brings a time of increased domestic responsibility that is often accompanied by a period of personal obscurity. Often the family or one of the parents places an extra burden of responsibility on the native. During this period the native may become involved in business concerned with real estate, building, farming, mining, ecology, food or domestic products.

If Saturn makes harmonious contacts while transiting the fourth house, domestic affairs will be stabilized in domestic affairs, resulting in greater security for the native and his or her family. Professional, partnership and group activities may take place in the home which can entail additional work for the native and his family. One may advantageously paint and paper the walls, lay carpeting, or perhaps paint the outside of the home or business buildings while Saturn transits this house. It is also possible for an older person to move into the domestic scene; one assumes the responsibility of an older person in some related way.

Saturn is in its detriment while transiting this house; consequently, the reflex action of the tenth house often makes it difficult for the native to attain career success because domestic and family problems may interfere with professional advancement. The difficulties resulting from obscurity and loneliness associated with this transit of Saturn may initiate a deeper degree of spiritual maturity. Saturn afflicted while transiting this house may promote a tendency toward emotional depression and despondency.

Transit Saturn Through the Fifth House

Saturn transiting the fifth house usually indicates a time of increased responsibility related to children. If Saturn is afflicted in the natal horoscope and makes adverse contacts while in his house, and if one is the right age, there could be an unwanted pregnancy. This is not a good time for speculative financial investments. During this transit, however, the native may become involved with a business concerned with a theater, stock market investment, education or teaching. Those involved in the creative and performing arts may be more disciplined and better organized in their work. This transit by itself however does not provide creative inspiration.

Many natives complain about a lack of romance while Saturn transits this house. Romance, if it does occur, may be with an older, more mature or established person, or someone with whom the native has had previous connections. This is not an easy period because if Saturn's accidental detriment in this house; therefore, loved ones may become cold and unresponsive. Romantic involvements may have heavy obligations connected with them. If Saturn is afflicted there can be a major disappointment in love. On the other hand, if Saturn is well aspected, it can cement a love relationship.

Transit Saturn Through the Sixth House

Saturn transiting the sixth house indicates a time of increased responsibility in one's work. However, if Saturn is well-aspected in the natal horoscope and makes favorable contacts while transiting this house, the native will manifest skill, efficiency, good organization, patience and thoroughness in work. Although the native will feel secure in his or her job, there will be a greater work load with more responsibility.

Care should be exercised with diet, as this house has a tendency to restrict the flow of digestive juices in the same way that it does in the first house. Greater caution is needed regarding health; sensible dietary habits should be followed, as these are especially important during this period for the native's well-being. Under this transit of Saturn, chronic illness could interfere with the native's ability to work. During this period, if Saturn is afflicted, the native may be subjected to bone, skin, knee, or kidney disorders. Sprains and breaks in particular are likely to occur. Recovery from disease is likely to be slow, since the vitality is apt to be low. Often this transit of Saturn brings about an opportunity to work at something related to the medical field.

If Saturn is afflicted in the natal horoscope and makes adverse contacts while transiting this house, there can be problems of unemployment or overwork. The native may be forced to perform difficult, objectionable or menial tasks. There is also danger of becoming ill or injured as a result of overwork or occupational hazards.

Transit Saturn Through the Seventh House

Saturn transiting the seventh house of the horoscope indicates a time of increased responsibility regarding personal relationships, especially marriage and business partnerships. Under this transit the native is forced to consider the partner or the other fellow, especially this person's needs and wishes. If marriage occurs under this transit, it is apt to be to an older or mature person or to be one who is well-established and career oriented. Saturn transiting this house can bring about a karmic marriage or can delay or prevent marriage. This of course depends upon how Saturn is placed in the natal chart. If Saturn is well-aspected in the natal horoscope and makes good contacts while transiting this house, its influence can give stability and reliability to marriage, business or other close personal relationships. However, if the native harbors selfish motivations while Saturn is in this house, he or she will suffer unpopularity and loss due to the reaction of others whose sense of justice is violated. The native is also apt to have a strong sense of justice at this time. While Saturn transits this house, the native may become involved in professional matters related to law, arbitration and public relations.

If Saturn is afflicted in the natal horoscope and makes adverse contacts while transiting the seventh house, there can be difficulties and burdensome responsibilities involving marriage, partnerships, public relationships and lawsuits. There can be heavy obligations in relationships with people in general, but particularly with those connected with the government or those within the native's own profession.

Transit Saturn Through the Eighth House

Saturn transiting the eighth house usually indicates a time of increased responsibility regarding joint finances, taxes, insurance and corporate affairs. During Saturn's transit through this house, the native can become involved in professional, group or partnership matters related to insurance, taxes, accounting, corporate finances or businesses related in some way to death. If Saturn is heavily afflicted, one may even be married to someone who may be or become a financial burden. There can be problems with taxes, insurance, inheritance, partner's money, corporate financial affairs or alimony.

In some cases the native may develop a serious, philosophic interest in occult subjects, especially those relating to life after death and reincarnation. A serious interest in scientific investigation of the fundamental energy forces of nature may also develop under this transit. The native is likely to give serious thought to questions of life after death. Thoughts may also turn to making out a will, inheritance, legacies or purchasing insurance. Often transiting Saturn in the eighth house brings about the death of an elderly member of the family or perhaps a friend. If Saturn is afflicted in the natal horoscope and makes adverse contacts while transiting this house, there can be a morbid fear of death or the actual death of a loved one.

Transit Saturn Through the Ninth House

Saturn transiting through the ninth house usually indicates a time of increased, serious interest m higher education, especially in studies that will give the native status and career advancement. One's attention is drawn to religion, law, philosophy, history or foreign cultures. Often the native develops a strong ambition to achieve some special intellectual or cultural distinction in the form of writing, publishing or lecturing in the fields of religion or philosophy.

If Saturn is afflicted in the natal horoscope and makes adverse aspects while transiting the ninth house, there may be difficulties while on long journeys or while in foreign lands. The native may be confronted with difficult or uncongenial university studies if at an institution of higher learning. Also, there may be obstacles involving publication or communication.

Transit Saturn Through the Tenth House

Saturn's transit through the tenth house usually indicates a time of culmination of the native's ambition for career, position and status. Increased responsibilities arise in the native's profession or job. There can also be increased responsibility through relationships with superiors, as well as with established governmental or corporate institutions. In general Saturn's transit through the tenth indicates a time of increased work and social responsibility. The native will be very busy with the affairs of the world in which he or she moves. While Saturn transits the

Midheaven and the tenth house, the native will receive fame and recognition deserved s a result of past positive motivations and actions. This result of course depends to a great extent upon how Saturn is aspected in the natal horoscope and the contacts it makes while transiting the tenth house. If in the preceding years the native shirked responsibilities or acted with selfish motivations, this transit may bring a time of public disgrace, fall from high position or some form of social deprivation and difficulty. On the other hand, if in the past the native has worked with patience and self-discipline and has acted with altruistic motives, Saturn's transit through this house may bring a time of professional public honor or public recognition.

If Saturn is afflicted in the natal horoscope and makes adverse contacts while in the tenth house, there can be a lack of recognition. There can also be difficulty gaining the favor or support of people in positions of power and authority. There can also be problems with unemployment or the lack of adequate opportunities in professional pursuits.

Transit Saturn Through the Eleventh House

Saturn transiting the eleventh house indicates a time of increased responsibility generated by friendships and group associations. In some instances the native may be called upon to act as a counselor or advisor to others. The native may assume the role of leadership or responsibility within a group or organization.

This transit corresponds to Aquarius, and Saturn is accidentally dignified in this house. If Saturn is well-aspected and strong in the natal horoscope and makes favorable contacts while transiting this house, the native is apt to develop serious philosophic, scientific and humanitarian interests that may lead to friendships with older, more mature or serious-minded individuals. The native may also become involved with groups and organizations that have similar goals. This association may lead to a broader and deeper understanding of life and its worthwhile accomplishments. In general when Saturn transits his house the native will try to understand life more in terms of universal laws and principles.

If Saturn is weak in the natal chart or makes adverse contacts while transiting the eleventh house, the native may enter into friendships or group activities with ulterior motives relating to status, career or monetary advancement. Since like attracts like, the people with whom the native associates are likely to have the same motives. Naturally, such associations will last only as long there is the possibility of personal gain. This eventually may lead to indifference, dislike or even enmity.

Transit Saturn Through the Twelfth House

Saturn transiting the twelfth house in the horoscope indicates a time of withdrawal from the outer affairs of life, and serious attention is directed toward introspective, spiritual disciplines. This transit of Saturn through the twelfth house may be a time of obscurity during which the native's ambitions are thwarted. During this time the native will work quietly behind the scenes, and may become professionally involved in some form of secretive organizational or even governmental activity, or might undertake some form of monastic, spiritual discipline. The native may be especially drawn toward retreats or monasteries.

Often under this transit the native develops a professional interest in psychology or medicine, perhaps becoming submerged in a large, impersonal institution or organization. The native is apt to work in hospitals, universities, prisons or in an area pertaining to religious organizations. If Saturn is strong in the natal horoscope and makes favorable contacts while transiting this house, the native may experience deep, spiritual realizations that give an inner peace of mind. In general this is a time for a spiritual search that probes the evolution of the meaning of past experience. The native should work to make conscious the contents of the unconscious mind.

If Saturn is afflicted or weak in the natal horoscope or makes adverse contacts while transiting the twelfth house, the native may succumb to moodiness, depression, negative thinking and emotional despair. If carried to extremes, these attitudes may lead to a nervous breakdown. If Saturn is heavily afflicted, the native may be tempted to use devious, secretive or underhanded means to obtain money, status or a professional position. The native might also have to bear some private sorrow or be subjected to hospitalization or imprisonment. In some unusual cases, the native may even become a political prisoner.

Transit Saturn Through the Quadrants

One of the most valuable contributions to the field of astrological prediction theory is the interpretation made by the late Grant Lewi of Saturn's major cycles from the Nadir to the Midheaven and from the Midheaven back to the Nadir as this planet transits through the houses of the horoscope.

During the period of Saturn's transit from the Nadir to the Midheaven through the western sector of the chart there is a gradual rise in fortune with respect to public recognition and professional status. Conversely, during Saturn's transit from the Midheaven to the Nadir the native goes from a time of culmination of personal ambition to a time of personal obscurity.

Saturn's transit through the tenth house indicates a period of peak activity with regard to career and personal material ambition. During the period of Saturn's movement from the tenth house to the first house the native must gather sufficient material to work with during the time of personal obscurity when Saturn goes from the Ascendant to the Nadir During this obscure period, when Saturn moves through the first quadrant of the horoscope, it is difficult for the native to gain new opportunities for career advancement and to achieve status in the eyes of the world.

When Saturn by transit reaches the Nadir the native experiences a low ebb where personal fame and fortune are concerned. During this period the native is thrown back upon his or her own resources and must go it alone in terms of acquiring material security and the necessities of life. This period of trial is followed by a gradual increase in personal and material security. This is the result of a realization of the necessity for greater personal resolve and self-discipline. The pangs of the social loneliness experienced while Saturn transits the fifth house and the hard work necessitated by Saturn's transit through the sixth house leads to the new start in the seventh house.

When transit Saturn enters the seventh house and crosses the Descendant the native no longer has to go it alone. At this time opportunities arise for partnerships and for some degree of cooperation from the public with respect to career ambitions. The reason for this is that Saturn has reached the house of its accidental exaltation. As time goes by outlets are found for the native's abilities in terms of larger public demands.

There is the a gradual increase of personal recognition and material security, culminating in Saturn's conjunction with the Midheaven and entry into the tenth house.

Transit Saturn Conjunctions

The conjunctions of transiting Saturn to planets usually indicate a time that calls for work, self-discipline and acceptance of responsibility in the affairs of the native's life ruled by the planet that Saturn conjuncts and the signs and houses that the planets rule. The native may have to work harder than usual to achieve results. If the native is willing to work and organize the affairs of the Saturn conjunction, it may lead to constructive and lasting accomplishment. However, Saturn conjunctions may also bring about frustrations and delays that promote a pessimistic outlook.

Transit Saturn Conjunction Sun

Saturn's transit over the native's Sun may increase the native's ambition for self-sufficiency and independence. It may also delay or thwart personal ambition. This can be a critical point in the development of the native's career and reputation in his or her social environment. This transit may affect the native in various ways depending upon how Saturn and the Sun are aspected in the natal horoscope. It may strengthen the native's resolve and self-discipline, or it may merely cause depression and a negative attitude. In any event the native's strength, patience, endurance and self-discipline will be tested. In the long run this transit has a maturing and strengthening effect on the native's character.

There are likely to be problems and difficulties brought about through the affairs ruled by the sign and house in which the Sun is placed and the affairs ruled by the house in which Leo is found. This conjunction is apt to bring frustration and difficulties in matters relating to love and romance. During this transit there can be increased responsibility or difficulty with children or their education. It is not favorable for stock market investments, speculative enterprises or the pursuit of pleasure. The native is apt to feel that self-expression is being thwarted.

Transit Saturn Conjunction Moon

This transit is generally considered to be one of the most difficult in astrology. It usually brings a time of emotional depression often caused by family, domestic or financial problems of some kind. The native may be burdened by the responsibility of caring for a parent, an older person or a family member who is sick. Contact with such people may drain the native's vitality.

There can be health problems that are caused by sluggish digestion affecting the stomach because Saturn restricts the flow of digestive juices. There can be water retention and sluggishness of the lymphatic system; therefore, it is recommended that the native avoid heavy food at this time. Under this transit there may be a tendency to brood about unhappy experiences and misfortunes of the past, which has a disintegrating effect on the native's present emotional outlook. It is very easy for the native to wallow in self-pity or to develop a sour emotional outlook that drives others way.

Under this transit, however, practical accomplishments may be achieved in the realms of domestic improvements, real estate or fixing up and organizing the home. While under this transit the native should remember that it won't last forever.

Transit Saturn Conjunction Mercury

Saturn transits over Mercury indicate a time of increased mental work and seriousness. It is a favorable transit for writing and serious study of mathematics, science and scholastic pursuits, provided the native is capable of self-discipline. By itself this transit does not bestow mental originality, but it does increase organizational ability, discipline and depth for the kind of work in which the native is engaged. The native will take a more serious interest in health, work and education for the purpose of improving career abilities. Under this transit one has the ability to give and receive substantial advice.

Because of the double Aquarius significance of this aspect, the native may become involved in serious group or organizational activities, especially those activities that relate to educational or scientific work. If Saturn or Mercury is afflicted in the natal horoscope, the native may be prone to negative thinking, worry and depression. Saturn's transit over Mercury could make him or her critical or inclined to lack understanding of others. There could also be difficulties relating to communication or transportation. Under this transit the native should be very careful regarding contract agreements and the signing of documents.

Transit Saturn Conjunction Venus

This transit may be favorable for creative work as it gives an increased awareness of form, symmetry, rhythm and structure in time and space. Under this transit the native may be involved in business affairs related to the arts or luxury items. Because of the double Libra significance of this transit, there may be an interest in arbitration, public relations or legal affairs.

On the emotional, social and romantic level, however, this transit may indicate a time of frustration. The native and those with whom he or she comes in contact will be more cautious with each other. This aspect also indicates that relationships will lack warmth and spontaneity. This isn't a favorable transit for romance, and it can also put a strain on an existing marriage because of overwork or burdensome responsibilities. However, it does increase the native's sense of loyalty. This transit also may cause an old romance or friendship to reoccur in the native's life. If Venus is afflicted in the natal horoscope, this transit can indicate financial difficulty. However, in the long run, it can favor business through well-planned organization and hard work.

Transit Saturn Conjunction Mars

This transit may indicate a time of increased work and professional ambition. It has a double Capricorn significance, so the native may assume important responsibilities in political, governmental or corporate management. There is even the possibility of becoming involved some-how in military affairs. There can be considerable activity concerning machinery, construction or physical labor. Under this transit the native should avoid potentially dangerous or violent sit-uations.

The native should avoid developing a hard, unsympathetic attitude at this time. On the negative side there can be a tendency to abuse others for the sake of personal ambition which can lead to resentment and conflict. If this transit is constructively used, it may lead to honest work and worthwhile accomplishments. Under this transit one learns to use personal energies in a wiser, more disciplined, practical and well-organized way. If Saturn or Mars is afflicted or weak in the natal horoscope, the native may experience frustration of desires that in turn may lead to anger and resentment and, in extreme cases, violence. Under this transit there may be difficult rela-tionships with government officials, bosses or those in positions of power and authority. This strife may be the result of the native's own attitude or the attitude of others, although it is more likely that both parties will be responsible.

Transit Saturn Conjunction Jupiter

This transit usually brings about a period of serious attention to business, educational and do-mestic affairs. The native is forced to examine plans for growth and expansion in these areas in a more realistic and practical way. This period favors steady progress in established, stable busi-ness enterprises because the native is apt to become more serious-minded and industrious. This is not a time for speculative business ventures, however. During this transit the political, philo-sophic and religious views of the native are apt to become more conservative. It is a favorable transit for educational endeavors designed to enhance the native's career potential.

In general this transit brings a time of serious self-examination of long-range goals and pur-poses, especially in respect to the affairs ruled by the signs and houses in which the conjunction occurs and which Jupiter and Saturn natally occupy and rule. If Jupiter and Saturn are afflicted in the natal horoscope, this transit may mark a time of financial difficulty and the placement of obstacles that block the native's professional advancement. The law of compensation is evident in this transit because much depends upon the native's past actions. If in the past the native has worked efficiently, honestly and constructively, this transit may mark a fulfilling time of worth-while and solid accomplishment.

Transit Saturn Conjunction Saturn

This transit marks the end of a cycle of experience and the beginning of a new one. This occurs for the first time in the native's life at about age twenty-eight. The culmination of the Saturn cy-cle indicates a period or arrival of adult maturity or an astrological coming of age. By this time transiting Saturn has made every possible transiting aspect to every planet in the natal horo-scope, releasing into manifestation every possible karmic experience.

The new cycle, represented by transit Saturn contacting its own place, is an important critical point in the native's ability to establish a career. It is at this point that the native either flounders or achieves stable professional security and status. The outcome of course depends on the discipline, work, application and perseverance that the native has set forth in the past. This transit marks a period when one usually becomes more serious and conservative in basic outlook. Under this transit, something transpires which makes the native think deeply about what direction his or her life should take, and this decision affects the life for a long time to come.

The second return of transit Saturn to natal Saturn occurs when the native is fifty-six to sixty years of age. This cycle indicates the beginning of the latter part of life and a reorientation to more serious philosophical pursuits. For some natives this marks the culmination of professional ambition and work and an arrival at true social status and respect.

Transit Saturn Conjunction Uranus

Because of the double Aquarius significance of this transit, there may be important developments in the native's friendships, groups or organizational associations. Old friends may reappear, or the native's friendships may be with established with older, more serious-minded, wise individuals. This is an excellent transit for work, scientific study, research, engineering and construction, and especially those areas related to machinery or electronics. This also is an excellent transit for the serious study of astrology. The native is motivated to work so that goals and objectives may be realized. Under this transit the native may make an effective effort by putting creative, inspirational ideas into practical use. The native may develop new and original ways of making use of that which is old and well-established. Under this transit the native may change jobs or embark on a new professional or business endeavor.

If Saturn and Uranus are weak or afflicted in the natal horoscope, and if the native has misused freedom and status in the past, he or she will be in for an unpleasant shock. This transit can precipitate karma (reaction of past actions) in strange and unexpected ways. The reverse is also true. This transit may bring about rewards past actions because Saturn always gives us exactly what we deserve, no more, no less.

In general the effects of this transit may be very positive or very negative, depending upon the native's motivations, capacity for self-discipline and past actions.

Transit Saturn Conjunction Neptune

This is a powerful but very subtle transit. If the native disciplines himself or herself to understand the subconscious mind in a conscious and organized way, very beneficial results may be obtained in terms of psychological insights into self and others. It is a good transit for the study of psychology and mysticism. However, it is a very dangerous time to indiscriminately experiment with seances or to contact astral plane entities and related beings since there is the danger of possession by negative entities under this transit.

The native's ability to reflect and meditate deeply and profoundly may be increased. As a result, the native can acquire a deeper, intuitive wisdom and understanding of life. The stabilizing influence of Saturn helps the native to quiet the mind and emotions and hold his or her attention steady in state of pure self-awareness. This process is a prerequisite for attaining deeper levels of intuitive experience.

The native with an afflicted natal Saturn, Neptune or twelfth house should avoid brooding and dwelling on the misfortunes of the past. Due to the psychological implications of this transit, depression and irrational fears that could lead to a psychological breakdown requiring institutionalization may occur.

This transit can also bring to light the past misdeeds of the native, resulting in public scandal and disgrace. There can also be problems with secret enemies that have had past karmic connections with the native. This is a good time to remember that one's real enemies are negative attitudes, fears and psychological tendencies.

Saturn Conjunction Pluto

This transit has a deep metaphysical significance that brings responsibilities of profound, far-reaching importance into the native's life. For the native whose horoscope reveals a tendency towards clairvoyant awareness and interest in the hidden forces of nature, this transit may bring spiritual experiences that give deep insights into the fundamental laws of the universe. The native could also develop an interest in magic or occult forces. Under this transit, meditation and spiritual self-development with an unselfish motive is an especially good path to follow. This transit often brings about the end of an old cycle of experience and the beginning of a new one in socially important or profound areas of the native's life.

If Saturn and Pluto are strong and well-aspected in the natal horoscope, the native may be capable of great concentration, focused purpose and self-discipline. This is a good transit for mathematical, scientific and occult study, work and research. Professional activities may include secret work involving government sponsored programs of scientific or engineering research and development on the forefront of technology. Under this transit the native is apt to have professional or business dealings with such matters as inheritance, taxes, corporate finances, and the goods of the dead.

This is a transit that can build or destroy a person's professional standing and reputation, depending upon past actions and motivations. Profound and irrevocable changes may occur in the native's life, particularly relative to career and important personal relationships. This transit often brings the death of someone significant to the native such as a close friend, parent, spouse or mentor. It may bring an end to something that is in some way connected to the house that Pluto or Saturn rule.

Transit Saturn Sextiles

The sextiles of transiting Saturn to natal planets indicate opportunities for steady progress involving work and organization. The intellectual nature of the sextile promotes the development of ideas and ways that advance the native's ambitions and improve the efficiency and effectiveness of work.

The third house connotation of the sextile aspect indicates that the native is apt to be involved in important communication with respect to business affairs, partnerships, professional activities, groups and organizations.

Mercury's rulership of the natural third house and its Aquarius exaltation involved in these sextiles of Saturn may also indicate that the native will undergo a program of organized study or research relating to the profession. Opportunities to join groups or organizations related to the native' career activities may result because of the eleventh house connotation of the sextile.

In general, transiting sextiles of Saturn improve the native's mental capacity in the affairs ruled by the planet to which Saturn is forming the sextile aspect. This is especially true in matters regarding the organization and management of information and communication.

Transit Saturn Sextile Sun

This transit brings opportunities for personal advancement and recognition for those who are willing to work hard. It is especially favorable for business and professional activities related to communication, media, arts, entertainment, children and their education. Often it brings personal recognition and distinction when the native has merited it through past work and training, and is thus beneficial to people working in politics or community affairs. In the case of the upper, approaching eleventh house sextile, the native may assume added responsibility and leadership in a community, political or professional organization. In general this aspect bestows more ambition and willingness to work and apply discipline in the important areas of the native's life. The native is inclined to pursue a goal that will help achieve something of lasting value.

Transit Saturn Sextile Moon

This transit stabilizes and increases awareness of family responsibilities. It is not a glamorous transit, but it may incline the native to make home improvements and become more conscientious regarding efforts directed toward domestic affairs. This transit also favors moderate and steady economic growth in a well-established business, especially those relating to food, household or domestic products, buildings and real estate. This can also be an advantageous transit for dieting or reforming one's existing dietary habits because there will be a greater capacity for self-discipline with which to start a new regimen. In general it favors stability in business and professional partnerships as well as in domestic matters.

Transit Saturn Sextile Mercury

This transit is excellent for all serious, intellectual disciplines such as formal educational programs, writing and research, and particularly those disciplines relating to mathematics and science. This is an excellent time to enroll in a university course or read an important book about which the native has been procrastinating. This is also a good time to write letters, term papers, articles or responses that have been neglected. The native will manifest a greater degree of patience, mental discipline and organizational ability. This transit will not necessarily confer originality, but it is excellent for helping the native organize thoughts and ideas. There may also be important communication regarding professional matters and group or organizational work. The native may also enter into a partnership that is related to intellectual work or communication. Friendships may be established with older, more experienced or serious-minded individuals from which the native may derive definite educational benefits.

Transit Saturn Sextile Venus

This transit brings opportunities for stabilizing social and business relationships. There may be opportunities to enter into a business partnership that is possibly related to the arts or luxury items. Works of art produced under the influence of this transit may show maturity and refinement, especially if there are simultaneously good aspects from other planets that confer creative inspiration. This is a good transit for serious work in the creative arts because Saturn confers a good sense of form, rhythm and structure coupled with the necessary discipline to turn one's inspirations into concrete manifestations. This is a good transit for cultivating relations with mature, well-established individuals who can stimulate social and professional advancement. This transit may help the native organize and stabilize financial affairs. Because of the double Libra significance of this transit, it is favorable for handling legal affairs or other matters requiring arbitration and diplomacy.

Transit Saturn Sextile Mars

This transit is favorable for hard work in professional affairs, especially those relating to construction, engineering, machinery, and all work requiring physical exertion. The native tends to acquire a more disciplined attitude toward the acceptance of physical exertion and discomfort. It is a good transit for embarking on physical fitness programs through which one can overcome indifference, laziness and inertia. This transit may also help the native develop qualities of endurance, strength and leadership. Because of the double Capricorn significance of this transit, there may be a definite energy outpouring in the direction of the native's professional work and ambitions. There is a no-nonsense attitude that gets the job done. The mental nature of the sextile also enables the native to organize such efforts more efficiently. In general under this transit the native is capable of exercising more willpower and discipline in his or her actions.

Transit Saturn Sextile Jupiter

This transit brings a time of increased work and progress with respect to business affairs, cultural activities, education, religion and philosophy. The native will become more serious-minded and philosophical, but this will be done in a practical way; consequently, the native is apt to work to merge religious and philosophical ideas into practical affairs. The native also will be more capable of exercising sound, practical judgment relating to significant business matters. This can be accomplished with a stable attitude that does not fall prey to excessive optimism or pessimism. This is a favorable time for organizing and handling corporate affairs or legal or governmental matters. Under this transit the native will be more aware of the need for honesty and integrity; consequently, the native can improve his or her reputation and standing in the community at this time. The transit also favors educational and organizational work relating to the native's career advancement. This is a good time to originate business and partnership agreements because all parties will show a greater degree of responsibility and integrity.

Transit Saturn Sextile Saturn

This is a favorable period for steady, purposeful, well-organized career activities that are advanced along established, traditional lines. It indicates a time of consolidation with respect to important areas of the native's life and responsibilities, especially those related to reputation, profession, marriage, partnership and group activities. This is a good time to consolidate, organize and perfect those activities and obligations that have already been formulated or contracted. If the native works conscientiously, he or she may gain the cooperation and favor of people in positions of established power and authority.

Transit Saturn Sextile Uranus

This aspect has a triple Aquarius significance and is excellent for participation in work and leadership related to organized group activities, especially those activities that revolve around scientific endeavors and career aspirations. This s one of the best transits for all forms of scientific work and research. Under this transit the native may establish worthwhile friendships with responsible, mature individuals who are reliable and can benefit the native. Through this cooperative activity much worthwhile work is accomplished which would be impossible for a single individual to undertake. The native has the opportunity to put creative, original ideas into practical, concrete expression, often combining the best elements of the old with the new. This is an excellent transit for the serious study of astrology and occult philosophy. The native may gain profound, intuitive insight by quieting the mind and thus being able to intuitively link with a transpersonal, universal level of consciousness. This is a favorable time for beginning business and professional endeavors and for initiating new partnerships and alliances.

Transit Saturn Sextile Neptune

This transit is favorable for gaining a more profound level of intuitive awareness. The native may bring to light hidden knowledge, often from the distant past, by tapping the resources of the subconscious mind. The stabilizing influence of Saturn makes it possible to achieve deep states of meditation with consequent expanded wisdom and insight into universal, spiritual principles. Under this transit the native may also gain deep, psychological insights into self and others that can be especially helpful in the fields of psychology and counseling. There also may be opportunities for professional endeavors involving work for hospitals, religious or charitable organizations, or some form of spiritual or religious psychology. Under this transit, however, the native's career activities may involve an element of secrecy. Often the job can relate to secret government or organizational projects. Information entrusted to the native should be kept secret.

Transit Saturn Sextile Pluto

This transit may inspire profound spiritual realizations if the horoscope indicates a degree of spiritual awareness. As with transit Saturn sextile Neptune, this transit to Pluto indicates that professional activities may be of a secretive nature, perhaps relating to research and development. The native is capable of exerting willpower and discipline that may be directed toward programs of self-improvement and regeneration. This energy could be directed toward spiritual growth, career advancement or both. There is also the possibility of benefit through inheritance, insurance or business dealings related to taxes, insurance, finances and the affairs of the dead. In some cases the native makes an organized effort regarding a new beginning in important affairs, especially those areas that deal with partnership relations and career activities.

Transit Saturn Squares

The squares of transit Saturn have a special significance because of the tenth house, Capricorn and Saturn connotation of the square. Consequently, squares of transit Saturn indicate very important periods of testing that result in overcoming obstacles in the native's evolutionary development. This should not be interpreted in a negative sense because transit squares of Saturn may increase the native's ambition, determination and discipline. This will in turn help the native achieve something of significance, especially as it relates to career, goals and objectives. This square requires a great deal of patience, discipline and hard work, but in the long run the results will be very rewarding.

If Saturn is weak in the horoscope and the native lacks willpower, the increased responsibility and the necessity to overcome obstacles may seem oppressive, causing the native to become depressed and, therefore, develop a negative attitude. The native can develop a harsh, Spartan attitude that drives other people away and generally makes the native unpopular, or the native may be rebuffed or discouraged by other people who have a harsh attitude and make heavy demands on him or her.

Under the squares of transiting Saturn, it is difficult to gain recognition and support from people in established positions of power and status. Usually the native must undertake a heavy work load of responsibility with respect to the profession. In short, transiting Saturn squares test one's strength and endurance.

Transit Saturn Square Sun

Transit Saturn square the natal Sun usually brings a heavy work load and obstacles that impair the native's self-expression. It also inhibits the native's vitality, thus creating a sense of weariness. One should avoid overwork that could lead to extreme fatigue and emotional depression. Under this transit it is a good idea to take care of work that has immediate importance.

Heavy career responsibilities may interfere with the native's social life, love life and pleasurable pursuits. While under this transit the native is apt to complain of overwork and no relaxation. Employers or other authoritative influences may tend to restrain the native's self-expression, thus creating a sense of frustration and resentment. It also could work the other way, and the native could have a similar attitude toward others, thereby creating unpopularity that produces a sense of personal loneliness. Transiting Saturn square the natal Sun is not a favorable time to seek the support, favor or recognition of those in positions of power, status or authority. This is not a good time to make speculative financial investments or to engage in stock market activities because there may be financial loss through investments.

In some cases children can become a heavy responsibility under this transit. Children undergoing this transit may have difficulties with their school work and are apt to feel unloved.

Under this transit egoistic and authoritative attitudes should be avoided.

Transit Saturn Square Moon

This is one of the most difficult transits as it tends to stimulate negative emotional experiences of the past and the native becomes moody and depressed. One can easily get trapped in past memories and lose sight of the here and now. This behavior inhibits the positive avenues of self-expression that are open to the native. This transit may also bring serious family and domestic problems, as well as financial difficulties that affect the home. The native may have to care for a parent or an older family member who is experiencing ill health or has negative, rigid mental and emotional attitudes. This saps the native's vitality. There also can be estrangements and lack of warmth in family relationships. The native should avoid harboring a negative emotional attitude which tends to lead to further personal isolation and loneliness. This transit does not last forever, so the native should try to remain positive. In some cases the native will experience hardships and limitations, but he also should realize that the transit trine follows the transit square.

Transit Saturn Square Mercury

Transit Saturn square natal Mercury is apt to bring about a period of mental worry and responsibility. The native may experience delays in communication, in studies or in other mental forms of work. Under this transit there may be tension in the nervous system that could also bring about problems with digestion. While under this transit the native should get a reasonable amount of rest and pursue sensible dietary habits. There may be problems because of unemployment, or the native may be subjected to occupational health hazards. There may be difficult interpersonal relationships at work caused by a breakdown of communication or overwork, which may also lead to ill health or nervous exhaustion. There also is the possibility of succumbing to negative thinking, which in turn blocks the native's progress.

Transit Saturn Square Venus

Transit Saturn square Venus usually brings about a period of personal loneliness, difficulty or estrangement in close personal relationships. The native is afraid of not being accepted by others and tends to act in a shy, awkward or defensive manner. During this transit the native is apt to be consciously or unconsciously reminded of painful emotional experiences of the past which can interfere with the ability to be content in the present. Transit Saturn square Venus is unfavorable for business affairs; thus, it tends to bring about a time of financial difficulty. It is not a favorable time for artistic endeavors either, because the native will feel depressed and lack inspiration. This transit may be a difficult period for romantic, marriage and business relationships or partnerships. There is general difficulty in expressing and receiving love.

Transit Saturn Square Mars

Transit Saturn square Mars is likely to frustrate the native's desires and ambitions, causing anger. Under this transit the native finds it difficult to adjust to career responsibilities. Often the native is required to assume heavy, unpleasant, strenuous and sometimes dangerous tasks. At times this transit marks the death of someone meaningful to the native. In some cases the native is forced to undergo conditions of hardship, or even physical danger, which may result in accidents and injuries. The native should try to stay away from situations of danger, and may tend to utilize energy in a sporadic way. There are apt to be conflicts with the boss, government, father or other stern, unsympathetic authority figures, or the native may assume an unsympathetic attitude toward people under his or her authority. In general the native should avoid hard, cold, egotistical or defensive attitudes.

Transit Saturn Square Jupiter

Transit Saturn square Jupiter usually brings a time of difficulty in the native's business and financial affairs. Professional and domestic affairs are apt to be adversely affected. Any attempts to correct problems in one area often create or aggravate them in another. Under this transit the native is often faced with a moral crisis pertaining to important social, ethical or religious problems with which he or she is attempting to cope. This is a difficult period for travel and higher education, and often these pursuits are blocked by a lack of money. The native's status and reputation may suffer because of his past mistakes or because the inability to cope with current problems.

Transit Saturn Square Saturn

Transit Saturn square Saturn usually brings about a period of difficulty and crisis with respect to the native's responsibility in marriage, partnerships and other close personal relationships, including career affairs. It is difficult to gain the cooperation of others or to make professional advancement; therefore, the native should guard against pessimistic, negative attitudes that make cooperation with others even more difficult, and which further impede success. The lower fourth house square is apt to precipitate home, family, domestic and parental problems. The upper tenth house square is apt to cause professional career difficulties.

Transit Saturn Square Uranus

Transit Saturn square Uranus may bring about sudden, unexpected setbacks and difficulties relating to career, close personal relationships, public relations, friendships and group activities. During this transit the native is apt to feel frustrated because unexpected obstacles appear that block the achievement of goals and objectives. The native or friends or both may have ulterior motives in their associations, which create an atmosphere of mistrust. It is possible for the native to suddenly lose a job or suffer a serious blow to status and reputation, especially if the motives are not pure. The native or associates may have unreasonable, dictatorial attitudes that demand hard work and discipline from everyone but themselves. This results in unpopularity and a deterioration of friendship and cooperation.

Transit Saturn Square Neptune

Transit Saturn square Neptune may bring about an onslaught of neurotic problems. This transit also tends to stimulate emotionally painful incidents in the native's past. The native experiences a free-floating anxiety that is hard to pin down or diagnose. The native's professional standing, reputation and important relationships may suffer due to gossip, rumors, hidden enemies, skeletons in the closet or concealed information that leaked out. Often the native is burdened by professional secrets that weigh heavily on his or her mind. Use of drugs, alcohol or other harmful forms of emotional escape are particularly dangerous under this transit. Under this transit one should not experiment with psychic practices because of the danger of contacting negative astral influences. If Saturn and Neptune are very afflicted, this transit could bring imprisonment or institutionalization due to mental illness.

Transit Saturn Square Pluto

Transit Saturn square Pluto may bring heavy problems and responsibilities that the native feels are more than he or she can handle. The native generally feels that he or she has to struggle against something very sinister and foreboding. These problems and responsibilities may arise as a result of large-scale social, political or economic changes over which one has no control. There may be difficulties encountered through inheritance, alimony, taxes, corporate finances and other people's money. The native's reputation and career ambitions may be disrupted by evil circumstances or forces. If in the past the native was guided by selfish motives, there may be heavy karmic retribution at this time. Under this transit the native should concentrate on gaining a spiritual understanding of the law of death and rebirth, and at this time the native may experience the death of someone important in his or her life.

Transit Saturn Trines

Trines of transiting Saturn bring about periods of time when the native may make steady progress in the career and in the realization of goals and objectives. However, the trine must be stimulated by an active willingness to work and organize one's life. Trines of transiting Saturn help the native to accomplish creative work and make educational advances possible. There is usually a definite growth which leads to maturity and an ability to assume responsibility. The native achieves a more organized, practical and profound understanding of life. The native is apt to have more patience, self-discipline and common sense, which in turn bring harmony and progress in marriage, partnership, professional advancement, friendship and group associations.

Transit Saturn Trine Sun

Transit Saturn trine Sun is favorable for advancement in the native's career and public reputation. Under this transit the native may gain recognition from people in positions of power and authority, and thus may improve his or her status. This transit favors politicians or those running for public office. It also confers good business judgment, and is favorable for sensible financial investments and initiating business enterprises. This transit is a favorable period for formulating contracts and handling legal affairs. Leadership and managerial skills are heightened. It is a favorable time for teaching and working with children, and it is a good time for the native to pursue higher education that is geared to improving the career. The willpower is increased in terms of the native's capacity for work and self-discipline.

Transit Saturn Trine Moon

Transit Saturn trine Moon is favorable for business affairs related to farming, real estate, food, domestic products, building and home improvements. Under this transit the native will receive more cooperation from family members, thereby enabling him or her to improve and stabilize family and domestic affairs. The native will be emotionally stable and able to work patiently and diligently to achieve goals and objectives, and may be a little more reserved than usual. The mother, an older woman or another mature individual will help the native organize personal affairs and in some way this will enable the native to make significant progress in career achievements. This is a favorable transit for progress and stability in business and financial affairs due to the Moon's exaltation in Taurus.

Transit Saturn Trine Mercury

Transit Saturn trine Mercury is a favorable time for the pursuit of formal education and serious study. At this time the native's mind is more precise, organized, practical, mathematical and scientific. If other factors in the natal horoscope supply originality and inspiration, this is an excellent transit for writing, lecturing, teaching, researching and inventing. The native can advance his or her career by advancing education and by writing and developing more efficient work procedures. Organization will improve, and paperwork, planning, communication and account keeping will benefit. This transit favors the formulation of contracts and the handling of legal documents. During this period the improved efficiency and accuracy in communication will favorably influence friendship, group activities, partnerships and public relations that in turn will make it easier for the native to realize goals and objectives. The native may profit through business related to printing, writing, teaching, education, publishing, transportation, communication and media.

Transit Saturn Trine Venus

Transit Saturn trine Venus is a favorable time for the pursuit of business affairs, business partnerships and public relations. This transit favors business affairs related to art, law, public relations, luxury items, arbitration, counseling, psychology and music in the classical tradition. This transit also helps to stabilize friendships and marriage affairs. The native's manners will be somewhat more conservative, cultured and refined. Under this transit the native's tastes and artistic skills are permeated with a sense of composition and structure. The native is apt to become more quiet and introspective because of the exaltation of Venus in Pisces stimulating a deeper level of emotional and spiritual understanding. The native will evidence many of the desirable qualities of the sign Libra. The native may be more considerate and cooperative, which may lead to greater social acceptance and the consequent opportunities for business success and career advancement.

Transit Saturn Trine Mars

Transit Saturn trine Mars indicates progress toward and the realization of career ambitions through energetic action and hard work. Mars provides the desire and energy to accomplish something while Saturn gives organizational capacity and discipline. The native is apt to become more efficient and resourceful in achieving goals and objectives, and may seek educational activities to improve skills and career potential. There is also the possibility of enlisting the aid of similarly inclined friends or partners in the accomplishment of a practical ambition.

However, this would have to be mutually beneficial to all concerned in order to succeed. This transit is especially favorable for work related to construction, building and machinery. It is a good time for artistic pursuits such as sculpture which requires physical building and the use of tools. In general there is firm determination and discipline to bring to fruition the projects the native has initiated.

Transit Saturn Trine Jupiter

Transit Saturn trine Jupiter indicates a period when the native may make progress in business, professional and financial matters. The native is apt to acquire a more conservative, philosophical outlook which brings favor and recognition from people in positions of power and authority in established educational, religious, social, corporate or governmental institutions. This is also a favorable transit for handling legal affairs, business contracts and agreements. The native's work may relate to the business and financial affairs of schools, universities, hospitals and religious institutions. The native acquires a moderate outlook that avoids extremes of pessimism and optimism. This even temperament allows the native to work evenly and steadily toward the realization of goals. Under this transit the native is more conscientious with regard to personal honesty and integrity, and therefore stands the chance to attract partners and group associations of similar character. This transit also helps to stabilize domestic circumstances and family relationships. Religious or philosophical inclinations toward everyday practical, ethical values are likely to be prominent during this transit.

Transit Saturn Trine Saturn

Transit Saturn trine Saturn brings a time of steady professional advancement that is usually a reward for good work performed by the native in the past. Business and professional partnerships formed under this transit tend to have lasting and enduring loyalty. This is a favorable transit for advancement in politics and public life along traditional, conservative lines. This transit is apt to bestow more patience and steadiness in the native's endeavors, and because of this, he or she will probably achieve something of permanent or lasting value. Under this transit the native's sense of honesty and integrity are enhanced, and he or she will tend to be more reliable and responsible, basing attitudes on sound ethical principles.

Transit Saturn Trine Uranus

Transit Saturn trine Uranus provides an excellent setting for the native to put creative, inspirational, original ideas into practical application. It is an excellent transit for all mental, scientific and philosophical pursuits, especially those related to mathematics and engineering. Good organizational ability is combined with originality at this time. Because of the double Aquarius, eleventh house significance of this transit, it is a favorable time for the native to work with groups and organizations and to establish new friendships. Friendships may be established with older, more mature, serious-minded individuals who impart scientific or occult knowledge and wisdom. The native may become a counselor to others. This is a good transit for the study of astrology and other occult disciplines. This is because there is a deeper understanding of the fundamental laws that govern the universe. The reason for this is that Uranus penetrates to the realms of unseen energies, while Saturn provides an organized understanding of these super-physical realities. In some cases old friends and acquaintances reappear in the native's life and have a beneficial influence. The native may also assume a position of organizational responsibility within a club, group, lodge or professional organization. Friendships and organizational contacts may help the native advance career and professional ambitions. This is a favorable time to make changes and improvements and to initiate new activities in the career and professional life.

Transit Saturn Trine Neptune

Transit Saturn trine Neptune brings about deepening and steadying of the native's perceptions; consequently, it is excellent for all types of spiritual work that require serenity, steadiness and concentration. Professional affairs may relate to institutions such as hospitals, universities, asylums, religious organizations, retreats, charitable organizations and sometimes governmental organizations, especially those involving an element of secrecy. Under this transit the native's profession also may involve spiritual or psychological counseling. The native may become interested in psychology or an organized program or discipline to explore the unconscious mind and deeper levels of consciousness. Often under this transit the native has the ability to draw upon past experiences stored in the unconscious mind, which enables him or her to solve practical problems. In general this is a favorable time to pursue meditative disciplines, and in some cases there can be memories of previous incarnations or an interest in scholarly, historic pursuits based on an unconscious memory.

Transit Saturn Trine Pluto

Transit Saturn trine Pluto brings a time when it is possible to gain a profound level of insight into the unseen superphysical forces behind existing reality. This may take the form of meditation, yoga or occult disciplines or investigations or scientific pursuits such as advanced mathematics or medicine. There can be important and extensive advances through professional activities and career ambitions. Affairs related to the career often involve an element of secrecy and are sometimes linked to secret government research and investigations. Under this transit the native is capable of a deeper level of concentration and willpower expressed as seriousness and purposefulness which brings about changes. Often the native has to deal with some form of intrigue or could be involved in combating corruption or foul play in some form. This is a favorable transit for meditation, and the native can improve clairvoyant and intuitive faculties.

Transit Saturn Oppositions

Transit Saturn's oppositions to natal planets usually indicate that there may be longstanding problems that involve responsibility in relationships and partnerships. Often there is an unequal distribution of work and responsibility so that the native or others surrounding the native feel overburdened, put-upon or used. In these cases the native should examine the situation in order to seek greater justice and balance. In some cases heavy professional burdens and responsibilities may interfere with important relationships because they stand in the way of fulfilling other responsibilities It seems to the native that no matter what he or she does, something inevitably suffers. There is a need to exercise patience and to see issues from all sides. The native is forced to realize that the harvest does not come without considerable effort and that harmony may be achieved only through an equal exchange of energy and acceptance of responsibility.

Often the native is forced to develop a more realistic attitude toward ambitions, and must learn to choose friends and associates more wisely. In some cases the native is forced to cope with a relationship involving a negative or oppressive person, or may have a similar attitude toward others. In any case, estrangement and a lack of warmth usually results. These problems may only be overcome by giving and demanding responsible cooperation within the relationship in question if it is to be continued.

In some cases, the native feels trapped in an association that is continued only because of karmic necessity and unavoidable responsibilities rather than because of any freely determined inclination on the part of one or both partners. An example of this would be estrangement in a marriage that is continued merely because of economic reasons, responsibility toward children or social mores.

Transit Saturn Opposition Sun

There are two oppositions of Saturn to the Sun in the natural zodiac. One is expressed by the Sun's exaltation in Aries and Saturn's exaltation in Libra, and the other is indicated by the Sun's rulership of Leo and Saturn's co-rulership of Aquarius. This transit often indicates a period when personal freedom and self-expression is limited by an authority figure or by the native's employer. Often the personal ambition of the native, associates or both result in a power struggle for status and supremacy, especially with respect to partnerships, career advancement and group or organizational leadership.

Personal egotism and self-expression are always held in check by social pressures and collective power. Thus, we have the archetypal struggle between individual will and self-expression on the one hand, and the limitations imposed by socially established traditions, authority figures and organizational structures on the other. This may result in a struggle on the native's part to overcome those people who represent these limitations in the native's life, or the native may cultivate ego identification with the established order whereby the native seeks to subject others to his ir ger own authority in the name of law and discipline. This of course results in arousing resentment and opposition in those the native seeks to control.

Only by a democratic and cooperative attitude that demands equal rights and privileges for all concerned can this difficulty be overcome. The native should expect only the respect and rewards earned through his or her own work and discipline. In this way the native can be free of blame and, therefore, respected by others.

In the case of children this aspect may indicate that there may be difficulties relating to parental authority.

This is not an advisable time to seek the favor of persons in positions of power and authority or to aggressively pursue one's political career advancement by seeking distinction or asking favors. Neither is it a favorable time for speculative financial investments, romantic and pleasurable pursuits, or for entering into a marriage or partnership. The best course to take is to perform the routine responsibilities that are necessary and wait for a more favorable time to initiate major changes.

Transit Saturn Opposition Moon

This transit often brings difficulties and estrangements in family and domestic relationships. Emotional depression that is the result of dwelling upon past relationship failures gives the native a negative, cold, pessimistic, emotional attitude toward others. This attitude perpetuates a vicious cycle of loneliness and social unhappiness. The native must consciously work to have a more optimistic, friendly and positive attitude if other are expected to respond in a socially pleasing manner.

Since there is a natural opposition of the Moon and Saturn indicated by the Moon's rulership of Cancer and the fourth house and Saturn's rulership of Capricorn and the tenth house, there often is a tug of war between domestic and professional responsibilities that can be emotionally and physically exhausting for the native. The single mother who must work to support her children, and also care for them and her home, is a typical example of this plight.

Often this transit is linked to a breakdown or failure within the network of family relationships. This is often caused by a broken home, divorce, death, or some kind of enforced separation. Family problems may obstruct the native's career advancement.

Often the home life is made difficult by financial limitations, which is indicated by the Moon's relationship to Taurus, in which it is exalted, and Saturn's relationship to career and profession. Lack of professional opportunity or difficulties at work may cause financial limitations which adversely affect the domestic scene. This transit is especially unfavorable for businesses related to real estate, building, food, farming and domestic products.

Because of the Moon's rulership of the etheric body, this transit may have an exhausting effect on the native's physical vitality. There may be problems with sluggish digestion and water retention in the tissues. Physical lack of energy and fatigue are a major contributing factor in an emotionally negative outlook that promotes periods of ill health that interfere with the native's ability to work. The process may, however, work in reverse; boring and dreary work may result in a lack of enthusiasm and energy. Fortunately, this transit does not last forever, although sometimes it seems as if it will.

Transit Saturn Opposition Mercury

This transit often indicates that there may be relationship problems that are caused by a breakdown of communication; messages may be stopped or delayed. This of course interferes with cooperation in partnerships and professional responsibilities. The native may also be burdened in work by oppressive legalities and red tape. There may be a negative attitude on the native's part toward the ideas of others or on the part of others towards the native's ideas. This leads to frustration, resentment and the lack of effective cooperation. The native's negative mental outlook also interferes with friendships and group cooperation. The native tends to be overly worrisome, and this results in a negative, pessimistic outlook. Preoccupation with problems and difficulties prevents the native's mind from arriving at constructive solutions to problems.

Transit Saturn Opposition Venus

Transit Saturn opposition Venus brings about emotional disappointments in romantic relationships and close personal friendships. There may be difficulties and burdensome responsibilities through marriage and other partnerships; these are often caused by financial misfortunes or limitations. These problems also may be the result of one or both parties being overly preoccupied with their career responsibilities. Sometimes forces beyond the native's personal control about enforced bereavement or separation from a marriage partner. There even may be unrequited love in which the native receives a cold, hostile or indifferent response. This often results in depression, hurt and a bitter, resentful outlook.

In the case of purely business or financial relationships there may be losses through lack of cooperation or failure to assume one's fair share of responsibilities. The obstinacy may be on the part of the native or someone else. There may be business lawsuits or other legal difficulties occurring under this transit. This is not a favorable time to initiate legal actions or enter into partnerships or marriage. Under this transit the native will get a cold response in dealings with the public. This is a difficult transit for artists, entertainers or people whose success depends upon their creative ability and personal charm. The native is apt to feel unpopular and socially rejected.

In general there will be a lack of social self-confidence and a shyness that is apt to be interpreted as aloofness and snobbishness by others.

Transit Saturn Opposition Mars

Transit Saturn opposition Mars is considered one of the most difficult and dangerous transits because it involves two malefic planets. There is a possibility that there may be a conflict with the native's employer or business partner, and this may even involve the law or government officials. This is not a favorable transit for pursuing personal career ambitions in an aggressive political way. Under this transit the native may become involved in political conflict, or he could be victimized by political oppression.

The native is likely to come in contact with people who frustrate and oppose his or her desires and ambitions, which in turn leads the native to feel and express anger and resentment. If the native has a tendency toward an authoritarian personality, he or she may assume a disagreeable, mean, dictatorial and oppressive attitude toward others. This of course leads to enmity, resentment and opposition from others. Any aggressive action on the part of the native may bring the native into conflict with established authority figures and, in extreme cases, the police. If the conflict is carried to an extreme, violence could be the result.

All safety precautions should be scrupulously observed with respect to occupational hazards and dangers; extra care should be used in handling firearms and machinery. Under this transit the native should avoid violent or disagreeable people, and should stay away from circumstances in which physical violence and danger could occur.

Transit Saturn Opposition Jupiter

Transit Saturn opposition Jupiter brings a time of difficulty involving important relationships dealing with business and professional affairs. Under this transit the native may be prone to involvement in lawsuits, red tape and legal difficulties. Legal difficulties may arise as a result of bankruptcy or some other financial crisis. There also may be conflict between family and professional responsibilities.

There may be bad timing in the pursuit of professional ambition or in approaching employers or those in positions of power and status who can grant favors. Under this transit there may be confusion about ethical and moral issues that have an important relationship to the native's life. The native may have to deal with people who are too conservative and traditional so that they oppose worthwhile ideas or may be prone to such attitudes. The native may alternate between extreme attitudes, from unrealistic optimism to extreme pessimism. There may be obstacles and difficulties experienced through university studies, travel, religion, organizational work and in dealing with established businesses and governmental institutions. Under this transit the native should try to maintain the status quo of professional, educational and domestic responsibilities. At best, the native should wait to pursue more aggressive ambitions after this transit is over.

Transit Saturn Opposition Saturn

Transit Saturn opposition Saturn occurs when the native reaches approximately ages fourteen and forty-two. Transiting Saturn is conjunct its own place in the horoscope when the native reaches approximately age twenty-eight. This fourteen and twenty-eight year cycle is repeated throughout the native's life. It marks a time of crisis with respect to relationship responsibilities involved in marriage, other important relationships, groups and organizations. This transit often is associated with feelings of personal inadequacy which result in a herd consciousness or self-imposed social conformity regardless of the costs.

Fourteen-year-olds are known for their feelings of social awkwardness and rigid conformity to the social standards of their peers. It is at this age that the first serious thought is given to one's choice of profession. At age forty-two there is conformity to middle class, social and professional standards, at which time family, home and professional responsibilities make themselves felt. At this time, adult social responsibilities are at their height and are generally linked to a more conservative attitude.

Transit Saturn Opposition Uranus

Transit Saturn opposition Uranus often indicates a crisis in the maintenance and pursuit of personal freedom in the face of social pressure and professional responsibilities. These responsibilities are often externalized in the form of a relationship problem with a person who represents the attitude and the authority of the established social structure. The native may assume the attitude of either Saturn or Uranus, becoming either oppressive toward others or rebelling against authority and seeking personal freedom without regard to duties, responsibilities and the rights of others. There may be a hypocritical attitude that expects complete freedom for oneself and, at the same time expecting disciplined sacrifice and hard work from others. Although the native may be a reasonable person, he or she may be forced to deal with someone of this temperament. Under this transit, what the native may consider to be brilliant may actually be a series of impractical and unworkable ideas.

The native may have to deal with friends and group associates who are oppressive or who have selfish motivations relating to money and status. The native may have similar ulterior motives involving friendships that naturally results in estrangement from friends and an inability to cooperate on the job or in a group. When carried too far these negative attitudes may result in the native's loss of a job or fall from a high position, which results in a loss of status and even social ostracism. If in the past the native had selfish motivations or used dishonorable tactics for the sake of personal ambitions, this transit may bring a sudden and unexpected reversal of fortune.

Old acquaintances often reappear at an awkward or embarrassing time, making life more difficult for the native.

Transit Saturn Opposition Neptune

Transit Saturn opposition Neptune tends to stimulate painful, unconscious memories and negative emotional experiences of the past that color the native's attitudes toward present relationships. As a result, the native is apt to respond to other people in a mistrustful, fearful or neurotic way. Under this transit there is the danger of deception and insincerity being present in important business, marital and family relationships. This often manifests as a tendency to play along with a meaningless relationship in a half-hearted way rather than risk expressing one's honest feelings. This pattern of behavior may be initiated by the native, by those with whom the native has contact or by both. Neurotic problems and deception may also interfere with the native's professional success and efficiency at work. Under this transit the native may experience a vicious cycle of loneliness which is the result of others shunning him or her due to a detached and depressing emotional attitude.

During this period the native who has had a prior tendency toward mental illness should exercise the will to be happy and adjusted, because in extreme cases this is a period when one could be thrown into a complete psychological breakdown with consequent institutionalization. Brooding, self-pity and blaming others for misfortunes should be avoided at all costs. The native should avoid negative astral psychic practices, drugs and alcohol. Accordingly, the native should stay away people who may influence him or her to become involved in these activities.

Transit Saturn Opposition Pluto

Transit Saturn opposition Pluto brings with it the danger of the native coming in contact with people of sinister and evil character. Negative occult practices and influences should be avoided but not fear, as fear will only invite them. Under this transit there can be difficulties and possibly lawsuits incurred through matters pertaining to inheritance, goods of the dead, insurance, taxes, business finances, alimony and other people's money.

The native may have to deal with oppressive, authoritarian officials and organizations, at which time he or she may be forced to defend individual rights. There may also be betrayal or oppression at the hands of an employer or false friends. As the native or his or her associates may manifest contrary, dictatorial tendencies, such attitudes or contacts should be avoided. Under this transit one should not try to force his or her will or authority on others.

VIII

Uranus Transits

Transit Uranus Through the Houses

Uranus transits through the houses of the horoscope indicate the department of a person's life in which unusual and unexpected events are likely to occur. In these affairs the native is apt to depart from traditional modes of behavior and express his or her own unique individualism. The actions pertaining to these matters will be characterized by a desire for freedom and independence of expression. The native is apt to employ unique and original methods in activities. These affairs will bring into the life new friendships and group associations. In some cases the native will employ scientific methods and will be involved with humanitarian works pertaining to the house that Uranus is transiting.

Transit Uranus Through the First House

As Uranus passes over the Ascendant, the native is apt to undergo a radical change in self-awareness arid personal outlook on life. In some cases the native may become interested in occult subjects such as astrology, or may have clairvoyant experiences for the first time in his or her life. In any event, the native is apt to undergo a sudden awakening to a higher level of consciousness. The native will manifest a desire for greater personal freedom and independence of action. Consequently, the native is likely to radically change many of the familiar patterns of life and strike out in different directions. This may be accompanied by the dropping of old friendships and establishing new contacts. The native can take an interest in ultramodern or extremely old ideas and cultures. This interest can take a scientific bent or can be related to humanitarian group activities. In general the native will be inclined to sacrifice security for the sake of freedom and exciting new experiences.

If transiting Uranus makes favorable aspects while in the first house, there will be much personal gain, excitement and happiness. New and worthwhile contributions can be made to society at this time.

If Uranus is afflicted while transiting this house, the native is apt to be eccentric, unreasonable and uncooperative to the point of alienating friends and making worthwhile accomplishments difficult, if not impossible. In such a case, good advice goes unheeded. There can be a tendency toward impatience and erratic behavior, making it difficult to finish useful projects.

Transit Uranus Through the Second House

The Uranus transit through the second house is likely to bring about erratic fluctuations in the native's financial affairs. If Uranus makes beneficial aspects while transiting this house, there can be new ideas in scientific pursuits and sudden gain through ingenious business endeavors. This transit is especially favorable for those who make money through group and organizational work or through inventions. For such people there is apt to be much financial activity that would be related to corporate enterprises, partner's money, government money, insurance, taxes and inheritance. The reason for this strong eighth house emphasis is that Uranus is exalted in Scorpio. In any event, financial endeavors are apt to involve group efforts and other people's money.

If Uranus is afflicted in the second house, the native may experience sudden financial loss or an inability to cooperate with others, which may result in financial setbacks. If the motives are selfish, the person's plans are apt to backfire disastrously. The native can experience difficulty through impatience and impractical, unrealistic ideas. The native can be too erratic, independent and impatiently headstrong, making it difficult for him or her to listen to good advice or follow plans through to completion. In general this transit will bring home lessons of detachment with respect to material possessions and the proper use of money and resources.

Transit Uranus Through the Third House

The Uranus transit through the third house is likely to bring important changes in the native's thinking and manner of communication. Many old ideas and concepts will be discarded and new ones adopted under this transit. The native will not accept any ideas on the basis of hearsay, but will want to evaluate them on the basis of his or her own experience and observation. The native is apt to become involved with scientific, humanitarian and occult areas of interest. Interesting relationships can develop with brothers, sisters and neighbors, or these relationships can undergo radical changes.

Restlessness and much coming and going accompany this transit. The mind becomes more keen and intuitive, and ideas are arrived at through sudden flashes of intuition. This transit acts as a strong intellectual stimulus because of the natural affinity between Mercury and Uranus. The native's thinking is subject to changes due to the influence of friends and group associations, and in like manner the native will influence the thinking of those with whom he or she associates. These changes in the native's thinking often bring about alterations in goals and objectives. Interest in electronics and electronic communication media can develop under this transit, and some natives develop new scientific theories or inventions or make unusual discoveries. Often, a new course of study is undertaken, generally in pursuit of occult knowledge. This is a favorable transit for the study of astrology.

If Uranus makes adverse aspects while transiting the third house, there can be mental vacillation, inability to listen to advice, impractical ideas and extreme nervousness and restlessness. If Uranus is a afflicted while in the third house, it is very unfavorable for signing contracts or making written agreements, as they will not turn out as planned.

If Uranus makes favorable aspects while transiting the third house, the native can be inspired with new and original concepts that will help to realize goals and objectives. This is a favorable aspect for writing on scientific, astrological or occult subjects.

Transit Uranus Through the Fourth House

This Uranus transit often brings major changes in the native's family and domestic conditions. There can be several changes of residence while under this transit. Under the influence of this aspect, the native's home will be frequented by new and unusual friends and group associations. In some cases the home will be used as a setting for group and organizational activity. Many persons undergoing this transit will renovate the home or improve it in some unusual manner. At best there will be major changes in the domestic sphere before this transit is over. Family members can become scattered, or there can be unusual events with respect to family members. There can also be changes in the native's attitude towards his or her family background and national heritage. Before Uranus leaves the fourth house, profound mental changes will take place in the native's consciousness that will be caused by events affecting the roots of his or her being. The native will want to be free to come and go as he or she sees fit in the domestic environment. The native's freedom in this respect will depend upon whether the person has learned the lessons of Saturn and self-discipline concerning home and profession.

If Uranus is afflicted while transiting this house there can be disrupting conditions in family affairs and instability in the domestic scene.

If this planet makes harmonious contacts while in the fourth house, there will be great personal freedom in the home. There will also be exciting and unusual events taking place that help the native attain goals and objectives.

Transit Uranus Through the Fifth House

The Uranus transit through the fifth house often brings unusual and exciting romances. Whether these relationships will be permanent depends upon the aspects of Uranus while it transits this house. In any event the native will demand and express greater freedom and power in all manners of self-expression, whether this expression be of the body or mind.

If Uranus makes unfavorable aspects while transiting this house, there can be heavy losses through financial speculation, foolish expenditures or pleasures. Transit Uranus in the fifth house, if afflicted, can bring about unusual disruptive conditions pertaining to children and their education.

If Uranus makes favorable aspects while transiting this house, this can be a favorable time for artistic creativity of all kinds. There is apt to be an active social life and any new and exciting friends as a result of it. The native may become involved with theatrical groups or social or artistic organizations whose members feel they have a message for humanity. Under any circumstances, Uranus in the fifth house will bring new and unusual methods for self-expression and pleasure-seeking.

Transit Uranus Through the Sixth House

Transit Uranus here produces new and interesting experiences through work, employment, service and health matters. If Uranus is well-aspected while transiting this house there will be an opportunity for unique and exciting work that could be connected with electronics, technology or humanitarian pursuits. There will be increased opportunities for realizing goals through employment. New friendships and group associations are apt to be formed through the work environment, and employment can come through friendship or group association. The native will manifest creativity and originality in developing new methods and more efficient techniques for productivity at work. This transit is especially favorable for engineers, scientists, astrologers and those connected with medicine and the occult. An interest in unusual or advanced methods of healing can occur. This healing can take the form of acupuncture, massage and various forms of spiritual healing. Astrology could be employed as a method of medical diagnosis.

If Uranus is afflicted while transiting the sixth house, the native's health can suffer due to extreme nervousness or impulsiveness that can lead to accidents. At this time there is also the danger of various forms of extremism in diet or personal hygiene.

The native may be uncooperative on the job, thereby creating difficulties between employees, coworkers and employers, or may become eccentric, undependable and too revolutionary to hold a job. In many cases there arises some form of involvement with labor unions.

Transit Uranus Through the Seventh House

This transit indicates a time of instability and sudden changes in personal relationships, marriage and partnerships. If Uranus makes favorable transits while in this house, the native will seek out unusual, talented associates and partners from whom he or she will gain many new and valuable experiences. There will be interest in group cooperation and organizational work. Many old associations can be dropped in exchange for new and different associates and friends. This transit of the seventh house often bring about divorce if it makes unfavorable aspects, especially if the natal horoscope shows relationship instability. There can be sudden marriage or short-lived infatuations. Although the native may be interested in active personal relationships, he or she will not want to be tied down or restricted by these relationships. During this transit any indications of jealousy or possessiveness on the part of others is likely to repel the native and cause him or her to break off all association.

If Uranus makes unfavorable contacts while transiting this house there can be an unreasonable attitude with regard to others. If Uranus is well-aspected while transiting this house, goals and objectives can be realized through cooperation with others or through group endeavors. Money can also be made through business partnerships involving joint finances and corporate enterprises. This transit of Uranus will bring major changes in the native's awareness of others and in the manner in which he or she relates to them.

Transit Uranus Through the Eighth House

This Uranus transit indicates matters related to joint finances, insurance, money and inheritance. It also brings about increased awareness of and an interest in occult mysteries. If Uranus makes unfavorable contacts while transiting the eighth house, there can be sudden deaths among the native's family or friends. If the rest of the horoscope bears it out, the native's life may be endangered. This transit can indicate the death of old conditions, which often include worn out friendships. There may be a shift in the native's goals and objectives caused by a new perception of reality which makes old concepts give way to new. In general this is a powerful position for Uranus because of its accidental exaltation in this house. Occult or mystical experiences or other sudden erratic experiences often cause a major shift in the native's sense of values. Usually there is a strong lesson of detachment of some sort to be learned under this transit.

If Uranus makes difficult aspects while transiting this house, these occurrences can be a shattering experience for the native. There is the possibility of sudden inheritance or unexpected business opportunities. However, if Uranus is afflicted, matters will not go as planned.

If Uranus makes harmonious contacts while transiting this house, these experiences can have an inspiring, uplifting effect. In either case the result of this transit will depend upon the native's attitude and level of awareness.

Transit Uranus Through the Ninth House

The Uranus transit of the ninth house brings important changes in the native's philosophic outlook, spiritual perceptions and goals pertaining to higher education. In some cases, the native will have startling religious experiences or meet people who have a profound effect on the spiritual and philosophic outlook of the native. There are unexpected opportunities for travel or interesting meetings with people from faraway places, and the native becomes more receptive to occult ideas and philosophies. New states of awareness can motivate the native to seek higher education in scientific, humanitarian or occult fields. The native is apt to be attracted to foreign cultures, philosophies and religions, and could for example develop an interest in yoga as a system of Eastern self-development. New mental and spiritual horizons act as a spur to greater ambition and desire to achieve worthwhile goals that are motivated by idealistic and humanitarian sentiments. Whether these goals or ideas are practical depends on the horoscope as a whole.

If Uranus is afflicted in the ninth house the native can go to extremes in pursuit of some newly adopted religious or philosophic ideology. There can be tendency to take off on ill-considered journeys merely for the sake of adventure or some unrealistic goal.

If Uranus makes favorable aspects while transiting the ninth house, new insights into the ultimate purpose of life can increase the native's understanding of his or her goals and objectives. Journeys made under favorable Uranus ninth house transits will be productive and may bring many unusual, exciting and worthwhile experiences. In general there will be new educational, religious and spiritual opportunities for the native toward unrealized areas. This is a favorable transit for the study of astrology and other occult subjects. There can be a greater humanitarian concern with matters concerning the general social order.

Transit Uranus Through the Tenth House

Uranus transiting the tenth house brings sudden and important changes in the person's profession, status and relationships with people in positions of power. Much depends upon the nature of the aspects made while Uranus transits this house. Friends and group associations will help the native attain professional and status-oriented goals, or the native will do the same for friends.

The native has the opportunity to gain the friendship of people in power and authority who in turn can further the native's ambitions. Often such professional dealings will involve business or government financing, research, insurance, taxes and legacies.

If Uranus makes adverse aspects here, there can be sudden reversals of fortune and loss of employment and status. If the motivations are not pure there can be scandal and public disgrace. There is also danger that such activities could be carried out with ulterior motives.

If Uranus makes favorable aspects while transiting the tenth house the native has the opportunity for interesting and original professional work. The native is likely to originate new and unusual methods to achieve professional goals and ambitions.

Transit Uranus Through the Eleventh House

The Uranus transit of the eleventh house is important because Uranus is accidentally dignified while transiting the house that Uranus rules. This transit brings important and sudden changes in the native's friendships, group associations, goals and objectives. In some cases, the native can enter into a new and more intuitive state of consciousness, and there may be original ideas and new insights into scientific, social and spiritual conditions that will open new avenues of expression.

If Uranus makes favorable transits while in the eleventh house the native will establish worthwhile friendships with interesting and unusual people. The native is apt to become involved in group and organizational activities that have humanitarian or scientific goals.

If Uranus is afflicted while transiting the eleventh house there can be sudden disruptions in friendships and group associations; these are often caused by the native's own unpredictable behavior and attitude. If the native has ulterior motives while Uranus transits this house, plans will backfire and cause failure and unpopularity. Such partnerships will last only as long as both parties feel they are getting something out of the arrangement.

Transit Uranus Through the Twelfth House

The Uranus transit through the twelfth house indicates a period of sudden change and upheaval in the native's private affairs. Forces stemming from the unconscious mind erupt, causing changes in the native's secret motivation. This is a favorable transit for meditation and the development of clairvoyant abilities.

If Uranus makes favorable aspects while transiting this house, deep wisdom and knowledge can be brought to light that proves invaluable in problem solving. Such inspiration could also be a spur to artistic creativity of some kind. The native can be prey to sudden irrational impulses that stem from the subconscious mind. There can be a tendency to be drawn into secret societies and organizations. The native may become involved in secret alliances that may not be in his or her best interests, and so-called friends can turn out to be secret enemies.

Transit Uranus Conjunctions

Transit Uranus Conjunction Sun

This transit brings about a period of rapid change in the native's life because the native is apt to assert his or her independence and originality. There is a general impatience with old conditions that have become commonplace and that no longer serve as a creative stimulus. The native therefore starts new activities that give a greater scope to his individual expression.

Many new friendships are formed at this time, and often unexpected love relationships develop under this transit. The native may meet someone who is unusual and dynamic. New group associations are formed at this time, and the native may become the center or leader of group activities if abilities and basic inclinations permit. Friends and group associations often create situations that help the native realize objectives. Often this transit brings about an interest in astrology or other occult pursuits. In some cases the native has unusual clairvoyant experiences. Under this transit one is apt to initiate business enterprises or other activities involved with joint finances, corporate money, insurance or government funding. Such business activity often relates to technological endeavors. The native will never be the same after experiencing this transit. It brings about an altered and in most cases expanded consciousness. Personal magnetism and leadership abilities are intensified. However, if the horoscope shows tendencies toward irresponsibility, the native may mistake this freedom for license, thereby dissipating energies and resources in eccentric and nonproductive pursuits of pleasure. If the natal horoscope shows health difficulties, overexertion should be avoided during this transit.

Transit Uranus Conjunction Moon

This transit brings about sudden changes in domestic affairs and family relationships. There are likely to be sudden changes affecting the home, and the native is apt to move or make alterations in the domestic environment. Also likely to occur is the sudden reactivation of deep-seated, emotional tendencies based on past experiences, especially those from early childhood. Emotionally erratic tendencies may be prevalent. This transit can spark the creative imagination and bring out hidden knowledge that resides within the subconscious mind. Under this transit women will experience greater personal magnetism, originality and sparkle. Men undergoing this transit can establish exciting relationships with unusual, fascinating women. This transit often brings about unexpected financial conditions in the native's life. This can pertain to personal finances, partner's finances, inheritance, taxes, insurance or business enterprises. If other factors in the horoscope concur, there can be an unexpected removal of a family member. In other instances there can be new additions to the family, or close friends will be like family members. The home can become the scene of group or organizational activity. This transit often brings sudden changes in a woman's health. Often these variations are stimulated by motional factors.

Transit Uranus Conjunction Mercury

This transit brings about new ideas and a new state of awareness. This is an especially favorable transit for writers, teachers, scientists, inventors and those who work in communication fields. This is also an auspicious time to study astrology and other occult subjects because the native may attract new ideas that come in sudden flashes of inspiration. The mind works faster and more intuitively at this time. The native will develop friendships with neighbors and coworkers, and is also apt to establish group associations that will introduce new concepts and expand mental horizons. There are unusual job opportunities or interesting and mentally stimulating work. Those who are scientifically, electronically or mechanically inclined are apt to produce new inventions. In some cases the native will become interested in diet, the occult, healing and medicine. Interesting and unusual communication with brothers, sisters, neighbors and friends is common at this time. There is apt to be much coming and going under this transit, and the native should therefore have rest periods. Otherwise the native is apt to become nervous and high-strung.

Transit Uranus Conjunction Venus

This transit brings unexpected opportunities for love relationships, which would likely occur under unusual circumstances. Whether the relationship endures, however, depends upon other factors in the horoscope. In any event there will be a strong attraction to the other person, bringing excitement and sparkle into the relationship. This transit can bring about the proverbial "ideal" relationship. This is a favorable transit for marriage, providing other factors in the horoscope indicate stability. The native with artistic and musical inclinations will be inspired to produce works of greater originality and creativity, and is likely to receive deserved recognition and financial reward. Because of Venus' exaltation in Pisces and because Uranus rules the super-conscious mind, this can be a period of intuitive, spiritual inspiration which usually finds expression through the arts, humanitarian endeavors, friendships and other relationships. There can be original insights into more effective ways to earn money, especially in businesses dealing with the arts or public relations. In general the native will be happy and magnetic, drawing people to himself or herself because of the sparkling quality of personal expression. The native often establishes new friendships and business partnerships under this aspect.

Transit Uranus Conjunction Mars

This transit brings about a period of increased energy, initiative, willpower and a desire for independent action. The native may become more aggressive, and a strong creative impulse may be expressed. Under this transit the native has the will and courage to initiate action to realize goals that seemed impossible to attain before. There will be increased personal energy which the native will direct and consolidate in order to attain professional ambitions. The native often sparks new activities among friends and group associates. However, there will be a propensity to become egocentric, headstrong and impulsive, which may cause the native may alienate friends. New enterprises involving corporate money, partner's finances, government funding, insurance, taxes and the goods of the dead will materialize. There is also a possibility of an unexpected inheritance. Rehabilitation programs for the native or others could be initiated under this transit. Carelessness in driving, handling of machinery, firearms and electricity can cause severe accidents and even death. In some cases, the native will be forced to deal with violent or dangerous situations. Rash actions should be controlled at this time. This may inspire one toward an active involvement in occult pursuits. It is a favorable transit for engineering and scientific endeavors, providing safety rules are strictly observed.

Transit Uranus Conjunction Jupiter

This transit brings about new and expansive experiences connected with the native's social, cultural, religious and philosophic outlook. Mystical experiences and new friendships may suddenly and radically alter the native's outlook, but this is usually for the better. Under this transit, one becomes more tolerant, optimistic and receptive to ideas that often relate to educational, humanitarian, spiritual or occult interests. The native will be more generous towards others, and will also cooperate with friends and groups for humanitarian and spiritual advancement. This is a time of general good fortune and unexpected fortuitous events. These are apt to come through friends, group associations, inheritance, corporate or partner's money, educational institutions or religious establishments. It is a time of progress and expansion in the realization of goals and objectives. There can be sudden unexpected good fortune through opportunities for higher education, new enterprises and long journeys. Opportunities for unusual activities connected with hospitals, universities or religious institutions may arise. The native may become interested in the cultures, religions and art forms of distant countries. Friendships may be cultivated with people from distant places. Unexpected journeys to faraway places may occur under this transit.

Transit Uranus Conjunction Saturn

This transit can bring about sudden and unexpected changes in the native's career and public standing. Whether these are favorable or unfavorable depends upon the native's past motivations and other aspects occurring at the same time. There is likely to be a sudden change and a disintegration of the crystallized conditions in the native's life. These changes are apt to affect professional activities, public standing and reputation. Corporate enterprises, friendships and partnerships will also be affected. With this transit, if these experiences are handled in a constructive manner, the native will gain valuable insights into new methods of accomplishing career objectives and work responsibilities. And, at this time the native has the opportunity to give concrete practical expression to inspirational ideas. If Saturn is afflicted in the natal chart and the native's motives are selfish, reversals of fortune, public disgrace and fall from high positions may occur. At this time the native feels a greater sense of responsibility and loyalty toward friends and group associations. New friendships with older, well-established or more mature people are apt to be formed at this time, or old friends may reappear. Sudden deaths of friends or family members could bring new situations into the native's life that involve additional responsibilities for him or her.

Transit Uranus Conjunction Uranus

This transit occurs at approximately the 84th year of life. It usually has an occult significance, making the native aware of superphysical realities. Life after death and reincarnation have a new meaning for the native. Because Uranus is exalted in Scorpio, the native can realize the continuity of life and the fact that birth and death are two sides of the same coin. This is an aspect of true freedom that enables the native to explore and experience many new and unusual things. There is a sense of spiritual freedom that is generated by this transit, and the goals of the native's life change in accordance with a growing sense of spiritual detachment. There can also be sudden changes in the person's life concerning friendships and group associations.

Transit Uranus Conjunction Neptune

This transit brings unusual, sudden, mystical and sometimes clairvoyant experiences that give one deep insight into life's inner, spiritual mysteries. Large-scale cultural changes of a social, economic or political nature have a profound effect on the native's affairs, goals and objectives and state of consciousness. Many deep, unconscious memories of the past may be brought to the surface. These can even be related to previous embodiments. In some cases there is contact with those who are discarnate. Under this transit sudden inspirations can spark creativity in the realms of science, art and mysticism. The native's powers of visualization and mental creativity are greatly heightened under this transit. This is a favorable aspect for the study of astrology and all other occult subjects, especially those pertaining to psychology. There can be unusual and sudden occurrences in the home or in matters relating to insurance, taxes, partnership or corporate money and inheritance. Old acquaintances can reappear on the scene, and can be friendly or unfriendly, depending upon other factors in the horoscope.

Transit Uranus Conjunction Pluto

This transit may bring profound changes caused by internal experiences that are based on large-scale forces in the culture to which the native belongs. There is often a sudden end to old conditions which brings entirely new circumstances. Things are never the same again, especially within the affairs of the house in which the conjunction takes place, as well as the houses that Uranus and Pluto rule in the natal horoscope. Matters relating to insurance, taxes, corporate money, partnership money, goals and objectives, friendships and group associations are apt to undergo drastic changes. Because of the double Scorpio and eighth house significance of this transit, there can be the death of someone. Death can occur in a subtle sense in terms of the death of old concepts and conditions and attitudes toward life. Properly handled, this transit can facilitate inner, spiritual liberation from materialism and sensory limitation. This usually takes the form of some kind of direct experience with the superphysical planes of existence. This is a favorable aspect of the study of the deeper levels of science or the occult. At best, there can be inspiration into ways and means of regenerating existing conditions in the native's life. Larger forces affecting the culture as a whole can drastically change the native's circumstances.

Transit Uranus Sextiles

Transit Uranus Sextile Sun

This transit indicates a period during which the native becomes more self-confident, inventive and creative. Intuitive insights and original ideas inspire the native to initiate new creative enterprises. It is a favorable transit for influencing people in positions of power and authority. It also inclines one to assume personal leadership in some new endeavor. New friendships and group associations are often formed under the influence of this transit. New opportunities arise that are connected with occult, scientific or humanitarian endeavors. Opportunities arise to make possible long-cherished goals and objectives. It is also a favorable time for business enterprises, business partnerships and government-supported projects. This is a favorable transit for love relationships and for theatrical and other artistic or creative endeavors. New opportunities can arise for an exciting social life, which can lead to new friendships and romances. This is also a favorable transit for reasonable financial speculation based on new ideas and concepts.

Transit Uranus Sextile Moon

This transit stimulates the imagination and brings to light hidden resources stored in the unconscious mind. It is favorable for home improvement projects and for making a new start in domestic and family relationships. Women often play an important part in the realization of the native's goals and objectives. There is often the opportunity for financial gain through the application of new ideas and original approaches to business. Such business enterprises can involve other peoples' money, corporate money, insurance, taxes or legacies. Businesses dealing with food, real estate, housing and products used in the home are especially favored by this transit. If the natal horoscope indicates intuitive abilities, this transit will intensify them. New friendships can be established with women, who influence the native toward a fresher and more open-minded outlook on life.

Transit Uranus Sextile Mercury

This transit stimulates the native's thinking and communication. Original and intuitively inspired ideas accompany this transit. The native gains new insights and establishes communication with groups and friends who stimulate the intellectual life. This is an especially favorable transit for work in occult subjects, scientific endeavors and communication, especially that dealing with electronic media. Work involving electronics in general is favored at this time. Under the influence of this aspect the native comes up with many startling solutions to problems that make it easier to realize objectives. Often an interest develops in health, diet and other means of improving one's physical body. Unusual and unexpected communication is often received during this transit, and these frequently involve brothers, sisters or neighbors. It often occurs that the native finds new and unusual ways of improving work efficiency, and the native is also likely to establish friendships among coworkers, employers or employees. This transit stimulates mental interests directed toward the study of astrology, reincarnation and other related fields. Some natives may experience mental telepathy during this transit.

Transit Uranus Sextile Venus

This transit brings exciting new personal relationships and love opportunities into the native's life. Under this aspect one is apt to be more optimistic, exuberant and joyous, which in turn produces greater social appeal. This is a favorable time for artistic pursuits. Inspiration and originality will manifest in the artistic expression. The native will have the opportunity to enter into exciting and profitable business partnerships or moneymaking enterprises which are often related to artistic pursuits or the sale of luxury items. At this time one is apt to realize goals for personal happiness and love relationships. Marriage can arise under this transit. The native is able to attract charming, unusual and talented friends who inspire greater personal happiness and creativity. The native is able to tap inner resources that give a deeper peace and a greater appreciation of harmony and beauty. These amplified feelings are often gained through quiet periods of inner reflection. In general this transit will enhance the native's popularity.

Transit Uranus Sextile Mars

This transit increases the energy and initiative of the native, who becomes more aggressive in carrying out plans to achieve personal ambitions. Often the person will employ unusual methods to achieve success. This is a favorable transit for pursuing business enterprises and for furthering career ambitions. Business engaged in during this period often relates to science, engineering, economics and management leadership. There is a strong will to succeed, which makes this a favorable time to spearhead new enterprises. At this time, energy and original ideas, combined with effective leadership and group cooperation can overcome obstacles and make significant breakthroughs. This is a favorable transit for all matters concerned with occult affairs, corporate money, insurance, inheritance and efforts towards the improvement and regeneration of existing conditions. In general, one's desires and energies are strongly directed toward obtaining goals and improving conditions surrounding one's life.

Transit Uranus Sextile Jupiter

This transit brings about a time of mental and philosophic expansion for the native, who becomes more open and receptive to new religious and philosophic ideas. Consequently, this is a favorable time for study and investigation of occult subjects. This often manifests as an interest in religious ideas that originated in distant parts of the world, such as those pertaining to yoga, Vedanta or Buddhism. This is also a favorable time for the study of astrology. Unexpected opportunities arise for higher education or foreign travel. New friendships and group associations will broaden the horizons. Domestic affairs are apt to improve, and new and ingenious methods of dealing with the home will be realized by the native. The home will be used as a gathering place for friends and groups. Relationships with family members can begin a new phase based upon a higher spiritual understanding. This is also a favorable aspect for corporate enterprises, financial affairs connected with partnerships and matters dealing with insurance and inheritance. The native may receive unusual or unexpected opportunities for advancement through universities, religious organizations, hospitals or other humanitarian institutions. At this time a regeneration in the individual's way of thinking can result from an internal mystical experience.

Transit Uranus Sextile Saturn

This transit brings about opportunities for professional advancement through original ideas and effective cooperation in the implementation of career organization, work and goals. The native gains insights into giving a practical expression to inspirational ideas by using present technology combined with new ideas to increase efficiency. One is able to gain the friendship of those in positions of power or leadership, thus helping to bring about the realization of one's goals and objectives. This is also a favorable transit for business and corporate enterprises as well as the constructive resolution of legal problems. The native tends to establish friendships with older or mature individuals or with organizations that have a serious purpose. These may be professional or fraternal groups, or organizations with scientific or humanitarian purposes. This is also a favorable time for serious philosophical and occult and astrological work or study. In general the native tends to combine originality with serious, diligent work to achieve goals.

Transit Uranus Sextile Uranus

This transit occurs at about age fourteen and again at approximately age seventy. In the first instance it produces an awakening to new ideas and an awareness of the interesting aspects of the development of one's self and one's culture. This sextile also corresponds to the age of puberty. This is very significant, as Uranus is exalted in Scorpio, the sign ruling sex. At this time young people begin to take an active interest in creative, original mental expressions and have their first introduction to the mysteries of science and the wonders of nature's workings. There is also a growing awareness of other people's values and the necessity for interpersonal cooperation for the sake of the larger society. At this time many young people ask serious questions regarding the nature of spiritual reality as distinguished from religious and social conditioning.

The influence of this transit has a connotation of Gemini as a third house sextile to its own place, depicting the awakening of the mind to a higher dimension of reality. At this time youngsters begin to establish their own intellectual friendships as distinguished from fifth house playmates. Under this transit, youngsters go further afield in search of new contacts. They are no longer restricted to brothers, sisters and near neighbors for mental stimulation.

By the same token, those who have reached approximately age seventy are freed from many responsibilities associated with family, children and profession. They are free to establish friendships and investigate higher spiritual realities. They are no longer exclusively bound to materialistic concerns and responsibilities. There is greater mental freedom and interest in exploring unusual possibilities of life. At this time the inner spirit begins its journey back to its source. This implies not necessarily a physical death, but rather an abstraction into a state of spiritual awareness that accompanies the last of life, for which the first was made.

Transit Uranus Sextile Neptune

This transit has a highly occult and mystical significance, as the native is mentally and intuitively introduced to deeper levels of spiritual reality. Although this does not mean that everyone who experiences this transit evolves into a mystic or sage, it does invariably help to bring out whatever innate intuitive and clairvoyant faculties are present. Through this sextile transit there is also the potential to gain considerable wisdom and understanding through tapping the deep memory reservoir contained in the subconscious mind. Through this drawing upon the subconscious mind, a new awareness is produced that can give a glimpse of cosmic consciousness. An interest can develop in occult subjects, or one can become involved in friendships or organizations which further this interest. Under this transit one can implement new ideas that will gain acceptance with respect to hospitals, institutions, educational organizations and scientific, humanitarian and fraternal organizations.

Transit Uranus Sextile Pluto

This transit brings about increased awareness of all matters pertaining to fundamental processes of regeneration and the mysteries of death and rebirth. The native becomes aware that many of the ordinary concerns of life are at most superphysical matters, experience with which results in growth. The native develops interests in understanding the fundamental energy and consciousness responsible for material manifestation and all of life's processes, and is therefore apt to delve into such subjects as astrology, occult phenomena, life after death and reincarnation. This increased depth of understanding often brings about important changes in the native's goals and objectives. If the natal horoscope indicates a potential for intuitive or clairvoyant abilities, this transit will tend to bring it out. This is a favorable transit for creative self-expression through art or the sciences. It also favors friendships and group activities that serve the purpose of regeneration and greater spiritual understanding and growth. The native becomes more resourceful and self-reliant in finding solutions and in realizing goals and objectives. There is increased awareness of one's self as a spiritual creative being. In the outer circumstances of life, this transit can be favorable to matters relating to insurance, corporate finances, taxes, goods of the dead and a partner's money.

Transit Uranus Squares

Transit Uranus Square Sun

This transit brings about a time of rebellion and demand of freedom for personal self-expression, regardless of the cost. This is a time when egotistical or headstrong tendencies can have serious and far-reaching consequences, and the native may throw away or destroy hard-earned gains for the sake of personal indulgence. Matters relating to friendship, group association, personal self-expression, love, speculation and personal leadership will be on an unsteady platform, although the native may be oblivious of this condition. Such a state of affairs will naturally have an adverse effect on the native's professional and family life. This is a time when one is apt to break off established friendships and family ties or leave a job for the sake of new adventures. In some cases external events beyond the native's personal control and that stem from forces operating in the larger society may disrupt the native's personal security and well-being. In most cases, it is the native's own attitudes that bring about adversity under this transit. The effect of this transit will be in accordance with the native's motivations, both past and present.

On the positive side, it should be remembered that even adverse aspects of Uranus have a liberating effect. They serve as a detonation of one's prison house, even though the native may be hit by a few of the flying bricks in the process. Such times are difficult to endure but are nevertheless productive of valuable experiences that expand the consciousness and lead eventually to greater strength and self-assurance.

In general, squares of Uranus should be handled in such a manner that the native does not initiate changes. However, if changes are forced upon him or her, the native should adjust to them gracefully and make constructive use of the new situation. In many cases the individual will have outgrown old conditions which require drastic events to make him or her go forward into new experiences. This transit seldom passes without giving the native a valuable lesson in spiritual detachment and correct motivation.

Transit Uranus Square Moon

This transit brings about drastic changes in one's financial, emotional, domestic and family affairs. Often it indicates a time when the lid blows off the contents of the native's repressed emotional problems related to past experiences and childhood. In the long run this transit can have a cathartic effect. While undergoing this transit the native will experience a state of unpredictable emotional turmoil. Women in particular will undergo extreme emotional stress. Regardless of sex, this is not a favorable time for relating to women or for involving oneself in problems pertaining to women. The native's emotional unpredictability is apt to alienate the native from friends and make it difficult for him or her to get along in groups or to adjust to family relationships. Some natives undergoing this transit sever family ties and strike out on their own. Because of the Uranus exaltation in Scorpio, there can be the death or removal of some family member. In general this transit tends to make one moody and unpredictable because of unrecognized, unconscious, emotional forces or outside factors beyond one's control.

Because both planets are involved with financial houses by exaltation, this is not a favorable transit for business enterprises, be they personal or corporate. Things will not be as planned, as unforseen contingencies will upset the person's financial security in some way. In some cases the home is disrupted by electrical or mechanical failures, or even by natural forces or ecological problems.

Transit Uranus Square Mercury

This transit brings about a period of mental uncertainty and confusion. Often this is brought about by new circumstances and information which force the native to change long-cherished ideas, attitudes and concepts. There is a tendency for the native to become headstrong and opinionated and obstinate. This is a time when one should be cognizant that we seldom know enough to make any conclusions final. The native may fancy himself or herself to be a genius, and may in fact be one, but at this time this genius may lack practicality, experience and adequate consideration of the ideas and opinions of others. All too often under this transit there is a tendency to jump to conclusions on insufficient information and considerations of what is involved. The native tends to be erratic in communication, which can be a source of annoyance to friends, groups, associations and those with whom the native has business dealings. Often the native changes his or her mind in an unpredictable manner, confusing others, while at the same time obstinately defending the newest mental stand. Under this transit the person can vacillate and take on the coloring of the friend or condition influencing him or her at the time. There can be disagreements, scandal and breakdowns of communication between brothers, sisters and neighbors.

Mental instability and nervousness can have an adverse effect on work and health, thus making it difficult to get along with coworkers, employers and employees. This is not a favorable time for travel, as one is apt to be erratic and impulsive in actions and decisions. Caution should be exercised while driving. This is also not a favorable time to sign legal papers or documents. Extreme care should be exercised in the event such a signing is absolutely necessary. Unforeseen factors can cause problems. Key individuals connected with the agreement may later change their minds. Under this aspect one learns to reserve judgment until sufficient information is available to make a sound decision. One also learns to exercise discrimination in speech and other forms of communication. Nervous disorders and digestive problems often accompany this transit.

Transit Uranus Square Venus

This transit brings about sudden romantic involvements and infatuations. These relationships are generally unstable and short-lived. While they last they are highly magnetic and emotionally intense, even to the point of blinding the native to common sense or consideration of the consequences. This transit is particularly precarious for those who are married, for it often brings about extramarital love affairs that threaten the marital stability and could lead to divorce. These relationships arising on the side are rarely permanent, and the native should be cautious since he or she could be left with no one when the transit is over. If the native is unattached, the consequences of this transit are not likely to be so devastating, providing the native can go through this period with an attitude of detachment, enjoying the good aspects of new relationships and experiences without expecting or demanding permanency from them. If there are no illusions of permanency or stability, there can be increased happiness, excitement and enjoyment of life. This transit is one of the most potent and sexually overpowering of all transits.

This transit can also increase social activity and general pursuit of pleasure. Care should be exercised so that this does not lead to overindulgence and excesses that could undermine the native's reputation and financial stability. There can be a dissipation of time and money without anything concrete to show for it all. Much depends upon the overall nature of the natal horoscope. This transit could be highly beneficial for one who is shy, socially inhibited, overly conservative or overworked. For those who are extroverted in a pleasure-oriented sense, this transit could increase these tendencies to a point of dissipation and excess.

This is not a favorable transit for permanency in friendship, and to some it brings many new and exciting contacts. This transit is not favorable for business or marriage partnerships or corporate dealings. The native learns that all that glitters is not gold. Business dealings under this transit are not likely to have real substance or permanence or practical value. One should be especially careful of get-rich-quick schemes. One's energies would be better channeled toward artistic creativity or appreciation of the arts.

Emotional needs stemming from the unconscious mind are often brought to the surface and lead to sudden extremes of behavior that can bring about the native's self-undoing. So powerful are the emotional forces released under this transit that the native can be temporarily oblivious to family, business and marital responsibilities. This transit can bring changes in the native's profession, home and partnership dealings. The circumstances of the native's life are rearranged by the time this transit is over.

Transit Uranus Square Mars

This transit brings about sudden extremes of action and possible violence in the native's life. Impulsiveness, impatience and headstrong attitudes can lead to serious accidents and disruption of personal, professional and business affairs. In extreme cases it can pose a threat to the native's life. There is a tendency to be harsh, quick-tempered and irritable. Extreme care should be used with electricity, guns, fire, explosives, automobiles and generally all situations in which serious accidents could occur. Egotism, self-centeredness and anger are apt to alienate friends and bring about arguments and disagreements and cause discord in matters relating to joint finances, partner's finances, inheritance and corporate matters. In some cases there can be the sudden death of a family member.

Aggressive attempts to further one's professional ambitions may lead to more harm than good at this time. The native should tread carefully when dealing with those in positions of power or authority. The natural tendency of this transit is to make one rebellious toward established power structures and authority figures. Attempts to use violent or coercive means will lead to resentment and opposition. The native should guard against self-centeredness where motivations are concerned. This could interfere with the realization of goals and objectives.

In some cases the native can be subjected to external conditions of violence, disruption and sudden change over which there is no personal control. This would be especially so if the native is caught in circumstances of social, financial, political or ecological upheaval in the larger environment. In such cases, considerable destruction can occur as the first stage in the creation of a new and better situation. This is not a time to precipitate changes, but if changes are forced on the native, he or she should be willing to make the necessary adjustments and prepare for a new and different order of things which ultimately will hold greater potential for good.

Transit Uranus Square Jupiter

This transit brings about a time of false optimism that can be dangerous. It is not advisable to take unnecessary risks or to be overconfident in enterprises. The tendency to take too much for granted can have disastrous long-term consequences. Many fortunes have been lost under Uranus' transiting square to Jupiter.

The native can become ensnared by impractical, eccentric cults and religious beliefs. There is a tendency toward wishful thinking and impractical idealism. This is not a favorable time for long journeys or religious pilgrimages because things will not go as planned or expected. The native's friends and group associates are apt to mislead even if they are well-meaning. The danger of hypocrisy also accompanies this transit.

Astrological or occult advice given at this time can be faulty. This is a time when astrologers should use extreme caution and care in making prognostications. Snap judgments are especially dangerous at this time.

Unwise business dealings and corporate investments can lead to lawsuits, especially where business money, partner's finances, inheritance, alimony, insurance and taxes are concerned. This is an unfavorable transit for discipline in pursuit of higher education. Many students take impractical and useless courses at this time, or drop out of college completely. This is also an unfavorable transit for dealing with hospitals, institutions and churches. In general the native should exercise caution, avoid extremes and be realistic and practical while under this transit.

Transit Uranus Square Saturn

This transit can bring about sudden and unexpected difficulties in partnerships, friendships, corporate affairs and business and career goals. If the native has been selfish in personal goals and objectives, severe reversals of fortune can occur as a natural consequence of karmic law. Ulterior motives can enter into friendships and group associations, either on the native's part or on the part of those with whom the native deals. Consequently, cooperation will last only as long as all parties concerned feel that they are making gains in some manner. Having no other larger purpose to achieve, such associations are usually unstable, short-lived and burdened with mutual suspicion and distrust. Only by strict adherence to principles of justice and fair play can one avoid these pitfalls under this transit. Even though present motivations may be good, the consequences of past misdeeds can come up for reckoning at this time.

This transit can cause erratic behavior that lacks the discipline necessary for the attainment of any long-range goal. There is a tendency to work spasmodically, vacillating between extremes of overwork and indifference to work. Plans and the security of the native in general are frequently upset by unforeseen circumstances that can bring to naught much effort and hard work. This is especially disturbing to those who have become accustomed to a routine and crystallized way of life. In many cases natives are forced to make changes against their will. In the long run, such changes will lead to greater growth and understanding. Under this transit one learns that life is a dynamic process and that everything is in a constant state of flux and change. Attachment to established conditions can only lead to disappointment under this transit. Lawsuits can arise that are connected with partnerships, business and professional matters, contracts, taxes, insurance, alimony or inheritance. Extreme or fanatical attitudes should be avoided. Displays of unreasonable, inconsistent or dictatorial attitudes should be avoided under this transit.

Transit Uranus Square Uranus

This transit occurs in the average person's life at approximately age twenty-one and again at approximately age sixty-three. In the first instance it represents the normal period of rebellion in youth. This lower square of Uranus indicates a time when the young people break away from their families and make their attempt at independence and self-sufficiency. This usually is accompanied by uncertainties and difficulties in establishing new friendships and group associations. This is a time when one must adjust to the larger financial world as represented by Scorpio, the seventh house and other people's money and values.

The age twenty-one transit coincides with the upper square of transit Saturn to its natal position. This indicates the struggle to acquire a job and to get a foothold in the professional world. The need for financial independence, itself motivated by a need for independence from parental ties, is represented by the transit of Uranus squaring its natal position. Consequently, the traditional time of coming of age is beset with uncertainty, difficulty and struggle.

The upper square of Uranus around the age of sixty-five indicates a time when one must learn to seek deeper spiritual values in life. This is a time when children are grown and ordinary professional ambitions no longer give sufficient meaning to life. The native must learn to adjust to new circumstances and social ideals which were not prevalent or acceptable during his youth. To get along in a changing world, an old dog must learn new tricks. This necessity may cause difficult adjustments for the native. Much depends on the natal horoscope and the signs and houses involved as to what departments of life will be affected. In these areas, the native will be forced to adjust to change.

Transit Uranus Square Neptune

This transit indicates a time when strong psychic stresses occur in the native's life. Many unresolved problems stemming from the subconscious mind can be brought to the surface. The native may be prey to irrational fears or astral influences of a deceptive and confusing nature. Spurious or impractical dabbling in the occult will produce negative results or no results at all.

Friends and group associations may be deceptive or impractical. Financial dealings involving other people's money, such as insurance, taxes and inheritances, are apt to be deceptive or illusory. In some cases natives will tend to drift off in a private planetary world that bears no useful or practical relationship to the ordinary affairs of life. These psychological tendencies can have a disruptive and confusing effect on family and domestic affairs. Social forces in the larger society may bring about confusion or loss into the native's life through the affairs ruled by the signs and houses which Uranus and Neptune occupy and rule. Such occurrences may be beyond the native's control.

Transit Uranus Square Pluto

This transit brings about a period of drastic change and upheaval in the native's life, especially with respect to the affairs ruled by the signs and houses which Uranus and Pluto occupy and rule in the horoscope. The change away from the status quo of these matters is drastic and irreversible. Because of the double Scorpio and eighth house significance of this transit, much occurs that seems to be destructive. At this time it is well to remember that birth and death are two sides of the same coin. Destruction of the old is a necessary first stage in the creation of the new. Social, political, economic and ecological forces beyond the native's personal control often play a major part in these transitional events. It should be remembered that when dealing with trans-Saturnian planets, individual destiny is linked with mass karma.

The successful handling of this transit requires detachment and an expanded understanding and vision that goes beyond the material plane. The native may have to contend with crises that tax the inner spiritual resources, and often becomes acquainted with death in some form. All of this can come through family, friends or mass events. This transit brings about a strong sexual impetus that can cause psychological problems and upheavals for the native. In general the native's goals and objectives and basic understanding of life are forced to undergo a drastic change. The native is often forced to combat corrupt people and circumstances. These confrontations may come through entrenched corporate interests, through economic situations associated with big business, or through friends.

Transit Uranus Trines

Transit Uranus Trine Sun

This transit brings about a favorable period for the realization of goals and objectives. It is an exciting time that often includes unexpected good fortune in some form. This transit increases self-confidence and gives the individual creative insight. The native becomes more energetic, positive and popular. As a result of this, the native receives opportunities to exert personal leadership and to acquire recognition for personal creative endeavors. Many new friendships are established under this transit. Unexpected love relationship opportunities present themselves as the native expands the social sphere.

This transit favors humanitarian work, scientific endeavors, inventing and pursuit of occult studies and activities. Because the Sun rules the natural fifth house, this aspect favors artistic endeavors and financial speculation. In some cases the native may receive gifts, grants, inheritances or opportunities for travel and higher education. This transit also increases the native's insight into occult and philosophic matters; this is one of the best transits for astrological work or investigation of other occult sciences. In general this transit increases the native's interest in new methods of self-improvement. This often takes the form of developing new areas of interest into new and untried realms of experience or adventure. Because the Sun is exalted in Aries, the sign of self-hood, and because Uranus is exalted in Scorpio, the sign of regeneration, some new form of self-improvement is tried at this time that helps to expand the native's horizons.

Transit Uranus Trine Moon

This transit is favorable for financial and domestic expansion and regeneration. During this time the native has increased freedom and insight with which to overcome the negative emotional habit patterns of the past. Unexpected benefits may come through the influence of women, and this transit also often brings romance into the life if the native is a man. This is an especially favorable transit for business partnerships and transactions involving corporate finances. Businesses dealing with real estate, food, domestic products, electronics and scientific research are especially well influenced. This aspect also has a beneficial effect on work related to ecological concerns. The native is fortunate at this time in finding new ways to improve family and domestic conditions. The opportunity can arise for improving the home itself or for moving to a better home environment. During this transit old friends reappear on the scene. Also, interesting and unusual friendships can be established with women at this time.

Transit Uranus Trine Mercury

This transit is favorable for all mental and intellectual activities. The native is inspired with many original ideas as the mind works faster and with increased intuition. This is a very favorable transit for creative work pertaining to electronics, communication, media and especially any facet of these fields that is involved with entertainment. Writing, lecturing, teaching, traveling, and studying through higher education are all favored at this time. The native can develop an interest in new methods of healing, including those that are related to occult practices. There are new insights into scientific work, astrology and occult subjects in general. A heightened ability to communicate in an original manner will facilitate establishing many friendships and group associations. The double Aquarius influence of this transit increases the native's concern with universal issues that affect human destiny and the well-being of humanity. Creative insight into new ways of improving work efficiency furthers the native's career and brings popularity and success in dealings with coworkers, employers and employees.

New and stimulating friendships often develop through the native's work. Unusual and interesting activities arise through neighbors or neighborhood activities that in some way involve brothers or sisters. This aspect has a beneficial influence on all matters dealing with transportation, including arriving at one's destination promptly, the condition of roads and highways and the purchase of means of transportation, such as a car. This is also a good transit for signing contracts and formulating plans. Because of the ninth house significance of the trine aspect and the third house significance of Mercury, this is an excellent transit for long journeys and pursuit of higher education. This is also a favorable time for writing and publishing. This is one of the best transits for the study of astrology or other occult subjects. It can also increase the native's business acumen, especially with regard to business finances, insurance, taxes, inheritance, grants and funding.

Transit Uranus Trine Venus

This is one of the most exciting and romantic of all transits. It can bring about love relationships and opportunity for marriage. Almost invariably there will be increased social activities that can bring about the realization of one's goals and objectives. This transit improves financial conditions and brings the native into contact with persons with whom he or she can form partnerships or have worthwhile business dealings. This transit produces a strong stimulus for improving artistic creativity and productivity. Consequently, it is very favorable for artists and entertainers of all types. Romantic opportunities arise suddenly and under unusual circumstances. An ideal love could also be brought into a person's life at this time. This is a very favorable aspect for marriage, providing the horoscope basically indicates marital stability. During this period the native will express a sparkle and effervescence that increases popularity and social contacts. Because of the second and eighth house connotations of this transit, the native can receive gifts, grants, inheritances or other benefits, and these could be connected in some way to business or corporate enterprises. This transit favors businesses related to luxury items, art, entertainment, electronics and fashion.

Transit Uranus Trine Mars

This transit brings a heightened vitality, energy and ambition to the native, who dares to attempt things for which the native would ordinarily lack the courage or initiative to tackle. This aspect is favorable for scientific engineering, electronic work and mechanical undertakings. There is often a strong desire to start new enterprises or to embark upon some kind of new creative work. Often the native's life takes an entirely new orientation, resulting from the native's formulation of new goals and objectives. Due to the double Scorpio, eighth house significance of this aspect, the native can have occult experiences which can alter values, desires, goals and purposes. There is a strong impulse toward regeneration and self-improvement at this time. The required willpower is present with which to initiate action that will regenerate existing conditions and thereby give a new start to the life. The native's change of consciousness and awareness of new powers and energies within brings about a new interest in philosophy, reincarnation, astrology and other subjects dealing with the ultimate purpose of life. Programs of self-improvement that are begun at this time often emphasize one's physical conditioning and can therefore involve exercising, athletics, yoga or dancing. The native may become interested in higher education, travel, art or sculpture and other forms of building as a creative expression. These interests are likely to bring about new friendships and group associations with dynamic and creative individuals. This is a favorable aspect for dealing with men, because there will be an inherent understanding of the male drive for action, ambition and accomplishment. Other eighth house matters, such as business, insurance, taxes, goods of the dead, joint money, grants and funding, are also favored at this time.

Transit Uranus Trine Jupiter

This transit brings unexpected good fortune and progress. If the native has been struggling to achieve something of worth for a long time, this transit can bring about the breakthrough. At this time there is a natural tendency to become more philosophical and spiritually inclined. However, this inclination will not manifest in the dogmatic and sectarian manner characteristic of many of the various Jupiter aspects. Under this aspect the native will be open-minded and receptive to new ideas and philosophies. Such tolerant understanding will be based on direct personal intuitive experiences that expand the consciousness. Consequently, the native will establish many new friendships and group associations with those who are similarly inclined. Such group activity will engender humanitarian and educational goals and purposes.

This is an excellent time for the pursuit of higher education, foreign travel and the study of foreign cultures, philosophies and religions. All occult and mystical studies and pursuits, such as astrology, reincarnation and meditation, will benefit the native at this time and will be a means whereby he can help others. This is a favorable aspect for work with hospitals, churches, institutions and fraternal organizations. The native can do much to regenerate existing conditions by initiating new programs based on broader understanding. The native may receive benefits through joint finances, inheritances, insurance, funding and established institutions. This is also a favorable transit for initiating corporate enterprises. There is an ability to look ahead and perceive developing trends.

Transit Uranus Trine Saturn

This transit brings about progress in the native's career, ambitions, partnerships and group associations. There is an ability to apply inspirational ideas in a practical way. The native's experience provides a basis for creative and original solutions to problems. At this time there is good organizational ability combined with farsightedness and originality. There can be unexpected good fortune during this period. The native can receive recognition and favor from established institutions and people in positions of power or authority. This is an excellent aspect for business, industry and governmental affairs. Gains can be made through research, engineering, electronics, insurance, corporate financing and government funding. This transit is excellent for work in the political field that deals with any reform and regeneration of existing political institutions of a business nature. This can be achieved through creative and intelligent work within the present system rather than by means of revolution. The excesses and outmoded methods of the traditional systems should be corrected at this time, while maximum use is made of their better features. This is a favorable transit for forming business partnerships and establishing friendships and group associations of lasting value. Friendships with older people or established persons will bring benefits to the native. Because of the double Aquarius influence of this transit, and because of Saturn's exaltation in Libra, this transit is favorable for all deep intellectual, scientific, mathematical and occult studies. This transit provides the ability for a steady focusing of concentration, which gives the native deep insights into the fundamental laws of the universe and their practical application.

Transit Uranus Trine Uranus

This transit occurs twice in the normal life span. The first trine of Uranus occurs at approximately age twenty-eight or shortly thereafter. This first trine of Uranus to its own place has a fifth house connotation. One arrives at a maturity of original, creative self-expression. This can bring a serious romance into the native's life. There can be new business enterprises, serious interest in the occult, and also new and exciting group associations.

The second trine occurs near age fifty-six and indicates a time of greater personal freedom for spiritual and philosophic expansion. This is a favorable time for long journeys, new adventures, cultivation of new friends and development of new group associations. This second trine is favorable for higher education and serious pursuit of higher spiritual understanding.

Under this transit, established individuals in business can make great advances. Gains through taxes, joint money, insurance, government funding and inheritance are favored at this time. This is an excellent time for humanitarian pursuits and programs designed to improve existing conditions that are of concern to the native.

Transit Uranus Trine Neptune

This transit has a subtle influence regarding the intuitive and imaginative faculties. It can also operate through external social conditions that are prevalent at this time. The native can benefit through a social, economic or cultural change occurring in society. In the case of those whose natal horoscope reveals potential clairvoyant faculties, this transit will bring out or amplify these latent tendencies. Because the imagination is increased at this time, this can be a favorable transit for creativity and inventing. Those in the teaching profession will have abundant ideas on how to reach and empathize with their students, enabling the teacher to realize his or her goals with students.

This is a favorable transit for all forms of humanitarian work concerned with uplifting and re-generating social conditions. The native may become involved with fraternal organizations, se-cret societies, churches, educational institutions, hospitals, asylums or religious retreats as a means of helping others. The home can become a place of group activity or spiritual endeavors. This transit can bring about an interest in occult sciences and astrology and especially in medita-tion or yoga. It can give prophetic abilities along with a concern for the ultimate destiny and well-being of humanity.

Transit Uranus Trine Pluto

This transit brings sudden and unusual changes in life that open up a new level of consciousness and new realms of experience for the native. Often there is a strong interest in self-improvement through some form of occult or spiritual practice. These interests often bring new friendships and group associations, or the influence of new friends can cause the native to become inter-ested in these subjects. This is a favorable aspect for work in occult subjects, especially astrol-ogy. This transit will tend to increase the intuitive faculties that are present. In some cases, a pro-found mystical experience can change the native's understanding of life. A strong interest in life after death and reincarnation is likely to be brought about by this transit. This is a favorable tran-sit for all eighth house matters, such as business finances, joint money, inheritance, insurance and goods of the dead. The increased clairvoyant perceptions and the general occult signifi-cance of this aspect are apt to bring about a deeper interest in religion, philosophy, higher educa-tion, foreign cultures and travel.

Transit Uranus Oppositions

Transit Uranus Opposition Sun

This transit is apt to bring about relationship problems caused by a clashing of the wills. The na-tive often wishes to dominate and remake others, while at the same time resents any interference in personal own affairs. This distorted view of interpersonal relationships is likely to cause sud-den estrangements in the native's life. Consequently, there can be a rapid turnover of friends and associations during this period. At this time the native tends to resent any threat to self-de-termination and has difficulty adjusting to any authority figure. This is a good time to try to see things from the other person's point of view.

Involvements pertaining to interpersonal love or romance are apt to be fascinating and exciting, but unstable and short-lived. The native may have to contend with others who are rebellious, un-predictable and eccentric. This is not a favorable transit for business partnerships, speculation or corporate affairs, as things will not turn out as planned. The native often experiences difficulties in getting along with friends and group associates, or he can attract friends and group associates who are unpredictable, eccentric and unreliable. There can also be difficulties through business funds, joint finances, insurance, taxes, alimony, inheritance and goods of the dead. Careful and impartial examination of both one's own motives and those of others is important under this transit.

Transit Uranus Opposition Moon

This transit is apt to bring about many emotional upsets and family difficulties. The native is often influenced by emotional habit patterns of the past which arise unexpectedly and in peculiar ways. These patterns interfere with the native's ability to relate to others in an acceptable manner, thus creating family difficulties and also financial problems if these relationships involve business. Under this transit the native tends to have difficulty in getting along with women in particular. The native may have to deal with eccentric and emotionally unstable women.

This is not a favorable transit for dealing with business partnerships, corporate affairs, insurance, taxes or goods of the dead. There can be family disagreements over financial matters or business affairs, especially those dealing with real estate, land, food or domestic products. Estrangements or separation from family or parents can take place at this time. In some cases, the home itself may be affected in some manner, forcing the native to move or make drastic alterations or repairs of the home.

Transit Uranus Opposition Mercury

This transit brings about difficulties in relationships resulting from communication problems. These problems can especially affect relationships between the native and employees, employers, coworkers, brothers, sisters or neighbors. This is not a good time to sign important papers or contracts of any kind. Unexpected occurrences often upset these plans and work to the native's disadvantage. Things do not work out as planned. Because one is apt to be nervous and irritable under this transit there is a tendency to make snap judgments. The native should avoid a "know it all" attitude and should listen to the advice of those more experienced. There is a dangerous tendency under this transit for one to take the advice of the wrong people and to use poor judgment in the selection of friends and group associates. At this time, what seems to the native to be new and unusual solutions to problems may lack practicality and acceptance where others are concerned. Nervousness and irritability can cause health problems that can affect the nervous and digestive systems. These problems can in turn interfere with the native's ability to function effectively at work.

Transit Uranus Opposition Venus

This transit brings about sudden and exciting romantic attractions which, however, do not stand the test of time. Many divorces, extramarital love affairs and emotional problems are precipitated during this transit. The native is apt to behave in an extremely willful and contradictory way where affairs of the heart and sexual behavior are concerned. At this time there is also the danger of indulging in luxury or useless social activities which deplete the finances. Although this transit can engender artistic inspiration, discipline and devotion can be lacking and this tends to result in a lack of concrete productivity. Under this transit one experiences extreme emotional instability and a touchy attitude where others are concerned.

This transit can bring about sudden financial losses which result from one's inability to cooperate with others in business dealings or one's bad judgment in choosing business associates. The hedonistic tendencies of this transit can make the native indifferent to practical responsibilities that involve discipline and sustained effort and which do not yield immediate pleasure and gratification. This attitude will work against success in business or marriage since true cooperation demands a shouldering of responsibility even when one is not so inclined. In any event, this transit will be characterized by a type of emotional impatience which makes it difficult to achieve a lasting success in relationships. For the person who is shy or overly conservative, this transit can be a good social catalyst for bringing new experiences into the life that give the person greater understanding and new values. At best, after this transit is over, one is awakened to a greater emotional expression and a heightened awareness of relationships.

Transit Uranus Opposition Mars

This transit brings about increased energy and ambition that is accompanied by a tendency to be overly aggressive and to disregard the rights of others. Impatience and an inclination to force one's will on others are apt to cause severe relationship problems that can lead to quarrels and, in extreme cases, to actual physical combat. The temper can be explosive, and the native's actions are apt to be impulsive and hasty. Even if the native does not personally express these tendencies, he or she will have to deal with those who have this kind of temperament. Extreme caution should be used in connection with electricity, machinery, firearms, explosives and motor vehicles, and situations of potential danger or violence should be avoided.

In some cases emotional tension is expressed through impulsive and reckless actions that can endanger the native's safety and the safety of others. Consequently, the native should exercise as much caution and self-restraint as possible. This is a time for cooperation with existing conditions and for not becoming entangled in pitched battles. This is not a favorable aspect for starting new ventures or for becoming involved in corporate or professional endeavors which involve other peoples' money. In general, the native should avoid initiating changes. This transit does, however, call for adjustment and cooperation in matters over which the native has no control. There could, for instance, be the sudden removal of close friends or associates under this transit, and the resulting situation could call for acceptance and adjustment on the part of the native.

Transit Uranus Opposition Jupiter

This transit brings about relationship difficulties that are caused by overconfidence and a know-it-all attitude. The native is apt to take too much for granted where family, marital, business, corporate and legal relationships are concerned. In general, there is a tendency to overreach oneself, thereby inviting social collapse and alienation of friends. In some cases, the native will espouse idealistic but impractical religious, social or educational views that annoy friends and make it difficult for the native to exist harmoniously in groups.

During this transit there can be an extreme restlessness and wanderlust. Faraway places and exotic experiences have a great attraction for the native. In pursuit of these, the native may neglect important responsibilities, and this can cause a breakdown in relationships. There can also be impatience and a desire to achieve large objectives without concerning oneself with the requisite work time, patience and perseverance. This can be a source of either annoyance or amusement to others. At this time, one should not overextend oneself financially or promise more than can be delivered, as the result of such extremes could be financial loss, business failure or lawsuits. Under this transit good judgment should be exercised in the choice of friends and group or business associates since one could be easily misled at this time. This is a time when it is wise to be more conservative than is normally the case. This is because one's expectations do not turn out as planned. There are always unforeseen difficulties which must be met.

Transit Uranus Opposition Saturn

This transit is apt to bring about sudden difficulties involving relationships connected with the profession. At this time any ulterior motives on the native's part or past misdeeds where one has taken advantage of others are likely to come out in the open and cause a loss of position and prestige. In some cases there can be removal or estrangements of friends and group associations, and open enemies or competitors are apt to cause conflicts at this time. The native should guard against high-handed and autocratic attitudes that will alienate friends and professional associates. Lawsuits and financial difficulties could possibly result under this transit. This is not a favorable time for dealing with joint finances, corporate money, insurance, taxes or goods of the dead. There can also be difficulties with employers, directors and people in positions of power or authority. Attempts to disrupt or overthrow the established order of things will result in frustration, disfavor and loss for the native.

During this transit there is a strong tendency to want to cut loose from all responsibilities and subordination to established authorities and systems. Such action is likely to leave the native without a means of support. This transit often brings about a crumbling of personal relationships and social, political and business connections which the native has depended upon for security. Such events are often unavoidable and beyond the native's control. In such cases the native should adjust to the change, release the past and take advantage of the new opportunities that present themselves. In many cases, economic forces beyond the native's personal control can cause loss of employment. In the long run, such events can make the native stronger, more independent and resourceful and can provide many valuable experiences. Much depends on the purity of one's motivations as to the effects this transit will have. An impartial, objective examination of the motives of others will help the native to use good judgment in the handling of important relationships.

Transit Uranus Opposition Uranus

This transit occurs once in the normal life span and at approximately age forty-two. It can be a time of uncertainty and difficulty where friendships and group associations are on an unstable footing. Because of the natural opposition of Leo to Aquarius, which is ruled by Uranus, this transit is known for the tendency of middle-aged men and women to suddenly become involved in extramarital affairs or other ill-advised pleasure-seeking adventures. This is also a time of financial insecurity which is often coupled with difficulties with one's children who are entering the difficult adolescent stage. It is not a favorable time for business enterprises or financial speculation unless other factors in the horoscope outweigh this influence. Major decisions made under this transit have far-reaching consequences that affect the native well into the future. There can be unanticipated frustrations and difficulties in attaining one's goals and objectives. Under this transit, one should be realistic and use moderation in the choice of action in any important matters. This transit can teach the native an invaluable lesson in spiritual detachment and universality. At this time especially, conduct should have its basis in universal principles.

Under this transit, friends could become hidden enemies or could either intentionally or unintentionally confuse or mislead the native. The person's unrealistic attitudes and poor judgment at this time can bring about self-undoing and a subtle chaos, which could in turn lead to neglect of home, family and domestic affairs. Even under the best conditions, this transit can bring about upsetting dreams and psychic experiences.

Transit Uranus Opposition Pluto

This transit is one of the most drastic and, in a sense, disruptive for the native. Established conditions will undergo sudden complete changes. As with Uranus opposition Neptune, large-scale forces affecting society at large can disrupt the life of the native. The double eighth house significance of this aspect indicates considerable danger to the native and his friends. The extent of such danger will depend upon other factors in the horoscope as well as prevailing conditions. During times of war or social or ecological upheaval, such dangers would be heightened.

In general, there is the possibility of estrangement from friends and group associations. This is not a favorable time for the realization of one's goals and objectives. Nor is this the appropriate time to initiate changes, for during this transit one should gracefully adjust to whatever changes occur beyond one's personal control. This transit brings a strong lesson in detachment. One learns that material things do not provide security and the only thing that is certain is change itself. On the positive side, this transit can bring about startling and enlightening experiences with relationships that can permanently alter the native's values. Spurious and dangerous occult practices are especially ill advised during this period.

IX

Transits of Neptune

Neptune transits are apt to bring about subtle changes in a person's life which are not obvious at first. Their effect is like the slow rise of the tide. This does not mean that they are not powerful in the end result. Like the tide, the Neptune transit can inundate a whole area of a person's life. The reason for this is that the effects of Neptune transits are worked through the unconscious mind and stimulate the inner psychic sensitivity of the native. A Neptune transit brings about a subtle change in attitude which in the end becomes strong enough to completely alter the direction of a person's life.

This explains why Neptune is said to be insidious, especially if it affects the native in an adverse way. If the effect is a constructive one, it eventually raises the native's consciousness to a point where he or she becomes directly and personally aware of the existence of spiritual realms. This brings about an understanding of the greater evolutionary purpose of life and of the native's place in it. This, in time, will change the native's goals, actions and purposes in life for the better.

It should be remembered that when dealing with Uranus, Neptune and Pluto events are often brought into the native's life by forces beyond personal control which are related to mass, national, racial or worldwide karma. These events may take the form of wars or major economic, political and social changes.

The manner in which these events relate to the native's individual life is shown by the transits of the three outermost planets. The person's attitudes toward, and ability to deal with, such events are shown by the aspects of these outer planets in the natal horoscope.

Transit Neptune Through the Houses

The transit of Neptune through the houses indicates in what department of life the native experiences peculiar, mysterious, secretive, and, in some cases, psychic occurrences. These events are often linked to conditions related to the native's past in some manner. The native will become very sensitive with regard to the affairs ruled by the house which Neptune is transiting. These affairs will be linked with the affairs ruled by the houses where Cancer, Pisces and Sagittarius are found in the horoscope. When Neptune makes favorable contacts, the native can be intuitively inspired and guided in his choices, leading to great gain and beauty. If Neptune makes adverse contacts, there is apt to be confusion or even chaos, deception, treachery, laziness and muddle, which often leaves the affairs of the house which Neptune is transiting in shambles. In any event, there will be subtle but powerful changes of affairs in respect to the house in which Neptune is transiting.

Transit Neptune Through the First House

When Neptune transits the Ascendant or first house there will be a subtle but marked change in the native's self-awareness and perception of reality. He or she will become more sensitive to and aware of intuitive, clairvoyant perceptions, and unconscious impulses arising from the past tend to influence the native's present goals and behavior. Much depends upon how Neptune is aspected in the natal horoscope and what contacts Neptune is making by transit.

If these conditions are unfavorable, there is danger of self-deception, confusion and daydreaming. There will be a lack of purpose and direction. The native may be driven by some unrealistic goal or delusion of grandeur. In any event, Neptune's transit of this house will make the native more susceptible to influences coming from superphysical realms of existence. How these influences affect one depends upon a careful analysis of Neptune, Pisces and the twelfth house in the natal horoscope. Mercury, the planet of the logical mind, and Saturn, the planet of discipline and practicality, should also be considered in order to determine how well-grounded the native may be. The native may develop an air of mystery and secrecy concerning activities during this transit.

On the positive side, the native can gain deep insights of wisdom through increased clairvoyant, intuitive awareness, and often is more humane and sympathetic, with greater understanding of the needs of others. The increased interest of the native takes the form of an inner spiritual search, which often leads to meditation and an unfolding of the faculties of the imagination. In some cases the native may receive inspiration that leads to creativity in music or the arts. The imagination and ability to visualize are intensified.

If Neptune makes adverse contacts while transiting this house, the native may experience peculiar psychosomatic illnesses and neurotic conditions. In some cases, diseases that are difficult to diagnose and cure will plague the health of the native. If Neptune makes favorable contacts, there is the possibility of a spiritual healing. In any event, the native's psychological condition will have a more than usual effect on the health.

Transit Neptune Through the Second House

This transit brings about unusual conditions with respect to the native's finances. If Neptune makes adverse contacts, the native is apt to be confused, lazy and impractical concerning financial affairs. He or she will also be an easy mark for con artists, get-rich-quick schemes and so-called charitable causes that prove to be otherwise. The native's money will tend to evaporate in many mysterious ways, possibly resulting in a state of financial depletion. He or she may pursue unrealistic or impractical plans for making money which will often cost more than can be realized at the time. In other cases, the native may idly dream about grandiose moneymaking plans while doing nothing to actually put them into effect.

Much attention must be paid to the native's level of practicality as revealed in the natal horoscope and, in particular, by Neptune and the second house of the horoscope. If these conditions are favorable, and if Neptune makes favorable contacts while in the second house, the native may strike it rich through creative imagination applied to moneymaking, and may experience seemingly fortuitous circumstances or good luck which brings considerable financial security in unusual ways. The native's business may also relate to the financial affairs of hospitals or religious and educational institutions. In any event, the native's values regarding money and property will undergo a subtle change during the course of this transit. Often the native's financial dealings are clothed in secrecy.

Transit Neptune Through the Third House

This transit indicates subtle changes in the native's thinking concepts and manner of communication. The native will become more interested in studying and investigating mystical and occult subjects. Things which are mysterious and out of the ordinary will have a mental fascination.

If Neptune is natally afflicted and makes adverse contacts while in the third house, there is danger of mental confusion, impractical thinking, deception and daydreaming. In any event, the native is apt to be nebulous in formulating and expressing ideas, and consequently his or her judgment will probably be questioned. The native may fail to communicate with those around him or her, or communication may be garbled and unclear, thereby causing much confusion. There can also be deception involving brothers, sisters or neighbors. Extreme caution should be used in the signing of any contract or written agreement if Neptune is afflicted when in the third house. This is a time when the fine print must be carefully scrutinized with the help of a trustworthy and levelheaded authority. The native's thinking is apt to be colored by unconscious attitudes based on past experiences that are no longer applicable in the present context. Any tendency towards evasiveness and dishonesty should be avoided.

If Neptune makes favorable aspects, the native can be inspired by intuitive ideas gained through higher states of consciousness. There can be real vision and insight into the past and future that makes possible creative solutions to existing problems. The native may have inspirational ideas relating to institutions, higher education, writing and communication. Much wisdom can be gained through the study of occult subjects. Increased imagination can lead to creative writing on religious, philosophic or educational subjects.

Transit Neptune Through the Fourth House

This transit through the fourth house is of great importance because here Neptune is accidentally exalted. Strong psychic manifestations come into play that bring into sharp focus the native's basic roots and consciousness. These relate to family background, heredity and past experiences. The home becomes the scene of unusual and mysterious occurrences. In some cases the native can become a recluse at home in order to search his or her inner consciousness. Often this is accompanied by the development of intuitive psychic manifestations. The home is artistically decorated as a place of beauty and refinement that serves to uplift all who enter into it, and often serves as a place for helping those in need.

If Neptune is adversely aspected during this transit, the native may be institutionalized for some reason. In some cases the native may be absent a great deal from the home. The home could be used in an unusual way, or unusual conditions could exist in the home. This is not the most favorable time to buy a home. There is apt to be some hidden condition that makes it less desirable than it appears, such as water seepage or another condition that would not be immediately apparent. At times the native is apt to be moody and emotional, as many past memories in the unconscious mind are stirred up by this transit. The parents or some other important family member may become a burden on the native or manifest peculiar psychological tendencies. In some cases, there can develop interest in contacting deceased relatives. If Neptune makes good contacts while transiting the fourth house the native can experience deep spiritual realizations and interests. In any event, psychic ties with the family will be intensified.

Transit Neptune Through the Fifth House

This transit through the fifth house indicates a time of peculiar conditions with respect to the native's creative endeavors, romantic life and children and their education. In areas of romance in particular, things will not be as they seem because there is a danger of much confusion and deception. This tends to be a chronic problem if Neptune makes adverse contacts during this transit. Continual deceptions, illusionary hopes and disappointments can often lead to a bitter outlook on life, especially where affairs of the heart are concerned. Often, conditions from the past affect romance favorably or unfavorably, as the case may be. The romantic partner may be in some way mystically inclined. Conditions surrounding the romantic relationship are often mysterious, dramatic or unusual. If Neptune is afflicted, there can be deception and disappointment in love. This is also a very dangerous position for any form of gambling or financial speculation. An afflicted Neptune here can lead to great financial loss.

This transit is more favorable for artistic creativity because the creative imagination is intensified. This leads to productive work in the arts, provided the rest of the horoscope indicates a capacity for putting ideas into practical application. Even at best, the native will have a difficult time gaining recognition for his or her talents. If Neptune makes favorable aspects there can be ideal love, fortunate romance and an easier time gaining acceptance for one's creative endeavors. This aspect is especially favorable for those in the performing arts and film industries. Musicians are apt to experience much creative inspiration during this transit.

There may be peculiar conditions relating to one's children or their education. If Neptune is afflicted, children are apt to experience psychological maladjustments and difficulties in school. If Neptune is well-aspected, children will show creative imagination and talent.

Transit Neptune Through the Sixth House

This transit indicates a time during which peculiar conditions arise pertaining to the native's work and health. This is not generally a favorable influence where work is concerned. This is indicated by the fact that here Neptune is accidentally in its detriment. If Neptune makes adverse aspects while in this house, the native will be unrealistic and inefficient. In the case of an individual who is normally an efficient worker, upsetting psychological conditions are apt to distract him or her from the job at hand. The native is apt to be confused as to procedures and objectives. Often the intentions are good, but discipline and organization may be lacking. In some cases there is an unconscious dislike of the work, ill health, a sense of boredom, alcoholism or drug abuse, any of which tends to undermine the native's job efficiency. Often the native experiences difficulty in obtaining employment, especially suitable employment. In some cases secret enemies among employers, coworkers or employees stand in the way of job success, employment or security. When this transit is in effect, work is often associated with hospitals and institutions. there can be interest in natural diets, homeopathy, acupuncture and other forms of healing. There is special emphasis on psychological factors related to healing or mental health.

In general, the body is highly sensitive to any form of drug. Natural forms of healing should be used whenever Neptune is in this house. Extreme care should be exercised in the use of anesthetics, as these are apt to have a greater than normal effect while Neptune is transiting this house. The native can be prone to psychosomatic illnesses, conditions difficult to diagnose and development of chronic ailments. Often this can affect the nervous or glandular systems. During this transit, excesses with alcohol, drug abuse and improper diet have a debilitating effect on the health. This in turn interferes with the native's ability to work.

If Neptune is natally well-aspected and makes favorable contacts while transiting this house, the native may use imagination and intuitive abilities to solve problems related to work. In so doing the native could receive success and promotion. When intuitive abilities are used, work is often related to artists, psychologists or humanitarians. It is often linked with hospitals, institutions, churches or schools of higher education. In rare cases the work may relate to the use of psychic abilities. While Neptune is in this house, the native may manifest unusual habits with respect to clothing and personal hygiene. If Neptune is afflicted, the native may become slovenly and unkempt in appearance.

Transit Neptune Through the Seventh House

This transit indicates unusual conditions in marriage, partnerships, close personal friendships and alliances. The native's attitude toward people in general will undergo subtle changes. Many factors that are not readily apparent are apt to affect these relationships. Often the native will develop a strong interest in psychology as a means of understanding and helping others.

The native's important personal relationships are apt to have a basis in past relationships that can go beyond the present incarnation. In any event, the native's choice of close associates and attitudes toward those he or she contacts is strongly influenced by the intuitive or unconscious levels of the mind. If Neptune makes adverse contacts while transiting this house, there is danger that the native will deceive partners or be deceived by them. There can also be paranoid attitudes, distorted ideas and weird imaginings with respect to the spouse or other close associates. These can color the native's attitudes and responses in a harmful way. Often, the native hypersensitive, fearful or excessively shy. In other cases the native may be gullible or easily influenced by others. Unconscious attitudes based on past experiences can distort the native's judgment regarding prevailing relationships. In some cases, a business partner can be deceptive and dishonest, absconding with valuable assets or failing to uphold his or her half of an agreement, or the native himself may be guilty of such actions. In the case of marriage the native or his spouse may be unfaithful, engaging in secret romances. In any event, this type of behavior is apt to bring lawsuits and estrangements. In some cases, the partner or the native may live in his or her private dream world, thereby making communication difficult or almost impossible. If Neptune is well-aspected in the natal horoscope and makes favorable contacts while transiting this house, there can be an intuitive understanding of other persons and close rapport with the spouse and partners. Aesthetic and spiritual values will be important under this transit. These values will elevate the native's relationships to a higher level of understanding and enjoyment.

Transit Neptune Through the Eighth House

This transit indicates a period when strange and peculiar conditions arise regarding the affairs of the dead, inheritance, insurance, taxes, finances, corporate money and psychic phenomena. The native is apt to become interested in mysterious occult phenomena, spiritualism, life after death and reincarnation. If Neptune is afflicted, there can be fraud, confusion and deception regarding taxes, insurance, inheritance, corporate money and goods of the deceased. In extreme cases, bizarre and macabre circumstances can arise that have a sinister connotation or these can be imagined and feared by the native.

If Neptune is favorably aspected in the horoscope, clairvoyant abilities can be developed and used in a constructive way during this transit. The native is able to gain insights into life's deeper mysteries and become aware on higher planes of consciousness. The native can gain through inheritance and corporate business.

Transit Neptune Through the Ninth House

This transit indicates a period during which the native becomes interested in a search for higher spiritual values. In pursuit of this goal the native may become involved with religious or mystical cults, foreign travel, systems of meditation or esoteric studies. There will also be pursuit of higher education along philosophic lines.

If Neptune is afflicted here, the native is prone to religious fanaticism, delusions of grandeur, bizarre cults and guru worship. This transit can make one feel that he or she is the chosen emissary of masters or higher spiritual beings. The native's vision of the future can be distorted by the unconscious mind, which introduces irrational fears and unrealistic hopes and expectations. The native may find ways to avoid responsibility for making one's own decisions in life.

If the natal horoscope shows good judgment and Neptune makes favorable contacts while transiting the ninth house, the native can have real spiritual inspiration and prophetic insights.

He or she is apt to study under worthwhile spiritual or religious teachers whose precepts will be based on impersonal universal principles that uplift people to their true state as immortal spiritual beings.

Transit Neptune Through the Tenth House

This transit over the Midheaven and through the tenth house will bring about important changes in the native's reputation and professional life. If Neptune is natally afflicted and makes adverse contacts while transiting this house, the native's past misdeeds are likely to be brought out into the open in subtle, unexpected ways that will undermine the career and professional reputation. This is often brought about by hidden enemies of the past. The native's career and public standing will in any event be eroded by subtle and demoralizing influences. In some cases, this can bring about the native's disgrace and ruination. Any shady or dishonest professional dealings will backfire under this transit.

On the positive side, this transit is favorable for those in an artistic profession or those who are involved in movie making, the performing arts and, in some cases, politics. This transit will confer a kind of charisma or dramatic image that appeals to the public. It can also give intuitive insights into public trends, political situations, changes in style and other developments that relate to the native's profession. Such insights may seem uncanny at times. In unusual cases the profession may become involved with astrology or the occult. There is also possible involvement with hospitals, institutions or work in psychology. If Neptune makes good aspects while transiting the tenth house, there can be professional advances and public recognition brought about by unusual events and people. The native's life will become glorious and exciting.

Transit Neptune Through the Eleventh House

This transit brings about unusual and peculiar friendships and group associations. If Neptune is well-aspected in the natal horoscope and makes favorable contacts while transiting this house, the friends and group associations will have a constructive influence on the native's life, raising him or her to a higher level of consciousness and often inspiring creative work and humanitarian endeavors. The native may become a member of a secret mystical organization, fraternity or occult society, and new friends are likely to be highly creative, artistic and intuitively aware.

If Neptune makes adverse aspects while in this house, the native's friends and group associations can have an undermining influence on his or her life. Young people and their parents who have not found direction in life should be particularly cautious of such influences. This is the kind of influence under which a person could be introduced to drugs, alcohol or other types of questionable stimulants and related activities. The influence is apt to work in a subtle manner and would not be readily apparent. In other cases the person could be deceived or deluded by friends, or the friends could become overly burdensome on the native because of their own lack of direction and discipline. Such disorienting influences that prey on the native can take the form of a false sense of loyalty or sympathy.

On the positive side, Neptune in this house can bring about the realization of the native's hopes and wishes and can increase interest in the spiritual side of life.

Transit Neptune Through the Twelfth House

This transit indicates a period during which the native is apt to seek seclusion and privacy for purposes of introspection and inner search. There will be more than ordinary concern with the affairs of the past and the unconscious mind. On the positive side, this transit can lead to constructive meditation and inner spiritual realization. There can also be the recovery of much wisdom from the past and even memories of previous incarnations. These inner realizations can provide inspiration for worthwhile artistic accomplishments.

If Neptune is afflicted in the natal horoscope and makes adverse aspects while transiting this house, there is apt to be a sense of depression, loneliness or neurotic conditions stemming from the unconscious mind. The native is apt to have difficulties in relating to practical reality. If these tendencies get out of hand, the native may become psychotic and be institutionalized. In other cases this transit may manifest as a bizarre or out of control imagination, which makes the native seem preoccupied and out of the stream of normal living.

In its best manifestation, this transit gives the rewards of true spiritual living, manifesting as an inner strength and creativity that is the native's hidden support. Under this transit, many persons seek out spiritual retreats and places of meditation. The native may also become involved with work relating to hospitals, sanatoriums, religious institutions or places of higher learning.

Transit Neptune Conjunctions

Transit Neptune Conjunction Sun

This transit brings about an increased self-awareness as a spiritual being to the native. The internal effects of this transit will bring about mystical states of consciousness, increased awareness of beauty, an intensified imagination, vivid dreams and, in some cases, clairvoyant and telepathic experiences. There can also be an intensified memory of the distant past, even going back to previous embodiments. These changed states of awareness will affect the native's attitudes regarding the affairs where Neptune is transiting and where Pisces, Cancer and Leo are found in the natal horoscope. In some cases the native will tend to become preoccupied with the mystical side of life during this transit. The native may become interested in meditation, yoga, eastern philosophy or some other form of religious practice that has an occult or mystical coloring.

The outer effects of this transit are apt to make the native more artistic or creative in music and visual or performing arts. Neptune intensifies the imagination, while the Sun, the natural ruler of the fifth house, relates to the arts. The conjunction, by its nature, is a dynamic expression of one's potential. In some cases this transit can bring romance into the person's life, especially if the fifth house or its ruler is involved. There could also be an interest in children and working with their education. The native may have a desire to speculate, but this can be highly dangerous if the Sun or Neptune is afflicted in the natal horoscope. There can be increased interest in psychology and working with hospitals, schools, institutions, churches and retreats.

If Neptune and the Sun are afflicted by other transiting planets or in the natal horoscope, there can be loss resulting from unrealistic and impractical attitudes. This is not a favorable transit for those prone to allowing their unconscious fears and past memories to dominate them. This is a time that calls for the practical application of the imagination and a time for realism. The native should concentrate on using the imagination to accommodate what can be done in a realistic way, using the resources at hand. There is the danger of being impractical about the time, work and money required to actually accomplish what the imagination can envision. A good Saturn and Mercury are strong assets during this transit.

The native should avoid any tendency toward daydreaming or evasion of practical responsibilities. This is not to say that a reasonable amount of time should not be devoted to meditation and other forms of self-improvement, for this is an excellent time to make progress in one's inner development. During this transit the inner realization should be applied to daily living for best results. During this transit the unconscious mind is strongly influenced, thereby affecting for a long time to come the attitudes that will influence the native's way of living. Consequently, it is of utmost importance to program the unconscious mind in a constructive way and to refrain from negative or unrealistic thinking that will undermine the native in some manner in the years to come.

Transit Neptune Conjunction Moon

This transit is a strong influence on the unconscious mind, as Neptune and the Moon are concerned with the conditioning of the past. If the Moon and Neptune are afflicted in the natal horoscope, the native is apt to be moody and preoccupied with conditioning stemming from childhood upbringing, family and parental influences. In some cases, influences from past embodiments will subtly affect the native's moods and attitudes. The imagination will be highly stimulated and, therefore, care should be taken to remain focused on practical realities and responsibilities. Otherwise, the unconscious mind and the imagination may cause the native to be wrapped up in a private dream world to such an extent that he or she will be unable to cope with the realities of the present context. The seriousness of this psychological danger is dependent upon the overall tenor of the horoscope and the tendency toward introversion versus objective and practical living.

Family affairs and domestic matters may preoccupy the native's imagination. This preoccupation can be used in a constructive way by increasing the sensitivity to family and domestic interactions. The home can be used as a place of meditation and spiritual unfolding. This transit often brings one an increased emotional sensibility toward women and an understanding of their minds. The moods of women will especially be better understood. Under this transit the imagination can be constructively employed in business, especially if the business relates to artistic, dietary or domestic products. In general, this transit brings increased psychic sensitivity and an awareness of the spiritual realm of existence.

If the Moon or Neptune is afflicted in the natal horoscope, or if other planets make adverse aspects to them during this transit, there is danger of psychological imbalance, emotional hypersensitivity, a runaway imagination and, in some cases, a persecution complex. If carried to extremes, there is danger of these tendencies bringing about the institutionalizing of the native. In some cases this transit will cause the native to seek out a retreat, monastery or place of seclusion where he or she can conduct meditative spiritual pursuits. Because the Moon and Neptune rule water signs, this transit is a highly emotional influence that needs to be balanced with a rational mental outlook.

Transit Neptune Conjunction Mercury

This transit brings about subtle changes in the native's mental outlook. Whether these are constructive or not depends on the natal horoscope and transits made by other planets to Mercury.

On the positive side, this conjunction can bring important intuitive insights, interests in pursuit of mystical knowledge, telepathic manifestations and, in some cases, prophetic insight. An intensification of the senses takes place that extends their capabilities into the realm of extrasensory perception. The imagination is intensified in such a way that the native can internally, visually, auditorily or tactually experience sensations as vividly as if these happenings were actually taking place in the external environment. This increased sensory faculty often provides inspiration for poetry, creative writing, musical composition and many other artistic expressions or for problem solving in the native's work or health concerns. At this time the native becomes more sensitive to the more subtle forces that influence people's attitudes and communication. This awareness gives insights into important subliminal influences and unconscious telepathic interchanges that affect human relationships and a person's ability to cooperate effectively in work and to maintain good health.

On the negative side this transit can cause the native to retreat into a private illusionary dream world, thereby losing contact with everyday communication and attention to detail, which in turn affects work and health. The imagination can exaggerate mental impressions out of proportion to their actual importance, which can lead to petty criticisms and misunderstandings in communication. Any personal remark can be magnified to a point where it can interfere with personal relationships, friendships and one's ability to get along with groups. In some cases the native envisions grandiose plans and schemes, ignoring the practical realities necessary to achieve them. As a result, the native is apt to take on more responsibility than can be handled and thereby acquire the reputation of being an impractical dreamer. In extreme cases, the clear thinking of the rational mind may become so submerged by the influence of the subconscious mind that the native could be institutionalized.

Transit Neptune Conjunction Venus

This transit is a highly aesthetic and sensitive influence. It requires a refined person to make full use of its potential, and is highly favorable for all musicians and artists because it intensifies their sensitivities to beauty and expands the creative imagination, thereby giving ample inspiration for new creativity. Works of art produced under the influence of this transit are apt to have a subtle, refined and mystical flavor. This transit is apt to bring romance that is very idealistic and highly romantic. The individuals will feel as though they were meant for each other. The lovers often fancy that they have known each other before or that the relationship was ordained from the beginning of time. Love relationships under this transit are often associated with situations of beauty and luxury, giving a feeling of drama and mystical glamour. Whether this relationship is a lasting one or a moonlit fantasy which disappears in the light of the Sun will depend upon other factors in the horoscope, which may or may not give it stability. If the native is going through a period of hardships, this transit can give to an otherwise drab existence a sense of transcendent beauty that is spiritually uplifting and makes hardships easier to bear. In general the native will manifest increased interest in art, entertainment and especially music. One experiences the cultural side of life under this transit.

If natal Venus is afflicted and the native is accustomed to a life of luxury and ease, this transit may serve to increase self-indulgence and lack of responsibility toward dealing with practical reality, thereby contributing to a life of idleness and non-productivity. If Neptune and Venus are afflicted in the natal horoscope, the native is in danger of drifting off into a fantasy world, thus depriving himself or herself of the real joy that comes through practical accomplishments. Often, alliances and partnerships may be formed that are based on illusionary assessments of the other person's integrity, or the native may be deceitful or unreliable. In such cases the native can suffer considerable financial loss as a result of unwise speculation and careless business dealings. There are often hidden factors that are not revealed until later. This is especially true if Venus is afflicted in the horoscope and the second, seventh and eighth houses are involved.

Transit Neptune Conjunction Mars

This transit will bring about subtle changes in the native's self-expression, profession and financial dealings with others. There is more going on in the native's life than is obvious on the surface. The desires are apt to be influenced by factors arising from the subconscious mind. Actions are often carried on in secret or behind the scenes. Such activity may relate to business dealings, corporate enterprises and matters relating to the profession. If the natal horoscope indicates dishonest tendencies, this can be a highly dangerous and subversive transit because there is a temptation to do things in secret. In such cases there can be treachery, deceit and dishonesty with respect to personal sexual matters or professional dealings. The imagination can inflame the desires out of rational control, leading to dangerous and perverted acts. The native may also be the victim of such acts even if he or she does not commit them. However, this does not usually happen to the native without some valid reason. The native usually invites such treatment through unconscious desires. This transit can also indicate altruistic and spiritually oriented action carried out silently and effectively to achieve worthwhile goals. Much depends on the promise of the natal chart and other transits taking place concurrently with this conjunction. This transit can bring about the death of some close family member.

Transit Neptune Conjunction Jupiter

This transit is of a highly expansive, idealistic nature and is apt to increase the native's interest in religion, mysticism and education. The native can become imbued with an idealistic zeal that manifests as a desire to save the world. However, the ideals and ideas espoused are often tinged with sectarian fanaticism and impracticality. This transit has a highly emotional influence that lacks practical application unless other factors in the horoscope supply organizational inclinations and ability. Often, there is a strong urge to become involved with a guru or teacher who promises enlightenment and spiritual self-realization through his or her teachings. This transit is often associated with taking trips or pilgrimages to India or other distant places in search of truth. But this is often merely an escape from the seemingly hum-drum routine of everyday living. On the positive side, this transit does give a sense of awe at the immensity of God's power and creation. It can inspire one with reverence and respect for the universal laws that govern the universe and the native's part in it. This transit can have a constructive effect on the native's domestic life, bringing to it more harmony, love and beauty. Accompanying this transit is a sense of overwhelming spiritual destiny, and the native can receive the rewards of past good works, making it a time of great expansion and increase in the life.

Transit Neptune Conjunction Saturn

This transit brings about difficult and peculiar circumstances that affect the native's profession and reputation. Situations will arise that will be difficult to fathom. These conditions can cause the native considerable worry and anxiety. This is because the origin of the trouble is hard to locate and deal with in a direct manner. On a general psychological level, this can be one of the most difficult transits. The negative Saturn principle of fear often combines with Neptune, the principle of imagination, to create all manner of imaginary fears and anxieties. There is a sense of foreboding which is often based on subconscious memories of past experiences. At such a time the native should realize that we create our circumstances by our thinking. This is a good time to remember, "That which I have feared has come upon me." Positive thinking should be made the order of the day while under this transit. If the native has any skeletons in the closet that could affect the professional standing and reputation, this is the time when they are apt to be exposed. This often comes about as the result of hidden enemies who take advantage of any opportunity to undermine the native. Uncertainties are apt to affect the native's close personal relationships, partnerships, domestic relationships and professional dealings. This makes the native feel that he or she stands alone in the world with no one around on whom to rely for support. At this time the native should be scrupulously honest, as any deception will backfire disastrously.

On the positive side, this transit can bring about profound mystical experiences. This period can help one gain steadiness in concentration and meditation, with consequent gains in wisdom and understanding. This transit gives the native the power to stand alone when necessary. The native can become interested in cultural influences from the past. These interests could take the form of involvement in archaeology, ancient history or classical music.

Transit Neptune Conjunction Uranus

This transit brings about unusual and often unexpected occurrences in the native's life which affect goals and objectives, friendships, joint finances, group associations, corporate endeavors, home conditions and private affairs. It requires an unusually aware person to realize the full possibilities of this transit, since its effects relate primarily to the inner, occult side of life. For those who are sufficiently open to such influences, it will bing about increased clairvoyance and intensified activity in respect to esoteric work. This is often involved with some occult or mystical group or organization. In any event it holds the possibility of furthering the native's spiritual awakening. There is often increased awareness of the past, which can include memories of previous embodiments. Old friends can appear on the scene unexpectedly and bring changes into the native's life. This can be a time of remarkable new insights into how to achieve one's goals and objectives, which can bring about the realization of long-cherished dreams. It is as though a magical force is operating in the native's life. The native may have a breakthrough with respect to corporate financing or may unexpectedly inherit money or property. If Neptune and Uranus are afflicted in the natal horoscope, or if other transiting aspects are unfavorable with respect to this conjunction, there can be unexpected losses and difficulties. Much depends upon the purity of the native's motives. In some cases, the pattern of the native's life is drastically altered by large-scale social, economic or political forces. Here, the national or racial karma overtakes the native's relatively insignificant personal affairs. Such a transit can reveal how the native's personal karma is related to mass karma.

Transit Neptune Conjunction Neptune and Pluto

It is unlikely that anyone now alive will live long enough to experience this particular transit. If such a transit were to occur, it would have a highly occult and subtle effect on the native's life and would affect the individual through the general circumstances of the culture.

Transit Neptune Sextiles

Transit Neptune Sextile Sun

This transit brings the opportunity for the use of intuitive, creative inspiration. It favors all creative, artistic endeavors, especially those relating to the performing arts, photography and video. The imagination is so intensified that intuitive or clairvoyant faculties play a strong role in the thought process. Extrasensory phenomena can be experienced as vividly and graphically as external sensory input. The composer who actually hears a piece of music in his or her head as though actually listening to music being played is an example of one who undergoes this kind of experience. This increased awareness and sensitivity increases one's appreciation of beauty and one's capacity for enjoyment of life. There is a sense of drama and romance with this transit which often brings about the opportunity for new love relationships. The native's increased ability to envision new possibilities can inspire greater personal action and creativity in a number of ways. These will be beneficially influential through friends, group associations, goals and objectives, the native's domestic life and communication. Often there is increased memory of past experiences that can give insight into how to improve present conditions. There can be opportunities for creative achievements in education and for working with people in power and authority.

Interest in children and in their education will also increase. There is greater understanding of the young and empathy for them. This transit gives one the ability to understand a child's aspirations and dreams, thereby enabling the person to inspire the child to realize his or her potential. During this transit the native will have more opportunities for involvement in a social life that brings more opulent surroundings and an opportunity to meet those more established people who can help the native attain particular goals.

Transit Neptune Sextile Moon

This transit stimulates the imagination and gives one the ability to recall in a vivid manner useful information from the past that increases the native's ability to deal with present situations. This is especially true with regard to those situations that deal with domestic and financial affairs. During this period there is increased insight into the native's own psychological makeup. This extends to friends, business associates and family members. These insights can be used to improve important personal relationships and increase business opportunities. If the natal horoscope indicates a potential for psychic ability, this transit often brings it out, giving prophetic insight and knowledge of events with which the native has no direct physical or personal con tact. Increased understanding of the subconscious mind and its workings can bring subtle changes in the native's basic outlook on life, making him or her less vulnerable to automatic psychological responses that are evoked by memories of past experiences. This transit often increases the native's general interest in the study of psychology and psychic phenomena.

Transit Neptune Sextile Mercury

This transit increases the native's imagination and opens up new mental concepts that result in subtle improvements of the native's communication ability, work and health. The native who has a natural capacity for psychic awareness as revealed in the natal horoscope is apt to experience mental telepathy and clairvoyant knowledge of events which cannot be known by any other means. There can be memory of the distant past, which can include past embodiments. All of this will help the native to be less automatically influenced by the subconscious mind and the memories it contains. There can be an intellectual interest in studying subjects such as psychology, mental telepathy, psychic phenomena, astrology and reincarnation. This is a favorable aspect for creative writing where the imagination necessarily plays an important role, and the native can gain intuitive insight into ways of improving work efficiency. This transit can also bring an interest in spiritual ways of healing through such methods as homeopathy, color, sound or positive thinking. It can also give the native an increased insight into ways of healing chronic ailments. Often, the new intellectual interest and awareness which this transit brings results in new friendships and group associations which expand the native's outlook and increase his awareness. There are apt to be opportunities for work behind the scenes such as research or work in hospitals, institutions or churches.

Transit Neptune Sextile Venus

This transit is highly favorable for all types of artistic and creative endeavors, especially those relating to art and music. This transit is of a highly subtle and aesthetic nature, but it does not necessarily provide the discipline and work required for significant artistic creativity. However, if other influences in the horoscope, such as favorable aspects of Mars, Saturn or Mercury, supply the ability to work hard, then works of superior quality and refinement can be produced. This transit can bring opportunities for partnerships in marriage or business. There can be romantic opportunities which have a special ethereal beauty connected with them. Often these relationships increase the native's financial status, either through marriage or new social contacts. The native may attract circumstances of greater opulence and security that make possible the leisure necessary for the enjoyment of the arts or creative work. This good fortune is often the result of something the native has earned through correct action in this or a previous existence.

Transit Neptune Sextile Mars

This transit brings about increased psychic awareness that can provide valuable insights into more effective ways of carrying out personal, professional, domestic and corporate activities. Opportunities arise for subtle and secretive activities which further the goals and purposes of the native. These often give the native a competitive advantage or superior insight. Intuitive realizations can give an awareness of karmic law, which may improve the native's desires. This improvement in the quality of the desire nature will bring about wholesome and meaningful friendships and group associations. These associations will bring about new avenues of expression for the native that will affect the professional, domestic, corporate and psychological affairs of the native's life. The native will be more aware and capable of communication pertaining to desires and psychological drives within self and others, thus enabling him or her to constructively direct these desires to bring about improved conditions. An abundance of psychic energy can be directed for purposes of healing or inspiring others with greater optimism. This transit is somewhat similar to favorable transits of Jupiter to Mars in that it improves the emotional outlook and brings about greater motivation toward constructive action.

Transit Neptune Sextile Jupiter

This transit is favorable for increasing the native's spiritual awareness and capacity for a positive emotional outlook. Generally, this transit brings an increased interest in and awareness of the spiritual and religious side of life. The native expresses increased optimism, good will and generosity toward family and friends, which in turn expands social horizons. There is often an opportunity for travel or some form of higher education or religious study. There are opportunities under this transit for interesting associations with foreigners or hitherto unknown cultural influences that increase the native's understanding and enjoyment of life. This transit can also bring about the karmic rewards of past good action by expanding the native's social, educational and religious prospects. Opportunities for association with religious institutions, hospitals and universities arise that can benefit the native through increased understanding and wider social contacts. There are also opportunities for improving domestic family relationships that expand the home and activities in the home.

Transit Neptune Sextile Saturn

This transit brings a period of deep introspection within the native. Neptune and Saturn are of extremely different natures in that Saturn deals with material practicality and Neptune with visionary inspiration. Therefore, this transit is difficult to understand. It can help the native use intuition to find solutions to practical problems. This sextile gives the native a calmness and capacity for concentration that is highly beneficial for meditation and using the creative imagination in a practical manner. This transit often brings opportunities to work in secret or behind the scenes that could be connected with hospitals, institutions or unpublicized governmental work. It is also helpful for those involved with psychology because it gives insights into the subconscious motivations of those who are being helped or those with whom the native must deal. This transit is also conducive to gaining insight into effective strategies whereby the native can further professional ambitions. Often, opportunities will arise through peculiar circumstances based on experiences, conditions and acquaintances of the past.

Transit Neptune Sextile Uranus

This transit brings about opportunities for inner spiritual growth and development. Friendships and acquaintances may enter the life that stimulate the imagination and increase interest in understanding such subjects as astrology, extrasensory perception, meditation, occult phenomena and other related fields. There will be opportunities for involvement in new forms of technology, scientific research or scientific study. Those interested in psychology will gain valuable insights. This transit often brings friends and associates to the native who are helpful with regard to his endeavors. Under this influence the native can become interested in life after death and reincarnation. Opportunities arise in matters connected to the use of joint resources, corporate financing and insurance. New and novel methods can be introduced into these affairs.

Transit Neptune Sextile Neptune

This transit occurs in the life of every individual at approximately age thirty, depending upon how fast Neptune is traveling in its orbit. It represents a time of coming into spiritual maturity when the native begins to awaken to the full potential of his or her inner creative imaginative faculties. Much will depend upon the content of the native's subconscious mind as to what opportunities arise and what resources of hidden consciousness can be brought to the surface. It does represent a time when the native can make use of memories. This transit is favorable for those whose work involves music, art or writing where the creative imagination must be used. The native becomes more aware of how to use his spiritual heritage and family background to give direction to life. This can in some cases facilitate the awakening of intuitive clairvoyant faculties.

Transit Neptune Sextile Pluto

This transit produces a subtle influence that can engender intuitive awareness in those who are sufficiently awake to take advantage of it. For the average individual it may indicate benefits derived from general cultural advances. This transit can also give the native insight into how to make constructive use of seemingly dead and useless resources, conditions and circumstances, thus building a new start from the ruins of old conditions. Old friendships, resources and information may come to light that can be meaningful in new ways for progress and for the realization of the native's goals and objectives.

Transit Neptune Squares

Transit Neptune Square Sun

This transit brings a period during which the native is in danger of losing his or her grip on reality. Self-deception is the pitfall of this transit. There is danger of refusing to face practical responsibilities. In some cases this transit is accompanied by delusions of grandeur, and things essential to the well-being of the native are neglected. Egotism based on forces arising from the subconscious mind are often responsible for such neglectful behavior. The native can stray by seeking pleasure and romance that get in the way of realistic approaches to life. Alcoholism, drug abuse, gambling and sexual promiscuity are among the dangers of this transit. The native should avoid the company of irresponsible, eccentric persons during this transit as their influence is particularly unhealthy, and in some cases the native could be deceived. Often the native's profession can suffer because of promises that turn out to lack substance, and unwise financial speculation is especially likely to result in heavy losses. The native is apt to feel a confusing and senseless need to prove his or her self-worth by pursuing financial or romantic matters recklessly or amorally, and is apt to suffer disillusionment in love.

Those who have children may encounter psychological difficulties with regard to them. In some cases domestic relationships are subject to peculiarly upsetting conditions or there can be a general lack of emotional understanding in these relationships. There may be physical problems with the home itself, such as water seepage or gas leakage. There can be bizarre dreams or weird, inexplicable psychic phenomena that can have an upsetting effect on the native. Dabbling in psychic phenomena should be avoided at this time. These bizarre experiences are often based on unresolved emotional problems that are deeply rooted within the native's own subconscious mind.

Transit Neptune Square Moon

This transit is apt to bring about a period of emotional confusion. Impulses arise from the subconscious mind, and emotional problems that have their roots in family relationships have a confusing effect upon the native that in turn interferes with the ability to effectively deal with present responsibilities. This particularly applies to emotional problems based on difficult experiences with the parents, especially the mother, which occurred in the earlier childhood. The native can be prey to an overactive imagination, magnifying out of all proportion the small emotional disturbances or past experiences that no longer apply to the present. During this transit confusing conditions arise regarding family relationships and the home itself. Unrealistic fantasies can interfere with the native's ability to perform work, thereby affecting earning capability. There can be unrealistic attitudes with regard to financial affairs where money is spent without regard to future needs. Buying on credit or borrowing money should be avoided during this transit. The native is apt to experience strange dreams and peculiar moods that are difficult to explain in the context of present circumstances. If the native's horoscope shows a tendency toward psychic unbalance, hallucinatory phenomena may result. Relationships with women can be deceptive and misleading at this time.

Transit Neptune Square Mercury

This transit brings about a period of mental confusion, and the native is apt to notice some facts and ignore others. This often results in faulty judgment due to the subconscious forces that distort the reasoning processes. Absentmindedness and daydreaming are apt to interfere with one's communication and ability to accurately perceive things as they are. These tendencies will be a source of annoyance to friends and will stand in the way of achieving goals and objectives. These tendencies also interfere with efficiency and the performance of work, which in turn adversely affects the reputation and professional standing of the native.

Confusion in communication is apt to have an adverse effect on domestic relationships. The native should exercise caution while driving because the attention is apt to wander under this transit. Information communicated or received by the native is apt to be distorted intentionally or otherwise. Extreme caution should be exercised in signing contracts or making agreements while under this transit. The nervous system is apt to be under strain due to confusion and subconscious forces which are apt to be psychologically unnerving. These same stresses can result in digestive disorders, which calls for caution in dietary matters. Drugs and alcohol should be avoided because of the undermining effect they have on the native's thinking and perception, particularly at this time. There can be excessive anxiety where work and health are concerned. This in turn interferes with the ability to work effectively. Problems could arise concerning relationships with brothers, sisters and neighbors which could be difficult to deal with and define.

Transit Neptune Square Venus

This transit brings about a period of emotional, social and romantic confusion. There is likely to be deception where the affairs of the heart are concerned. This can take many forms, such as falling in love with someone who is indifferent, being deceived by or deceiving the loved one, or both deceptions could occur. If the native is married, this transit can have an undermining influence on the marriage because of the temptation to become involved in extramarital affairs. There can be involvement in social activities of a kind that dissipates the native's money and energy. In extreme cases this could mean social involvement where excessive drinking and drugs are used, which would have an undermining effect not only on the well-being of the native but also on the professional standing and financial conditions. During this time, partnerships are subject to difficulties of a confusing nature that eventually affect the relationship. The native should exercise extreme caution in financial dealings and should avoid get-rich-quick schemes. There is also the temptation to dissipate money and resources on unwise expenditures, luxuries and emotional whims. Artistic endeavors attempted under this transit are not likely to be the products of inspired genius, although one might think they are. In general, self-indulgence and laziness can be a pitfall of this transit. Emotionalism and sentimentality are apt to be out of control.

Transit Neptune Square Mars

This transit brings about a period in which the native's imagination stimulates desires that can lead to unwise activity. Such activity can adversely affect the reputation, professional standing and financial affairs that relate to other people's money. In extreme cases the native may be the victim or perpetrator of fraud with respect to corporate money, taxes, insurance, inheritance, partner's money or alimony. Suppressed anger and hidden resentments can have an adverse effect on domestic and professional relationships. In general, forces from the subconscious mind can cause the native to manifest peculiar and self-destructive tendencies. Hidden jealousies and resentments are especially destructive at this time, and covert manifestations of hostility may be perpetrated by or against the native. If one has hidden enemies, this is the time when they would attempt actions against the native.

Transit Neptune Square Jupiter

This transit marks a period during which the native is susceptible to impractical religious and philosophic ideas, attitudes and beliefs. There is a strong temptation to escape the responsibility of ordinary existence by becoming involved in a religious cult or educational, philosophic activity that is escapist and lacking direction. The native often professes great idealism and religious fervor but seldom helps mankind or self in any significant way. Often, there is a temptation to go on a long journey as a means of escape. This is often in the guise of a religious pilgrimage or educational endeavor. Educational endeavors attempted under this transit tend to be of an impractical nature and tend to be of little help in real life. In general this transit is characterized by emotionalism and sentimentality which do not serve a useful purpose. In extreme cases the native is subject to delusions of grandeur or vicariously partaking of the glory of a religious teacher or leader.

Transit Neptune Square Saturn

This transit indicates a period in which the native is subject to many irrational fears and phobias. These are based on subconscious memories of past experiences in the life. The imagination stimulates the negative fear principle of Saturn, paralyzing the ability to deal in a practical way with the work and responsibilities at hand. These morose tendencies will interfere with the native's partnerships, marriage, domestic relationships and professional ties. In some cases, obscure situations, hidden enemies or confusing conditions will stand in the way of the native's success and professional ambitions. If there are any skeletons in the closet, this transit is likely to bring them out in the open. Private problems in the life of the native often cause severe anxiety and worry under this transit. In emotionally unbalanced natives, this transit can bring about mental illnesses that could lead to institutionalization.

In general this is one of the most difficult of all transits. It can best be handled by practical action, leaving nothing to chance and refusing to let irrational fears and anxieties get the upper hand. Under this transit there is great temptation to run away from responsibilities. Often this is based on an irrational fear that the responsibilities are too great or that the situation is hopeless.

Transit Neptune Square Uranus

This transit indicates a period of strange upsets in the native's life. The desire to get out from under depressing memories and conflicts stemming from the subconscious mind can cause the native to react in a peculiar and erratic manner. There can be the tendency for faulty judgment in the choice of friends, group associations and goals and objectives. In some cases there can be deception and disloyalty to friends, or friends can turn out to be secret enemies. In extreme cases, the native may be subject to peculiar psychic manifestations such as hallucinations, weird dreams or premonitions that turn out to be faulty or altogether unreliable. There is also danger of involvement with astral entities of an undesirable sort. In some cases the native becomes involved with weird cults and secret societies that preoccupy him or her with activities and mind exercises that lead nowhere. These, in turn, can detract from proper handling of domestic and professional responsibilities. The native may pursue unwise and ill-defined goals, leading to failure and frustration. There can also be a morbid preoccupation with matters concerning death. Matters relating to insurance, taxes, joint finances and business affairs are apt to be in a state of disorganization and confusion.

Transit Neptune Square Neptune

This transit, which occurs at approximately age forty-five, depending upon how fast Neptune is traveling, marks a time of internal emotional confusion and uncertainty. These feelings are based on subconscious forces having their origin in the past. This inner emotional and psychic stress is apt to bring about a preoccupation of attention which can interfere with the native's domestic relationships and professional advancement. There can be an undermining situation of some sort that will be difficult to deal with. In extreme cases this transit can bring on hallucinatory phenomena and negative astral influences.

Transit Neptune Square Pluto

This transit indicates a period of subtle internal psychic stress. This can be brought on by subconscious forces arising from the native's past or by external conditions that affect civilization as a whole, or by a combination of these factors. Obscure situations can adversely affect matters related to insurance, taxes, partner's money, joint finances, inheritance or alimony. There can be a morose fear of death or fear of unknown psychic forces. Dabbling in dangerous occult practices should be avoided during this transit. Such activities could subject the native to undesirable astral influences. Under this transit the death of a family member or associate can disrupt the domestic and professional life. Unconscious desires for power can endanger the personal well-being and professional advancement of the native. In extreme cases, hallucination and bizarre phenomena of a psychic nature can cause the native anxiety and distress.

Transit Neptune Trines

Transit Neptune Trine Sun

This transit indicates a period of spiritual inspiration and creativity for the native, so this is a favorable time for artists, musicians and performers because the intuitive and imaginative abilities are greatly heightened and invigorated by the Sun's brilliance. In many cases the native can make use of past memories to achieve greater growth and unfolding in the present. This transit also favors romantic opportunities. It can bring an ideal love into the native's life. Involvements in the arts and the social life are increased, and these can present circumstances that are favorable for the development of a romantic relationship. Intuitive and sometimes prophetic inspiration can increase the native's interest in philosophic, religious and educational endeavors. The native can have opportunities for exciting travels and adventures, often coming into contact with interesting people from distant places or foreign countries. For those whose natal chart indicates the possibility of clairvoyance, this faculty will be intensified under this transit.

This is a favorable time to help children through the insight and psychological understanding of them that this aspect provides. The native is able to appeal to the imagination of children, thereby creating a deep and vibrant rapport with them. This aspect will increase the native's self-confidence in his or her creativity, and the native will rely more on his or her spiritual guidance and faculties ever before.

Transit Neptune Trine Moon

This transit increases the imaginative faculties and provides greater empathy and understanding with family members and people in general. It is especially favorable for relationships with women. The native can be inspired to new and creative ways of earning and providing for financial or material security. Businesses dealing with real estate, domestic products and food will be especially favored by this transit. This aspect is favorable for those working in the fields of psychology, astrology and extrasensory perception. It gives insights into conditions based on the past experiences of those they are attempting to help. For those whose horoscope indicates clairvoyance, this period will heighten this faculty. The native can find favorable employment and opportunities in hospitals, institutions, universities and schools. This is a favorable transit for working out emotional problems and psychological difficulties that have roots in family conditioning and past experiences.

Transit Neptune Trine Mercury

This transit indicates a time of heightened mental powers. The imagination is intensified to the point of enabling the native to discover unique ways of communication and self-expression. This aspect is very favorable for people working in the fields of advertising, creative writing, journalism and public relations. Some natives may experience mental telepathy under this transit. This period also favors other extrasensory faculties, such as psychometrics and foreseeing the future. During this transit the native may have interesting communication with foreigners or those from distant places. It also favors long and short travels. This is a favorable time to pursue higher education along philosophic lines. Subjects such as psychology, astrology and the occult are also favored. This is a beneficial transit for spiritual healing, improving the health and personal appearance and for maintaining good hygiene. It is a favorable transit for finding suitable and interesting employment. This employment can be related to hospitals, schools, universities, food, clothing, communication or publishing. Those in the writing or publishing fields will be especially favored by this transit, which is also favorable for establishing interesting friendships and group associations. The native will be able to use creative imagination to realize goals and objectives.

Transit Neptune Trine Venus

This transit often brings romantic opportunities, increased social activities and the possibility of marriage. It is highly favorable for all creative artistic endeavors, especially music. This transit has a strong Pisces connotation because of the Venus rulership and the Neptune exaltation in that sign. The deeper levels of consciousness are a wellspring of inspiration for creativity in the arts. The native becomes more sensitive to beauty and is intuitively opened to social contacts, which in turn lead to greater popularity, better relationships with the public, greater harmony in partnerships and, consequently, increased prospects for financial gain. This is a favorable transit for raising money through art, entertainment and luxurious or pleasurable products. It is good for vacations and long journeys, and these activities will provide many unusual and beautiful experiences. This is a good transit for higher education study in fields such as art and cultural history. In general, there will be increased opportunities for social life and romance. Romance occurring during this transit will be full of sensitive emotions, idealism and beauty. In some cases marriages during this transit seem to be preordained or fated by destiny. In general, the native's appreciation of the aesthetic side of life will be increased.

Transit Neptune Trine Mars

This transit is favorable for activity involving secret work, activities pertaining to hospitals and institutions, corporate endeavors and self-expression along mystical or occult lines. There is an abundance of psychic energy with this transit which can be used in healing or other forms of spiritual work. Intuition is active, and ingenious solutions in carrying out plans and strategies can be arrived at under this influence. This is a favorable time for artistic pursuits that require physical exertion such as dancing. The native acquires an air of fascination and mystery that can attract romance and secret adventures of an exciting nature. This transit can indicate good fortune through inheritance, corporate endeavors, insurance, government funding and joint finances. The native can become interested in life after death, reincarnation and other occult mysteries. In some cases a personal contact with the world of the unseen takes place. The native can draw on past experiences and the intuitive faculties to find means of furthering professional ambitions as well as to establish good relations with persons of power or authority. Intuitive insights can create interest in spiritual pursuits and religious or educational activities. The native may travel for professional reasons or for some kind of secret work. This is a favorable aspect for improving the domestic situation through a combination of intuitive insight and constructive work.

Transit Neptune Trine Jupiter

This transit brings much spiritual and religious inspiration, and the native becomes mystically inclined and interested in the ultimate purpose of life. The development of clairvoyant faculties may bring to the native a religious or mystical experience that increases faith and the understanding of spiritual reality. The native could go on either a long journey in pursuit of cultural inspiration or on a spiritual pilgrimage. This transit can bring the rewards of past good action in the form of expanded opportunities and greater social and financial benefits. The native will be more optimistic and generous toward those less fortunate. There will be interest in uplifting the prevailing social order. This often involves contributions to or work with religious, educational or charitable institutions. The native is likely to come under the instruction of a spiritual teacher or a philosophic or religious system. This is a favorable aspect for domestic harmony, as it brings a stronger sense of unity among family members. It is favorable for working with children and furthering their religious education. Expansion and good fortune are possible in the affairs ruled by the signs and houses in which Jupiter and Neptune are found or rule in the natal chart. This possible good fortune will also concern the house that Neptune is transiting. In general, the native can draw upon the resources of the intuitive faculties for inspiration and guidance.

Transit Neptune Trine Saturn

This transit is favorable for deep reflection and serious meditation. Intuitive faculties can be used to find solutions to problems connected with the career and important relationships in the person's life. The native is able to draw upon past experiences and the wisdom gained from them, which enables him or her to improve methods and find solutions, especially those connected with the career. This is a favorable transit for creative work, higher education and spiritual endeavors that require wisdom, maturity and experience. The native will exude calm self-assurance, patience, steadiness and the sustaining confidence gained from penetrating insights. This transit is favorable for endurance and reliability in marriage and business partnerships. These are often based on past cooperation and associations. This is a favorable transit for those who combine artistic creativity with practicality and cost considerations. Often, an older person with spiritual insights exerts a favorable and stabilizing influence in the native's life. The profession may require work in secret, with the possibility of travel that is connected with the profession. The native may receive favor from governmental institutions and people in positions of power or authority. This favor would be based on past good actions and works. In general, recognition and advancement can come as a reward for past achievements.

Transit Neptune Trine Uranus

This transit is of a subtle nature and will affect the average individual through advancements and improvements in society. For those whose natal horoscopes indicate developed intuitive faculties, this transit will bring an amplification of these faculties. In some cases, old friends and romantic contacts from the native's past will reappear. This is a favorable transit for establishing interesting friendships and pursuing creative and worthwhile social activities. During this transit, one is apt to become involved with mystical and occult groups and organizations. One is apt to become interested in life after death, reincarnation, extrasensory perception and clairvoyance. This period is also favorable for those involved with advanced science and technology, and this transit often provides insights into the subtle workings of nature. This is a good period for gain through corporate enterprises, insurance, investments, inheritance and joint finances. New and exciting interests can help bring family members closer together. In general the native will be more open to new and unusual creative inspirations. This is a favorable period for meditation and for increasing the native's understanding of life.

Transit Neptune Trine Neptune

This transit indicates intuitive wisdom that can be gained through maturity and quiet, inner reflection. The native becomes more aware of the spiritual side of life and the part he or she plays in it. There can be memories of the distant past and even of past embodiments, which provide insights into existing conditions and situations. This transit helps to stabilize the home life and makes the home a place for inner spiritual unfoldment.

Transit Neptune Trine Pluto

This transit is highly occult, and its subtle influence affects the average individual through the cultural and scientific advances in general society. The native gains deeper insights into the ultimate purpose of existence and the reality of spiritual realms. This can manifest as interest in reincarnation, life after death, astrology, extrasensory perception and occult subjects in general. Highly developed individuals can experience a heightening of clairvoyant faculties under this transit. Gain can come through corporate enterprises, joint finances, inheritance, insurance and institutions. This is a favorable transit for pursuing higher education along spiritual or advanced scientific lines. Often, the native becomes aware of some of the mystical and scientific factors involved in the existence of the seemingly material universe. In general, the native's past experience and intuitive prompting will give insights into ways of improving existing conditions around the native.

Transit Neptune Oppositions

Transit Neptune Opposition Sun

This transit brings difficulties in relationships in general and with romantic relationships in particular. The native or the person is apt to have illusions about the nature of the relationship and what is expected of the other party. Past experiences buried in the subconscious mind can distort the ability to see others as they actually are. The native is apt to project many of his or her own psychological problems on associates. In some cases deliberate or unintentional deception is practiced by the native or the other party involved. In either case, ulterior motives can be at the root of the difficulty. At times, the native can be indifferent, which aggravates others who feel the native should shoulder his or her share of responsibilities. The native is often absorbed in a private dream world, making him or her oblivious to others. This creates conflicts in relationships due to a lack of awareness and lack of proper communication.

The native is apt to be absorbed in creative, artistic pursuits at the expense of practical considerations, thus incurring the enmity of others who do not appreciate these actions. Often, such irresponsible attitudes cause financial difficulty with consequent aggravation of family relationships with those who must depend on the native for material support. In general this aspect can cause relationship problems because of an inflated and illusionary sense of self-importance. In order to derive the best results from this transit, the native should seek to be objectively sensitive of others and less involved with his or her ego problems of self-expression. The native must be willing to do a fair share of the work and make sacrifices to make relationships work.

Transit Neptune Opposition Moon

This transit brings about relationship problems based on psychological problems that have their origin in earlier childhood experiences. This is a time when the native is apt to act out a parent-child relationship in present relationships with others. This will be a source of annoyance for others who wish to be regarded as distinct individuals in their own right. This transit often makes one aware of family and domestic relationship problems which come up for solution at this time. The native runs the danger of relating to other family members exclusively in terms of past experiences with them. During this transit the native is confronted with financial problems stemming from his or her impracticality, extravagance and laziness. Such attitudes will further complicate domestic and family relationships. The native is apt to have a difficult time relating to and understanding women. Often, unconscious memories of difficulties with the mother will interfere with the ability to relate to women in a harmonious manner. One is apt to be moody and to imagine slights on the part of others where none is intended. This over-sensitivity can result in a persecution complex.

Transit Neptune Opposition Mercury

This transit indicates a period of mental confusion and difficulty in communicating with others. In some cases there can be deliberate or unintentional untruthfulness on the native's part or on the part of others. This often causes confusion, mistrust and bad relationships. Communication can be delayed, falsified or confused. This is not a favorable time for signing contracts or for making budding agreements, as hidden factors are likely to cause quarrels and separation. The native is apt to be confused in thinking, thereby making it difficult to relate to others in a clear, concise way. There can be difficult relationships with brothers, sisters and neighbors. Rumors and gossip could be a source of difficulty. Absentmindedness and lack of attention while driving can be a threat to health and safety. There can also be communication problems with employees, employers or coworkers. This, of course, will make for difficult relationships on the job. Lack of attention to detail in work situations can cause difficult relationships and inefficiency. All of these developments can contribute to nervousness and psychological stress, which can have an undermining effect on the native's health. Improper diet and neglected personal hygiene can make the native socially objectionable, as well as possibly debilitated or unhealthy. In general this transit is apt to cause the native to become too absorbed in his or her personal and psychological problems, with consequent breakdowns in communication and relationships.

Transit Neptune Opposition Venus

This transit is apt to cause emotional difficulties in romantic, marital and business relationships. Emotional over-sensitivity is apt to make the native open to disappointment and disillusionment. There is a tendency to bestow the affections on an inappropriate object or to refuse to recognize that the loved one does not have the same feelings towards the native. Consequently, this can be a transit of unrequited love. The native often refuses to be objective and realistic about his romantic concerns. In other cases, there can be deliberate deception involved in the romantic or marital relationship. This can be on the part of the native or the partner or both. This transit can bring financial difficulties as a result of extravagances, unwise expenditures and laziness. In business partnerships, sentimentality and emotional bias may lead to an un wise choice of associates. Domestic relationships can be characterized by maudlin sentimentality and unwise emotional attachments. In some cases the native can become absorbed in a fantasy world as a way of escaping unpleasant realities. So-called interest in aesthetic values may be a means of escape. Others may view the native as simply being impractical. To get the best results from this transit one must have a sense of realism, justice and truthfulness and an ability to see the other person's point of view in romantic and emotional relationships.

Transit Neptune Opposition Mars

This transit can be one of the most dangerous to deal with because of its powerful, undermining effect. The native or those with whom the native has dealings can have selfish or ulterior motives that can manifest through mechanisms of covert hostility. Desire for selfish financial gain through appropriation of other people's resources and money can be the root of many difficulties. All matters concerning joint finances, corporate money, taxes, insurance, inheritance and alimony should be handled with utmost care. One should be wary of hidden factors and should be scrupulously honest where one's own motivations are concerned. At times, desire for power and status can cause the native or others to use underhanded or unfair tactics. Under this transit, people are apt to profess friendship when in reality they are hidden enemies who will undermine the native. The imagination can inflame the desires and block out reason, which leads to actions and unsavory personal involvements that would not ordinarily be contemplated. Dishonesty and hidden resentments in family and domestic relationships should be avoided under this transit. In some cases the native is apt to harbor subconscious resentments that he or she is unwilling to recognize. Because everyone is more or less telepathic on the unconscious level, these unconscious emotional tendencies can interfere with meaningful relationships. To get the best out of this transit the native should be scrupulously honest about his or her feelings and use good judgment in the choice of associates.

Transit Neptune Opposition Jupiter

This transit is apt to lead to unwise involvements in social contacts and so-called spiritual and educational pursuits. There is a tendency to team up with people who are completely idealistic and impractical in their pursuit of the spiritual life, education and social improvement. During this transit the native and friends are apt to spur each other into greater expansion along impractical lines. At this time one is highly susceptible to sob stories and appeals for help for both worthy and not so worthy causes. During this transit, one must be wary of promoters and con artists. The native may pursue higher education, religious activities or foreign travel that would not be productive at this time. One is susceptible to spiritual teachers who may or may not be as saintly as they appear. There is the temptation to overexpand in the domestic sphere, with consequent difficulties in domestic relationships. Under this transit one can have too great an emotional dependence on other family members. In some cases the native can display an inflated sense of spiritual self-importance, pontificating while expecting others to take care of practical needs, or the native may be duped by others who have this attitude. To derive benefits from this transit, one should maintain a sense of practical realism and should equate spirituality with useful service and living.

Transit Neptune Opposition Saturn

This transit often brings difficulties in relationships as a result of anxiety and irrational fears. Mistrust of others is often based on subconscious memories of painful experiences of the past, which makes it difficult for the native to relate to others in an objective manner. The native lacks self-confidence at this time and is unable to inspire confidence in others. Much energy is wasted in negative thinking, anxiety and fear, which in turn interferes with the native's ability to succeed in professional pursuits, marriage and partnerships. Fear of failure and personal inadequacy can cause the native to avoid responsibility, thus creating difficult relationships with others. In extreme cases, deep-seated neuroses activated by this transit can lead to mental unbalance and institutionalization. If the native has been dishonest in the past, this transit can bring these matters to light, causing public disgrace and professional setbacks. Under this transit discretion should be used in the choice of professional associates. This aspect can indicate underhanded tactics on the part of the native or those with whom the native deals. Desire for power and status can lead the native or those with whom the native has professional dealings to use devious strategies. In either case the native runs the risk of acquiring secret enemies who undermine his or her activities. To get the best results from this transit, strict honesty, positive thinking and attention to existing conditions should be employed.

Transit Neptune Opposition Uranus

This transit is apt to bring difficult relationships and peculiar conditions with friends and groups. Unrealistic ideas entertained by the native or friends create difficulties in relating with them on a sound basis. There is apt to be confusion in goals, making it difficult for the native to effectively cooperate in group endeavors. Obscure conditions can interfere with the native's attainment of hopes and wishes. Distortions can arise from the subconscious mind that interfere with objective work and cooperation, making it difficult to achieve goals. In some cases the native can have an irrational fear of death that preoccupies his or her attention, interfering with worthwhile cooperation in the present situation. Deceptive circumstances are likely to arise with respect to insurance, taxes, joint finances, corporate affairs, goods of the dead and alimony. In general this transit can cause anxiety, producing adverse financial conditions. In many cases, the anxiety-producing circumstances are brought about by large scale social, political and economic upheavals within the larger culture. Under this transit one can be subject to weird and upsetting psychic phenomena. To get the most out of this aspect, practicality and realism must be employed in the attainment of goals that are well-defined and actually attainable. Discrimination should be used in the choice of friends and associates in general.

Transit Neptune Opposition Neptune

This transit represents a time of internal spiritual retrospection and a withdrawal from involvement with the active, physical world. In some cases this aspect is associated with senility and is characterized by the spirit withdrawing from physical incarnation, or the native may feel psychologically isolated and alone. Under this transit one can become absorbed in past memories, making it difficult to live in the present and relate to younger generations. This is not to say that this transit by itself means the end of life for every individual. In some cases the infirmities of old age can make a burden on other family members and thereby cause domestic relationship problems. To derive the most from this transit the native should recognize the eternal existence of spiritual realities and maintain an attitude of inner peace.

Transit Neptune Opposition Pluto

This transit often affects the average individual through problems that arise as a result of large scale changes in the general social culture. The native can be caught up in a mass struggle for survival brought about by political, social, economic and ecological upheavals. There can be difficulties concerning taxes, insurance, goods of the dead, corporate money and alimony. Unwise dabbling in occult practices should be avoided during this transit. In extreme cases, the native may experience hallucinations, disturbing dreams or other strange phenomena. To get the best results from this transit the native must be willing to cooperate with difficult circumstances in order to bring about the regeneration of existing conditions. During this period there can be fear of unknown or improperly understood occult forces.

X

Transits of Pluto

Transit Pluto Through the Houses

Pluto's transit through each house is apt to bring fundamental changes and transformation in the affairs ruled by the house that Pluto transits, thereby linking these changes to the affairs ruled by the houses where Scorpio, Aries and Leo are found.

Pluto often manifests as a leveling or dissolving agent, reducing that which it touches to its most fundamental energies and then recreating it in a new and better way. More than any other planet, Pluto rules the various experiences of death and rebirth. These experiences can be a severe shock for those who look to outward material things for their security in life. There is no true security to be found in material things. Change itself, hopefully constructive change, is the only permanent law in this material world and throughout the universe.

Transit Pluto Through the First House

This transit causes unusual occult experiences to occur in the native's life, and the native is apt to become more perceptive in some way, which can include clairvoyant abilities. The native may be forced to personally confront grave issues such as physical dangers or threats to one's life or personal well-being. This forces the native to develop attributes of courage and will-power. Usually there is increased self-awareness of oneself as a spiritual entity. This may result in the native's taking an active interest in occult or esoteric studies and programs of self-improvement. The individual's increased personal awareness of nature's subtle forces can arouse interest in advanced sciences. A self-transformation in the native is brought about which relates in some manner to the affairs ruled by the house where the sign Scorpio is placed.

Transit Pluto Through the Second House

This transit brings about major changes and transformations dealing with the native's attitudes and ideas concerning money and material wealth. This transit does not usually end without the native being forced to acquire an entirely new set of values. The relationship between one's personal wealth and the wealth of other people or organizations is brought into focus because of Pluto's rulership of the eighth house and Scorpio, which rule other people's money. If the native has selfish motivations regarding other people's money, he or she is apt to experience severe financial reversals resulting from the karmic consequences of his or her actions. Any past dishonest financial dealings will be brought to the surface regardless of how well hidden they may be.

The native does not finish this transit without learning that one cannot selfishly own anything, and that we are given the privilege to use resources only on the condition that they are used for the greatest benefit of all concerned. Resources come from nature, and to nature they must be returned and in some way multiplied and improved. If the native refuses to learn this lesson, then that which has been given will be taken away and the native will be forced in some way to make a new start. In the learning process, the native is apt to see great destruction of that which he or she holds dear. This will be especially true if Pluto makes adverse aspects while transiting the second house. Through these seemingly intense experiences the native learns invaluable lessons about non-attachment. In some manner the native will be forced to look to a spiritual source of all life for a truer sense of values. This value lesson will be related in some way to the affairs ruled by the houses where Scorpio, Aries and Leo are found on the chart.

Transit Pluto Through the Third House

This transit brings about fundamental changes in the native's way of thinking and communicating. The native often must deal with secret information or advanced forms of knowledge, and the management of this information can have far-reaching consequences. Often there is an interest in studying advanced forms of science or occult subjects, and the native is apt to experience mental telepathy while under this transit. Caution should be used while traveling. Care should be used in executing papers and contracts and in speaking and writing, because if information is divulged to the wrong people or in the wrong manner, the result can be serious.

Transit Pluto Through the Fourth House

This transit can bring upheavals and fundamental changes in the home, family and domestic life of the native. This can result in changes of residence. In some cases the home can be disrupted or even destroyed by war, revolution or riots. This transit can also manifest as an interest in ecological and geological concerns. If Pluto is well-aspected, this transit can bring about a rebuilding or improvement of the home. It can also cement family relations on a more spiritual basis. The native or a family member can have occult experiences or become interested in such matters. In some cases the native may become interested in genealogy, the family tree or deceased relatives, even to the point of having psychic contact with them. Somehow this transit through the fourth house will be connected to the houses where Scorpio, Aries and Leo are found.

Transit Pluto Through the Fifth House

This transit brings about a period in the individual's life when ideas concerning romance, sex, personal creative expression, speculative endeavors and gambling must be reconstructed. There may be matters of serious consequence where children are concerned. If Pluto makes good aspects during this transit, the children may manifest unusual talents and abilities, but if stress aspects are present, children will need careful supervision. In extreme cases, their lives may be endangered. The native is apt to experience strong sexual stimuli during this transit. This would be intensified if Pluto were to make contacts with Uranus, Mars, Venus or the ruler of the fifth house. At any rate, there will be an increased sex drive. Through this experience the native is forced to learn the difference between the constructive and destructive uses of sex. Romance during this transit are apt to be filled with intrigue, secrecy and, if Pluto is afflicted, even jealousy and foul play. In the case of highly creative people, this transit can bring about spiritually inspired works of art as well as other creative self-expressions. This transit of Pluto through the fifth house can link fifth house matters with the affairs of the houses where Scorpio, Aries and Leo are found.

Transit Pluto Through the Sixth House

This transit can result in work or employment which is secret and possibly involved with advanced forms of technology. The native is often forced to give serious considerations to health and ways of regenerating it. If Pluto makes severe afflictions, and if good judgment in matters of health is not used, there can be death as a result of illness. There can be many changes and transformations in the native's work and in the way it is approached. Often the native is required to revamp the work situation. If Pluto is afflicted during this transit, there can be danger of serious accidents or even death resulting from industrial accidents. It is inadvisable for the native to seek dangerous forms of employment or active military roles if Pluto is afflicted in the natal horoscope and makes adverse aspects during this transit. The native may undergo radical changes in dietary habits and manner of personal dress and hygiene when Pluto transits this house. This can be for the better or worse, depending upon the aspects Pluto makes. Pluto transits in this house are linked with the affairs of the house where Scorpio, Aries and Leo are found.

Transit Pluto Through the Seventh House

This transit indicates major transformation in the native's attitude toward people in general. Marriage and close personal relationships will undergo a transmutation of some sort. If Pluto is badly afflicted by transit or natally, the native could make some powerful and bitter enemies. The marriage or any partnership is apt to be with persons of strong will and secretive tendencies, and in some cases these tendencies will be of an occult nature. If the native is already married and Pluto is afflicted, there is danger of divorce resulting from a battle of the wills, sexual incompatibility or unfaithfulness in the marriage. There could even be a combination of all of these. Pluto, if afflicted while transiting this house, could enmesh the native in lawsuits or in situations that cause him or her to suffer public disfavor. This transit is likely to be linked with the affairs ruled by the houses where Scorpio, Aries and Leo are found.

Transit Pluto Through the Eighth House

This transit indicates a period in which the native becomes acquainted with death and the affairs of the deceased. This may be the result of a death of a close friend, an associate or family member, or the result of war or a natural catastrophe. If Pluto makes severe aspects during this transit, the native's life may be in danger, especially if the Sun or first house ruler is involved. This could also be the case if the Sun, ruler of the first house or first house cusp is in Scorpio or Aries, or if Mars, Saturn or Uranus are adversely involved by natal or transiting aspects to Pluto. These dangers depend upon the nature of the environment in which the native is placed at the time of the transit as well as upon age and state of health. During this transit there is apt to be increased interest in matters of the occult, life after death and reincarnation. There are apt to be serious matters concerning corporate money, taxes and insurance at this time. The management of these affairs is apt to have a far-reaching effect. If Pluto makes serious afflictions in this house during this transit there can be serious losses for the native and partners. There is apt to be strong sexual stimulus during this transit. If Pluto is afflicted, care should be taken regarding the health of the sexual organs. This would be especially so if Pluto were linked with the first, fifth or sixth house in any way. This transit of Pluto should be considered with respect to the houses where Scorpio, Aries and Leo are found.

Transit Pluto Through the Ninth House

This transit indicates a need to seek deeper and more fundamental values with regard to religion, philosophy, law and education. In many cases this involves a revamping and redoing of one's past educational experiences. The native is apt to have profound and prophetic insights during this transit of Pluto. Travel in faraway places is apt to bring unusual, profound, mysterious, and in some cases, occult experiences. The native could travel where there is great danger and chaos. If Pluto is afflicted while transiting this house, the native could be in personal danger while traveling. There will also be an interest in improving the social order and especially legal, religious and educational institutions. These ninth house matters are apt to be influenced by the affairs of the houses where Scorpio, Aries and Leo are found.

Transit Pluto Through the Tenth House

This transit indicates fundamental and far-reaching changes in the native's profession, reputation and relationship with the government and with people in positions of authority. The native's work can involve secrecy, matters dealing with advanced forms of technology, and serious life and death matters. At any rate, the native's work will be concerned with matters that are very consequential. There will be drastic changes of some kind in the professional activities of the native, or the native will seek to remold the way in which he or she works on a daily basis. If Pluto is afflicted in this transit there can be severe reversals in material fortune as well as public disgrace. These professional concerns will be linked with the affairs ruled by the houses where Scorpio, Aries and Leo are found. The native can be brought into contact with individuals in positions of power and authority. Often these people have a powerful will and occult abilities. If Pluto is afflicted, these people can be corrupt.

Transit Pluto Through the Eleventh House

This transit indicates that the native's friendships, group associations, goals and purposes will undergo fundamental changes. Many old friendships that are no longer meaningful will be discontinued. There will be new alliances formed with powerful and in some cases occult-oriented individuals. The native's goals will be revised, and what was once desirable will no longer hold precedence. These changes can be for the better or worse depending upon the nature of the aspects Pluto makes. The native is apt to become involved in secret groups and organizations, often of an occult nature. The consequences of these activities will be far-reaching in the native's life and the lives of other participants or those whom the native affects. These activities will be affected by the affairs ruled by the houses where Scorpio, Aries and Leo are found.

Transit Pluto Through the Twelfth House

This transit brings about a period during which the reservoirs of the unconscious mind are reactivated and must be purified and regenerated. The native is brought into contact with many powerful, hidden occult influences. If Pluto makes adverse aspects, the native can be subject to destructive entities and evil influences. There can also be danger from secret enemies. If Pluto is well-aspected, deep spiritual realizations can be gained from meditation and other spiritual disciplines. Many things from the past come up for review and regeneration through this transit, especially those habit patterns that lead to self-undoing. There can be an institutionalization of some kind during this transit if Pluto is afflicted. The affairs ruled by the twelfth house are affected by this transit and will be related in some way to the affairs ruled by the houses where Scorpio, Aries and Leo are found in the horoscope.

Transit Pluto Conjunctions

Transit Pluto Conjunction Sun

This transit brings major changes in the native's self-awareness. This often results in increased willpower and a desire to remake one's life through purposeful action and creative self-expression. Whether this manifests in a constructive or destructive way depends upon the aspects to the Sun and Pluto in the natal chart and upon the overall tenor of the horoscope. The native is apt to make drastic changes in lifestyle and will become more daring and willing to disrupt the status quo in order to achieve a desirable end. These changes often entail bringing up many powerful forces that stem from past conditions. The Pluto transit over the Sun forces the native to recognize and deal with, for better or worse, unresolved desires. It is much like a refining process in which the slag is brought to the surface. The native has a desire to make a new start and in some cases attempts to fulfill the unfulfilled desires of the past. Because the Sun is the natural ruler of the fifth house, and because Pluto is the ruler of Scorpio and Aries, there is a powerful sexual impetus, often resulting in new romantic involvements. In any event, strong changes are likely to affect the affairs ruled by the houses in which Aries, Leo and Scorpio are found and by the houses which the Sun and Pluto occupy in the natal chart. In cases of advanced individuals, Pluto's transit over the Sun can bring clairvoyance and intensified interest in the occult.

Transit Pluto Conjunction Moon

This transit indicates a time of drastic upheavals in the native's emotional and domestic life. This transit often is associated with the death of a family member, change in residence or some other drastic revision that affects the home and family life. This could be for good or ill. There is apt to be intense emotional agitation resulting from the reactivation of experiences in the native's past and early childhood conditioning. Women, or a particularly important female figure, are apt to have a major effect on the native during this transit. The house affairs ruled by the houses where Aries, Cancer and Scorpio are found, and the affairs ruled by the houses occupied by the Moon and Pluto will be strongly affected by this transit. Through this transit natural disasters and situations of mob rule can have an adverse effect on the native or the domestic scene.

Transit Pluto Conjunction Mercury

This transit indicates a period of intensified mental awareness, and the will to understand the deeper mysteries of life is intensified. The person may have experiences of communication by mental telepathy or may suddenly become aware that other persons are thinking about him or her. During this transit there is an interest in regenerating one's health and work through increased knowledge and understanding. The native may have to deal with secret information of grave importance for which he or she is made responsible. If Mercury or Pluto is natally afflicted, the native may indulge in scheming or conniving or other unfair practices designed to take advantage of others. Under this transit's influence the native may take up the study of some form of advanced physics or an advanced form of occultism. The native could become interested in business schemes involving corporate money, insurance, taxes or inheritances, as well as life after death.

Transit Pluto Conjunction Venus

This transit is apt to bring intense emotional and romantic experiences into the native's life. The love affairs that ensue can either degrade and debase the native or raise him or her to new spiritual heights. This will depend upon the natal aspects of Pluto and Venus and other transits that would be in effect at the same time. In any event, this transit will act as a strong sexual or creative stimulus, and in some cases will act as both. Such romances are apt to have a transforming influence on the native. They will be intensely emotional affairs, usually with strong sexual involvement. Often, a degree of intrigue is involved. Before this transit is over, the native experiences many important lessons in the proper use and understanding of sex and the emotions. Through this transit, natives with talent are apt to be inspired to new heights of artistic creativity. Important financial considerations can arise under this transit. Because Venus rules the second house of one's own money, and because Pluto rules the eighth house of joint money, important financial dealings can take place under this transit that can have far-reaching effects. These are apt to deal with insurance, inheritance, taxes, alimony, and the money of the marriage partner or business partners. It is necessary to examine one's own motives as well as the motives of others during this transit. The native will have a new sense of values by the time this transit has been completed.

Transit Pluto Conjunction Mars

This transit brings about a time of intensified will to initiate action into the native's life. The native generally becomes more aggressive, self-assertive and ambitious. Whether this increased energy is used constructively or destructively depends entirely upon the native's general character as revealed in the natal horoscope. In an unevolved individual this transit can intensify criminal tendencies, whereas in advanced individuals, it will give the will and energy to carry out creative work and to assume leadership for positive purposes. This transit allows new insights into more efficient ways of using energy or carrying out actions. In extreme cases, the native may be faced with life and death situations where he or she must show great courage and fight for survival. This transit can bring involvement in some form of engineering or scientific endeavor, which could involve advanced forms of technology. The desire nature and sex drive are often intensified under this transit. Good judgment should be used in the expression of this energy. The native is apt to discover new resourcefulness in the process of realizing goals. There is also a strong impulse toward self-improvement through action. This often results in efforts to improve the body through some form of physical exercise or athletic activity. Accompanying all of this will be a strong competitive drive to excel.

Transit Pluto Conjunction Jupiter

This transit indicates a strong impulse toward ethical and spiritual self-improvement and regeneration. Major conversions or spiritual points in a person's life often occur under the influence of this transit. The native is apt to radically alter religious, social, ethical and educational goals and outlook. There is an urge under this transit to expand one's spiritual awareness through some new or improved methodology. This often results in the native becoming involved in a spiritual organization or cult that the native feels imparts secrets and greater insights. Some natives will embark on a campaign to improve or regenerate higher education, reform the legal system or organize missionary efforts involving foreign countries. This transit can also give an interest in foreign religious cults. In its highest expression this transit can bring the native to the highest court, where he or she looks for the Master within. Clairvoyant or mystical experiences that have a lasting impact on the individual's ethical or philosophical inclinations often occur under this transit. The religious or educational interest triggered by this transit may cause the native to publish information designed to regenerate the educational or spiritual attitudes of the public. If Pluto or Jupiter is natally afflicted, the native may resort to religious fanaticism or could become involved in expansive business plans of an ethically questionable nature.

Transit Pluto Conjunction Saturn

This transit indicates a time during which the native undergoes severe disciplines in the interest of self-improvement. The willpower as applied to discipline and organization is greatly intensified. New methods are originated for handling work and professional responsibilities. The native may have to deal with grave responsibilities concerning matters of life and death that have far-reaching consequences. The native may have severe problems with other people's professional standards or need to buck the system. Often this involves having to contend with other people's vested interests or with a system which is outmoded, crystallized or insufficient. The native would feel a strong urge to regenerate and improve inefficiencies and abuses within the power structure. Often this regenerative work can involve secrecy. The native is apt to be concerned with matters pertaining to science, mathematics and the occult, which will be studied in a systematic, intensive and thorough manner in order to achieve a profound, detailed understanding. There may be concern over new systems for handling business finances, inheritance, taxes and insurance. Commitments made under this transit are apt to be enforced in an extremely binding way. If the natal horoscope is afflicted with Saturn and Pluto badly aspected, the native may be tempted to deal in a dishonest way with consequent danger of public disgrace or become involved in sinister plots or negative magic practices.

Transit Pluto Conjunction Uranus

This transit indicates the occurrence of sudden and dramatic events in the native's life that will have a profound effect. Often this brings about unexpected changes in the native's goals, objectives, friends and group associations. The native is apt to become interested in matters pertaining to science, the occult and astrology. This new interest comes about as a result of startling revelations. These drastic changes will be most noticeable in the affairs ruled by the houses where Uranus and Pluto are found and by the houses they natally occupy and rule. With this transit there is a strong desire for drastic changes combined with a resurgence of willpower that brings sudden changes and new conditions into the native's life. These changes can arise as a result of wars, revolutions, social upheavals or natural catastrophes. In some cases the native becomes a reformer or revolutionary who desires to remake the existing social order.

Transit Pluto Conjunction Neptune

This transit is apt to bring strong mystical revelations and experiences that cause the native to become interested in understanding the spiritual forces operating in life and throughout the universe. Deeply recessed memories and experiences of the past resurface from the depths of the subconscious mind for regeneration. Unfinished business and responsibilities that have been ignored in the past can no longer be avoided. This transit necessitates the attainment of a new spiritual sense of values. In the case of highly developed individuals the intuitive faculties will be intensified to such a degree that the native becomes a channel for spiritual wisdom and information needed for the regeneration of the present social structure. If Neptune and Pluto are afflicted in the natal chart, unusual delusions and astral obsessions can transpire.

Transit Pluto Conjunction Pluto

This aspect will not occur within a normal lifetime.

Transit Pluto Sextiles

Transit Pluto Sextile Sun

This transit is an opportunity for startling new expansions of consciousness, which can occur through purposeful thought and action that remolds the life. A clear mental understanding of the deeper purposes of life motivates the person toward renewed efforts of self-improvement. Often the individual begins some form of esoteric study or practice for the purpose of achieving higher states of consciousness, or this new orientation can take the form of discovering new ways of doing things through greater understanding of the principles underlying a creative self-expression or drive for significance. This transit inclines one to assume leadership in groups or social activities and engenders new ideas that can facilitate the growth and improvement of the group.

Transit Pluto Sextile Moon

This transit gives an opportunity for regenerating emotional habit patterns. The individual becomes more aware of memories and past experiences that dictate present behavior. Everyday common occurrences may include surprises that have deeper significance. This increased insight gives one the opportunity to gain freedom from negative emotional reactions. This transit affords the opportunity to improve home and family relationships. By making use of long-forgotten experiences, the native may find new ways to provide for financial needs or improve business. There can also be opportunities for better ways to handle joint finances, taxes, insurance and inheritance. The native may also inherit money under this transit.

Transit Pluto Sextile Mercury

This transit indicates an opportunity for increased mental awareness and study of deep subjects pertaining to science or the occult. The native is apt to experience profound insights under this transit. Sometimes this will take the form of penetrating analytic perception. The native finds improved ways to communicate and explain ideas and thus to accomplish goals. Under this transit those who spend a great deal of time traveling can find ways to utilize time and transportation means more effectively. Hidden or secret information that will in some way benefit the native is apt to come to light. Many persons with this transit will experience mental telepathy or improved sensory and clairvoyant faculties. There can also be insights into ways of improving the health and dietary habits.

Transit Pluto Sextile Venus

This transit indicates an increased inspiration and talent in those natives involved in artistic pursuits. Romantic opportunities and interest in pursuing are active under this transit. The social life of the native will improve and become more interesting. There could be opportunities for new and improved ways of raising money, which could involve partnerships or corporate endeavors. New partnerships formed are apt to be with people who are mysterious, intriguing or unique in some way. All partnership relationships can undergo improvement or changes that will bring about greater understanding. In some cases the individual will drop old alliances in favor of new ones with the purpose of eliminating those activities that no longer hold personal meaning.

Transit Pluto Sextile Mars

This transit indicates increased energy and enterprise, and willpower is focused in a purposeful manner in order to achieve desired goals and objectives. The native will have penetrating insights into how to accomplish his or her purpose in an effective manner. The native is self-confident, assertive, physically energetic and competitive, and will want to experience new things and thereby change his or her life pattern in fundamental ways. A strong desire for adventure and for conquering new realms of experience accompanies this significant transit.

Transit Pluto Sextile Jupiter

This transit brings the opportunity for expansion and growth along religious, philosophic and educational lines. There is greater resourcefulness and willpower to be creative in the realm of working with the prevailing social order. This transit is favorable for starting or expanding business or corporate enterprises, and for a successful outcome of any legal matters that may be pending in the native's life. This time will bring a renewed interest in spiritual self-improvement and may bring about a direct personal mystical experience. The native will experience a more positive mental outlook, and success will thereby be more likely because the native will be able to inspire confidence in others. This is a favorable aspect for pursuing higher education, religious studies, law and travel, and for working with and improving institutions and research or projects carried on in secrecy.

Transit Pluto Sextile Saturn

This transit is favorable for professional advancement through hard work entailing original ideas and careful analytic thought and the native can do precise work at this time. This transit furthers the willpower as applied to the mind and gives penetrating insights into new ways of organizing and achieving goals and objectives. It is a favorable transit for scientists, engineers, mathematicians, executives, researchers and scholars. Whatever professional advancement the native achieves under this transit is well-deserved, and this is a favorable transit for effective cooperation in business enterprises of all sorts. In both business and private affairs, it gives good organization and resourcefulness in the handling of joint finances, insurance, taxes and inheritances. For those engaged in occult studies, this is a favorable transit because of the increased willpower, concentration and insight it gives into nature's subtler forces.

Transit Pluto Sextile Uranus

This transit often brings about startling mental discoveries for the native. These discoveries take the form of new mental concepts often related to science, electronics, psychology or matters pertaining to astrology or the occult. New friendships with unusual or even mysterious persons may come into the individual's life under this transit. The native can suddenly become involved in a new form of group or organizational activities, and goals and objectives may undergo a change in the light of this new understanding. In some cases the native may unexpectedly receive an inheritance or business opportunity that is connected with corporate enterprises or joint financial endeavors. Because of the double eighth house connotation of this aspect, the native may become interested in life after death, reincarnation and other occult subjects. This may even be the result of a direct clairvoyant experience. In general this is an exciting transit that can bring many stimulating and sudden changes into the life.

Transit Pluto Sextile Neptune

This transit is an extremely subtle influence that usually requires a highly aware individual to make the most of what this sextile offers. It can bring insights into the native's inner levels of consciousness and can give easier access to an understanding of the contents of the unconscious mind. For the average individual, this transit may simply produce an increased interest in psychology and a greater understanding of one's motivations based on past experiences. This transit can also bring interest or involvement in new cultural advances affecting society as a whole. This may take the form of some program of higher education, or religious training, or scientific or artistic creative endeavors. For the spiritually awakened individual, this transit is excellent for meditation and the unfolding of higher faculties of perception. In such cases it may induce interesting mystical experiences.

Transit Pluto Sextile Pluto

This transit is favorable for helping the native to apply his or her will along the lines of creative mental endeavors. The native will gain insight into the more resourceful solving of problems. In general this aspect will give the native more determination to carry through whatever other constructive endeavors he or she is trying to achieve in this lifetime. This transit is also favorable for new starts based on past experiences and inherited resources. In general it will increase willpower and self-awareness and will give the native a greater sense of self as a spiritual being.

Transit Pluto Squares

Transit Pluto Square Sun

This transit indicates a time when the native must deal with severe problems that may involve matters of life and death. This is a time when courage and strength are required. Egotism and headstrong obstinacy must go by the board. The native must learn to be resourceful in order to meet emergencies, as nothing can be gained by forcing issues. Romantic involvements and financial speculation do not fair well during this period. This is a time when children need careful, firm but understanding supervision. Indiscriminate indulgences in pleasure can bring havoc in their wake. There can be difficulties related to matters of inheritance, insurance, alimony, corporate money and partner's finances. The native should avoid the wrong kind of dabbling in occult or magical forces, as these can have a very deleterious effect at this time. Dangers can be of a hidden and unexpected nature which require alert discrimination to uncover. The houses and signs that Pluto and the Sun natally rule and occupy, as well as the house that Pluto is presently transiting, will give clues as to where the danger lies. Look also where Aries and Scorpio are found on the natal chart. The home and profession are also areas where the native is apt to be tested. This is due to the fourth and tenth house connotations of the square aspect. For a responsible native this transit can be a great constructive impetus for developing strength, character, resourcefulness and willpower through the overcoming of obstacles in the life. As with all aspects of trans-Saturnian planets, the maturity and discipline of the native is more important than the technical, favorable or unfavorable nature of the aspect.

Transit Pluto Square Moon

This transit indicates a time during which the native is subjected to heavy emotional pressures and upsets usually connected with family relationships or past experiences. Often this indicates a time when the native is forced to make a decisive break with the past. In any event, all of the hidden weaknesses in his automatic emotional conditioning will be brought to the surface and the native will be forced to overcome or succumb to them. The native will no longer be able to afford the luxury of ignoring the unconscious mind. This transit will bring out the buried, unresolved problems of the past and bring them to a crisis point which the native cannot avoid. They will have to be dealt with somehow. If the native passes this test he or she will come away from the experience renewed, with much of the dead wood eliminated from his or her life. However, if the native succumbs to these experiences, it will leave him or her in a state of emotional devastation from which it will take a long time to recover. In some cases this transit causes the native's home and domestic life to be uprooted. This can be the result of external environmental forces over which the native has no control, such as natural catastrophes or social and economic upheavals. During this transit, in many cases, a member of the family passes from the scene. This could even mean the death of one of the parents. Women undergoing this transit should guard their health.

Transit Pluto Square Mercury

This transit indicates a time when the native is forced to change many of familiar ideas and concepts. During the duration of this transit the native will feel high-strung, nervous and mentally ill-at-ease. The native will undergo the shock of seeing many cherished ideas and concepts shattered under the impetus of new realities that cannot be ignored. If the native can maintain objectivity, this can be a very enlightening, although disturbing, experience. The native can experience physical side effects in the form of nervous and digestive disorders brought on by mental strain.

Relationships with brothers, sisters and neighbors are apt to be difficult, and in some cases these relationships will be severed permanently. This is a good time to remember that the only person you can change is yourself. The native should avoid being sarcastic and suspicious in speech, as this will only compound problems. At the same time the native should use extreme caution and good judgment in signing contracts and agreements, as these could work to his or her disadvantage and could be extremely difficult to discharge or terminate. In extreme cases the native may be in danger of being blackmailed.

There is also danger while traveling during this transit, and extra care should be used to prevent accidents. While undergoing this transit it is good to remember that more Americans have been killed in automobile accidents than in all U.S. wars.

The native will be forced to readjust ideas and methodologies in relation to work and profession, especially with regard to safety and communication with coworkers and employers. During this transit it is good to remember that communication of all kinds is apt to be confused, delayed, and in some cases, deliberately distorted. In some cases the native or someone else may deliberately try to falsify or hide the truth. The native may have to deal with matters of great secrecy and importance, and this could create mental stress. During this time it is of the utmost importance to maintain strict honesty and truthfulness in all dealings, while at the same time remaining alert to possible distortions on the part of others. When necessary, the native should defend what is right and just, while at the same time avoiding antagonistic and dogmatic attitudes.

If the native succeeds in using the positive attributes of this transit, he or she comes away from the experience wiser, stronger and with great depth of understanding that in turn can improve the health and professional life.

Transit Pluto Square Venus

This transit indicates a time when the native is in danger of becoming entangled in the wrong kind of social, financial and romantic involvements. Deceptiveness and dishonesty in the native's sexual behavior can contribute to the downfall. If the native is married, the temptation to become involved in extramarital love affairs will arise. If the native is single, he or she runs the risk of choosing the wrong type of sexual partner, who is apt to have a degrading influence on the native. The relationship is usually based on sexual attraction rather than real overall compatibility. Depending on the overall horoscope, the native may be responsible for dragging someone else down through sexual activities or be the victim of such activities, or both may occur.

During this transit one must beware of dishonest financial dealings that could involve inheritance, insurance, taxes, corporate and partner's money, alimony and business partnerships of all kinds. The native should examine carefully his or her motives and those of others before entering into any kind of business partnership or agreement. In some cases the native may be attracted to art forms and entertainment that is in bad taste or sexual perverse. However, for a talented artist this can be a time of inspired creativity that could involve hard work.

For the mature person who is willing to exercise strict honesty this transit can clear the air and bring all emotional attitudes out into the open so that important personal and business relationships start anew on sound principles. For the spiritually mature person this transit can bring detachments from the considerations of pain and pleasure, affording a clear, emotionally detached and objective view of reality.

Transit Pluto Square Mars

This transit indicates a time of intense impetus to action and increased energy. For the average individual this energy will be difficult to control. It is apt to break out in anger and dangerous, ill-considered, rash acts. The native should remember that force without wisdom to guide it brings destruction in its wake. The native should exercise extreme caution with firearms, explosives, dangerous chemicals, machinery, or any sharp instruments. Caution in driving is also a necessity during this transit because impulsiveness could endanger the native's life. This transit can also indicate that the native lands in dangerous conditions beyond his or her control such as military service. During this transit, anger, rashness and impatience should be curbed. The native should avoid dangerous situations and persons of a violent or criminal nature. Sexual involvements that tend to lead to jealousy and conflict should also be avoided during this time. Impulsive involvements in business-related financial dealings and ambitious new projects should be avoided, as the native is apt to become overextended or involved with undesirable associates, all of which could result in financial loss and professional disgrace. Ambition should be tempered by a rational and realistic assessment of the realities of the situation. Look before you leap is a good motto while one is under this transit. If this transit is used constructively, the native will gain valuable experience in handling difficult and dangerous situations, which will result in greater discipline and self-confidence. Additional ways of handling professional work and corporate affairs can be developed.

Transit Pluto Square Jupiter

This transit indicates a time when the native is inclined to attempt grandiose and unrealistic endeavors. These may relate to business, religion, educational or organizational endeavors. Furthermore, the methods which the native and others are involved are apt to be impractical and in some cases dishonest. This can also indicate a time when the native takes on an attitude of fanaticism that can be overbearing and aggressive, thereby rendering the native incapable of seeing other viewpoints. Often the native goes on a crusade to save the world without first reforming himself or herself. There can be the attitude that the end justifies the means so that the native professes lofty goals but uses questionable methods for attaining them, which in the end can undermine the entire effort. Under this transit one needs to learn greater patience and realism in pursuing goals.

In some cases the native is subjected to some form of moral test that will have a far-reaching effect on future development or evolutionary progress. If principles are adhered to, the native will be strengthened and gain wisdom because of the experience. If there is failure to do what is right under this transit, the result will be far-reaching. In any event, the stakes are high at this time because the issues involved affect society as a whole and consequently affect the native's reputation and effectiveness in society. The native should remember to not overlook small actions and deeds because this indicates the way larger issues will be handled. At this time it is well to remember that every large successful venture depends on the proper handling of small details.

The native can run the risk of having his or her vision so fixed upon some large goal that it is possible to ignore what is immediately obvious. The native's philosophic, religious and educational attitudes can undergo radical changes under this transit. If the native handles this transit in the right manner he or she will gain spiritual maturity and an ability to live realistically.

Transit Pluto Square Saturn

This transit indicates a time when the native must face severe problems and overcome grave obstacles where work and profession are concerned. This requires great patience and fortitude. In some cases the native may become overly ambitious and, consequently, emotionally hardened. In severe cases, desire for power can led to scheming, dishonesty and even perverted use of occult powers, or the native may have to deal with those who have such tendencies. The native may have to struggle against corruption in high places or powerful persons with dishonest, scheming motives. Under this transit, the native may be threatened, blackmailed or oppressed by persons in positions of power. All organizations that have political, financial or religious control of the masses may attract such selfish individuals. Depending upon the rest of the horoscope, the native could be victimized by, or implicated in, such plots and schemes, resulting in his oppression or degradation. If the plot becomes heavy enough, the native may be dealing in matters of life and death, mystery and intrigue with far-reaching consequences.

On the positive side the native can become a crusader for the reform of corruption and oppression. If the native handles this experience with good judgment, courage, fortitude and honesty, he or she can emerge with greater strength, wisdom, capability and deep understanding of the nature of good and evil.

Transit Pluto Square Uranus

This transit indicates a period of drastic upheavals in the native's life that have far-reaching and even permanent consequences. There is apt to be the termination of many old friendships and group associations. A new and unfamiliar set of circumstances will emerge. Under the influence of this transit, the native should not actively initiate change. However, the native must adjust to accept and make constructive use of whatever severe alterations of the basic life patterns that are thrust upon him or her. These can come about as a result of natural or economic, social or political upheavals beyond personal control. Goals will have to be revised in the light of new circumstances. During this transit it is wise to cultivate an attitude of spiritual detachment, which is not to be confused with apathetic, blind submissions.

One should realize at this time that the death of every old situation is also the birth of a new opportunity. The native may also become acquainted with death, due to the double Scorpio, eighth house connotation of this aspect. Properly used, such experiences can bring the native understanding of spiritual survival and life after death. Responsibilities concerning inheritance, taxes and corporate finances may be suddenly thrust upon the native, causing problems. The aphorism of this aspect is that the only thing we can be certain of is change. This transit will bring about the necessity for greater spiritual awareness and increased intuition. The emotions will undergo change, for better or worse.

Transit Pluto Square Neptune

This transit indicates a time when the native is faced with difficult and subtle problems of a spiritual nature. This can take the form of increased awareness of problems affecting the common destiny and survival of mankind as a whole which the native had ignored in the past by exclusive concern with his or her own problems. Personal concerns suddenly lose significance in the light of vast social problems which impinge on the native's life. This is also true of transit Pluto square Uranus. In the case of transit Pluto square Neptune, the effects will not be so sudden or drastic. They will be subtle, worrisome and gradually undermining. Often the effects of this transit are very complex, to the point of creative greatness transforming into utter confusion.

In some cases the native runs the risk of coming under the influence of negative psychic phenomena, or he may unwisely dabble in magic or psychic phenomena to his detriment. This is also a time when aberrations buried deep in the native's unconscious may be brought to the surface and cause problems. In extreme cases the native may be involved with a mysterious death or disappearance of an individual such as a child running away or death through drugs. This transit has the effect of forcing an individual to be realistic about life and self-undoing, should he or she refuse to think and live realistically.

Transit Pluto Square Pluto

This transit indicates and often precipitates severe problems of life and death on some level of experience. Due to Pluto's slow movement, this transit occurs late in a person's life and can often be connected with the native's own demise. However, this is not necessarily so if other factors in the horoscope do not concur. In any event, it forces the native to think about such issues as life after death and the relationship between body and soul. This often causes the native to study such fields as reincarnation and psychic phenomena. In some cases this transit can indicate a death of a family member. Old phases of life are brought to an end, and the native devotes time to more meaningful goals and spiritual realizations. Much that has served its purpose is eliminated from the life and only essential things are developed.

Transit Pluto Trines

Transit Pluto Trine Sun

This transit indicates a time when the native becomes more energetic and resourceful, thereby accomplishing much in the way of creative endeavors. The native also becomes inspired to find new and improved and more efficient ways of accomplishing his goals. This transit gives one a deep desire and ability for self-improvement and regeneration. The native will feel a compulsion to take action toward the realization of personal goals that he or she previously felt ill-prepared to accomplish. This transit also brings to the person a greater sense of courage, a self-assertiveness and a willingness to assume a role of leadership. Possessing the self-confidence to start on an enterprise of any sort is half the battle, since the determination to follow through accompanies the initial impulse once that impulse is given direction. A great deal of the specific nature and course of this profoundly creative impetus will depend on the rest of the horoscope. In some cases the native experiences clairvoyant or spiritual revelations due to the basically penetrative and occult nature of Pluto. These experiences often provide the insights which inspire commitment and efforts towards regeneration of one's self and the prevailing social order. This transit is especially beneficial to individuals who are involved in education, the theater, the arts, politics, law, corporate business and the occult.

Transit Pluto Trine Moon

This transit indicates a time when the native takes constructive action to regenerate the habitual emotional nature and domestic and family affairs. It is also good for businesses concerned with food and domestic products, real estate, building, mining, farming and activities related to the land. This transit often generates psychic or intuitive insight concerning the past family and social conditioning that has shaped the native's attitudes and automatic emotional responses. This realization can lead to a regeneration of personal attitudes and emotional and domestic conduct. Because of the Moon's exaltation in Taurus and Pluto's rulership of both Scorpio and the eighth house, this transit can also bring favorable circumstances into business and financial dealings of all types. In some cases the native may inherit real estate, personal property or money. Under this transit there is a strong desire to correct past mistakes, which often result in the native giving up self-destructive habits and relationships, or renewing old relationships of a more constructive type. This is a good time to give up drugs or alcohol because of the increased willpower and insights which Pluto affords. Many natives under this transit will take an interest in some form of mystical or esoteric work. Often there is an interest in studying reincarnation and life after death. Under this transit people will become more ecology-minded. Efforts will be made to improve the environment through the recycling of resources, improved industrial practices and proper treatment of trash, sewage and waste products. Often this transit results in improved health, with efforts being made to regenerate the health through proper diet, exercise and personal hygiene. This is particularly true in the case of women.

Transit Pluto Trine Mercury

This transit indicates a time of increased mental insight and desire to study and investigate subjects that were previously not understood, such as the occult or advanced aspects of science, engineering or mathematics, all of which will be of particular interest and significance to those with this potential in the horoscope. Some natives will experience mental telepathy, prophetic insights or other revealing experiences that are the products of what some persons call supernormal faculties. The native is apt to become interested in studying the powers of the mind as a means of regenerating life, goals, work and health. This can result in the person's enrolling in special schools, courses or programs that will help increase mental powers and abilities. Under this transit the native is able to establish communication and enter into contracts and agreements which were previously unavailable. A renewed interest in travel, religion or higher education can occur at this time. In some cases travel is undertaken to investigate knowledge or receive training not available in the native's immediate vicinity.

Transit Pluto Trine Venus

This transit indicates a period of inspired creativity, especially for the artistically inclined person, and it can bring romance and marriage into the life of the native. Often this transit renews the native's emotional outlook, in some cases inspiring a spiritual regeneration. Marriage in many cases improves the native's financial conditions because of the second and eighth house connotation of this aspect. For those involved in business, this transit can improve financial prospects, especially if the business is related in some way to the arts or to silken, luxurious or pleasurable products. Corporate partnerships that improve the native's material security are apt to be formed.

This transit is especially favorable for teachers, playwrights and those working with the mental aspects of the creative and performing arts. In the case of artists, musicians and performing artists, the creations produced often will manifest as spiritually uplifting messages. A talented artist is apt to produce a great work under this transit that will be long remembered and cherished for its excellence. Inspiration that is drawn from the soul memory of the person is often used in such works. Because of the double water sign connotation of this aspect, mystical tendencies are often manifest which can be expressed through art, music, religion or through interest in meditation, reincarnation and other esoteric pursuits. Often there is a desire to help the unfortunate, or there can be a decision to work in hospitals or in institutions in some capacity.

Transit Pluto Trine Mars

This transit indicates a time of increased energy and willpower directed toward constructive action. The Aries and Scorpio connotation of this aspect makes the native ambitious to achieve feats of strength and prowess. For this reason this is an especially favorable transit for athletes who are particularly intent upon winning any contest or establishing new records. The native will also feel a strong impetus behind professional interests. There is a desire to achieve positions of power and leadership. This is usually attained through developing new methods, combined with initiative, energy and hard work. The native's willpower and self-confidence will be at a greater height than what is normal. Consequently, the native will be more successful in new enterprises and projects initiated under this transit. While under this transit the native will possess a greater than normal capacity for leadership, charisma and courage. If the native has interests in higher education, travel or religion, he or she will manifest greater zeal in implementing his ideas and convictions.

Transit Pluto Trine Jupiter

This transit indicates an increased interest in religion, higher education, occult or esoteric studies, foreign countries, law or intellectual improvement. The native's normal spiritual, educational, religious, ethical and social interests are amplified by increased willpower and impetus toward constructive action. The native will take action to improve the conditions of those less fortunate. This will be done through programs of self-help and education. The religious conditions are often stimulated by mystical experiences which make spiritual concerns assume great importance. Because of these experiences, this transit gives a direct personal reality to what would otherwise be mere social conditioning. The native gains increased wisdom and insight through bringing to light many past experiences that may relate to previous embodiments. This transit produces an increased awareness of the continuity of life, and those working to bring about social, religious, educational and legal reforms will meet greater success. Travel is often indicated under this transit, for business, education or religious study. There can be work in institutions often with the purpose of somehow reforming them, and this is an especially favorable transit for educators, creative artists and those involved in law, religion and travel.

Transit Pluto Trine Saturn

This transit indicates a period of increased professional ambitions. It is especially favorable for those working in politics or seeking to reform existing institutions. The native will seek and demand justice for self and all people as a matter of principle. This transit is also favorable for handling legal matters and for obtaining justice in lawsuits. It will make the native appear more stern, severe and purposeful, and efforts will be directed toward a just and worthwhile goal. In general there is more willpower to do something about the important issues of life. Whatever the native's work, he or she will put more energy and discipline into it. There can also be the development of improved and efficient ways of performing important professional tasks. This is an especially favorable transit for doctors, lawyers, politicians, scientists, mathematicians and engineers.

Transit Pluto Trine Uranus

This transit marks a period in the native's life when he or she will seek to bring about major changes which break off old conditions and create entirely new circumstances. The native is willing to risk security for the sake of accomplishing something of fundamental importance that is unique as a new discovery or an advancement in the native's field. There can be sudden clairvoyant revelations that bring about fundamental changes in the native's outlook on life. Much that is hidden can come to light in unexpected ways. There is strong willpower to bring about constructive change and alter the usual life pattern. This is done in ways that are often irrevocable. The native may feel guided by a higher power. New friendships and group associations are likely to be formed which inspire the native to unique actions and creative endeavors. This is usually accompanied by expanded awareness and heightened consciousness. There can be insights into such matters as reincarnation and life after death under this transit. During this transit the native may also receive an inheritance. For those involved in business, major projects may be undertaken involving large sums of partnership money. These undertakings are usually associated with the development of new and unique services and products.

Transit Pluto Trine Neptune

This transit has a high esoteric and occult significance. Consequently, it requires a highly sensitive or advanced person to fully respond to its beneficial influence. In the case of such persons, there will be increased clairvoyant experiences. Greater access to the memory of previous incarnations and the wisdom that can be gained from such revelations will be realized. Under this transit people are likely to become involved in mystical or occult pursuits. There could be an increased interest in psychological or religious pursuits. On a more worldly level, those under this transit will take an interest in large scale cultural and scientific advancement that is of significance to humanity as a whole.

Transit Pluto Trine Pluto

This transit signifies spiritual insights and detachments from transitory physical concerns, and usually marks an increased interest in reincarnation, life and death, and related subjects. This interest is coupled with an increased spiritual awareness beyond the concerns of the physical body. In the case of highly advanced individuals it can bring about profound insights and wisdom that will be passed on to succeeding generations. It signifies the liberation of the soul as an immortal spiritual entity.

Transit Pluto Oppositions

Transit Pluto Opposition Sun

This transit indicates a period during which the native runs the risk of becoming involved with power struggles or a battle of the wills with other individuals who are important in his or her life. There is the temptation to be dictatorial or authoritarian when dealing with others, or the native may attract others who manifest this. During this time it is well to remember that relationships can only produce good results if they are carried out in a democratic manner and with a good sprinkling of cooperation. The native will be prone to all-or-nothing attitudes, which makes it difficult for others who would wish to cooperate. During this transit there is a tendency to want to remake others when home ground is where real work needs to be done, namely self-improvement on the self. There is also the danger of impulsiveness and headstrong attitudes that lead to false starts and serious mistakes. Much trouble can be avoided if the native is willing to compromise and consider the advice of others. There is also a tendency to be power hungry and egotistical. If the person is able to cooperate, the abundant and forceful energy of this aspect could lead to great accomplishments through cooperation with others. Difficulties in cooperation could cause trouble in corporate enterprises and with the finances connected with them. This is not a favorable aspect for romance. The individual is apt to be insensitive to the needs and wishes of the love partner. This indifference and highhandedness would lead to an eventual disruption or breaking off of the relationship.

Transit Pluto Opposition Moon

This transit is apt to bring about difficulties and disruption in the native's domestic, family and financial relationships. This usually occurs because of insensitivity and authoritarian attitudes on the part of the native or others in the native's environment. There is a tendency to run roughshod over the emotions and feelings of others, leading to resentment and estrangement. This is especially true in relationships with women. Tendencies arising from the unconscious mind based on unhappy experiences of the past are brought to the surface and adversely affect the native's ability to relate harmoniously to other persons, especially family members. In some cases the home itself is adversely affected because of the native's failure to take proper care of environmental and ecological concerns. At times, large scale cultural, economic or ecological problems with which the native is karmically connected threatens domestic and financial security. Under this transit emotional factors stemming from the past will be brought to the surface, forcing the native to deal with them in relationship to other people.

Transit Pluto Opposition Mercury

This transit indicates a period during which the native is mentally agitated and high-strung. There is danger of dogmatic and opinionated views that antagonize others and make communicating with others difficult. The native is apt to be too critical and caustic in speech and other communication, thereby antagonizing others to the point of causing a severing of relationships. Conversely, the native may have to deal with disagreeable persons who manifest these attitudes. These tendencies are apt to arise out of a desire to remake or reform the attitudes and understanding of others. In extreme cases the native may have to deal with, or may perpetrate, deliberate dishonesty, plotting or other devious behavior. One should be extremely careful in signing contracts or agreements of any kind while under this transit. Hastily made errors in judgment and breakdowns in communication can have unpleasant and far-reaching consequences. There can also be the tendency to become inquisitive and curious as to what others are thinking and doing with regard to matters that do not pertain to one's rightful concerns. This in turn leads to resentment and suspicion on the part of others, causing breaks in communication and mutual distrust.

At this time it is well to remember to mind one's own affairs and to become a good listener when communicating with others, thereby avoiding unpleasantness. If the native remains ethical and is wise in the choice of associations and diplomatic enough to effectively communicate much knowledge, then a great deal can be accomplished through a cooperative exchange of ideas. This transit and the mental strain associated with it can affect the digestion and the nervous system. This in turn can interfere with the efficiency of the native's work. Communication problems can arise in work situations due to inharmonious relationships with coworkers, employers and employees. This could adversely affect the health as well as the efficiency of the person's production. The native should also strive to be a careful and courteous driver during this transit. Courtesy on the road is essential, not only for good relationships, but also for safety. Under this transit, the native should be willing to cooperate with brothers, sisters and neighbors to insure good relationships with them.

Transit Pluto Opposition Venus

This transit is apt to bring about strong romantic and sexual involvements. The native can be drawn into questionable sexual and social activities. If the desire nature is not disciplined, this may take the form of extramarital love affairs or sexual perversions of various kinds. There is also danger of becoming involved in financial aspects of business partnerships that are not in the native's interest. These may even be associated with some form of unethical or illegal activity. In either case the native may be perpetrator of such activities or the victim of them. Activities of this type can lead to lawsuits, divorce and separations. During this transit the native may portray a general lack of social refinement. This will be particularly noticed by those women who must have social dealings with the native.

Because Venus is exalted in Pisces the native is faced with a relationship which has its origin in the past. This must be dealt with and resolved in some manner. So-called love at first sight can be explained by this opposition. Unfinished business relating to cooperation or separation is brought to issue and must be resolved. Because the opposition has a seventh house connotation, this transit does not have to be negative. It can mean the love of a person's life. However, cooperation with the other person and consideration for him or her are essential for a happy outcome. This aspect teaches one that we cannot grow in each other's shadow, but we can grow side by side in each other's light. The native must resist the tendency to want to dominate and remake the partner. This tendency could work in reverse, in which case the native would be forced to protect his or her personal integrity. It is well to remember during this transit that the only person one can truly change is oneself. Properly used, this transit can be an impetus to artistic inspiration of all kinds.

Transit Pluto Opposition Mars

This transit indicates a time when the native must use extreme self-restraint in order to avoid quarrels, arguments and battles of all kinds. This is one of the most difficult energies to control, and failure to control it can produce drastic, and in extreme cases, even deadly results. A few policies that should help during this transit are, think before you act, use reason and diplomacy instead of force, avoid all use of violence, and stay away from situations where violence is apt to occur. There is a tendency to get into a battle of the wills with one's associates at this time. Egotism, impulsiveness and any tendency to bully and push others around should be avoided. Patience is especially a virtue while one undergoes this transit. It is usually a good idea to remove oneself from the presence of ill-tempered, quarrelsome people rather than be drawn into conflict with them. Engaging in unnecessary conflict will only waste time and energy, and will also attract danger to the native. During this transit it is better to rely upon legally constituted authorities such as the police and the courts, rather than to take matters into one's own hands. Conflicts are apt to arise over joint finances, inheritance, corporate money, jealousy, love, professional positions and authority. This is not a good time to initiate joint activities or to throw one's weight around.

In some cases this transit could indicate that the native is unavoidably drawn in to conflict due to situations of war, fire, natural catastrophe or emergency in general. The native should avoid overexertion and extremely taxing work. Extreme caution should be exercised while handling firearms, machinery, cutting instruments, explosives and dangerous chemicals. Because of the double eighth house connotation of this transit, there is a possibility of the death of someone that is of consequence to the native. At best, this transit will bring about changes in relationships that can be constructive in the long run, although this change will be disruptive. In its positive expression this opposition can bring about effective cooperative efforts to get a job done and to produce workable results.

Transit Pluto Opposition Jupiter

This transit indicates a situation in which the native is apt to overreach with respect to partnerships and matters connected with expansion. A situation of this sort can be instigated by the native, associates or both. In any event there is a tendency to take too much for granted. In extreme cases, deliberate fraud and deception can be perpetrated by the native or associates. The native may antagonize others through fanatical attitudes relating to religion, education, law or his ideas on how the social order should be run, or become the target of persons with these tendencies. The native may instigate inadequately considered reforms and programs to remake everything in society except himself, all of which can result in unpopularity. If the native takes on the role of moral dictator in the household or neglects family relationships in favor of other pursuits, then this transit can cause disagreements and estrangements in the family life. The native's religious attitudes can be influenced by others, or the native may have to undergo unpleasant situations to protect himself or herself from unwanted pressure from others regarding religious and social views. In any event, coercion in the name of religion and moral or social reform is one of the problems of this transit. On the positive side, this transit can bring about better social conditions through effective cooperative action, which in turn will bring about a broader outlook for the native and those around him.

Transit Pluto Opposition Saturn

This transit brings about conditions where coercion and oppressive discipline are applied by the native, or where he or she is the recipient of such treatment. There is the danger of being associated with dictatorial, authoritarian individuals who go by the letter of the law but forget the spirit of the law. With this transit there is a danger of forced conformity, oppressively hard work and participation in dictatorial activities. In extreme cases, actual dishonesty, blackmail, coercion or selfish use of power to enforce compliance is used. There is likely to be an involvement with power-hungry, status-seeking individuals. At this time the deliberate use of occult powers for selfish ends is a danger. Under this transit, one may attempt to gain power under the pretense of improving the present power structure. Power struggles under this opposition often bring about lawsuits and the termination of contracts and partnerships. On the positive side, if the motives are pure and the judgment is good on the part of all concerned, a great deal of thorough and constructive work can be accomplished.

Transit Pluto Opposition Uranus

This transit indicates situations in which old partnerships are broken off and new ones are formed. These transitions are apt to be sudden and unstable. Many old goals are discarded in favor of new objectives. The native is apt to be confused as to who his or her real friends are and what his or her true goals should be. At times, revolutionary tendencies are in evidence, as there is a desire to remake or overthrow the existing social order. Many problems can be caused by impulsiveness and impatience. This is a time when one should not precipitate change. However, if change comes, the native should cooperate with the new state of affairs and make constructive use of the opportunities which the new situation affords. Under this transit the native should carefully examine personal motives and those of those with whom he or she is closely associated. It is also wise to think twice before taking major action or making a major decision. Irrevocable separations from old friends and group associations are apt to take place under this transit.

On the positive side, much that is useless can be eliminated from the life. This includes eliminating false values, useless associations and unworkable or worthless goals and limiting adherence to old concepts and conditions. The native can also gain a valuable sense of detachment and a fresh, unbiased outlook on life. This can be a liberating experience even though it is likely to be a difficult one. Under this transit one may be forced to gain a spiritual sense of values. There can also be the sudden demise of someone of consequence to the native. In any event, many old friendships and conditions will be changed to make way for the new.

Transit Pluto Opposition Neptune

This transit brings about peculiar, upsetting situations that often have a connection with relationships stemming from the native's past. Often, disturbing psychic and psychological phenomena accompany these difficulties. In many cases the situation is made more difficult by a sense of mystery which makes it difficult to pinpoint the source of the trouble. The native's own psychological distortions interfere with an objective assessment of important relationships and how to handle them. There is a need for a realistic and practical outlook while under this opposition. The individual should examine carefully all persons who try to influence him or her.

The native may possibly try to influence others through manipulation, or may be the victim of such treatment. In any event, it is well to be wary of such practices while this transit is in operation. Involvements of this kind at this time can bring entanglements with forces that can be very detrimental to spiritual growth. Difficult relationships that arise at this time are often of a karmic nature based on past experiences. One is confronted with situations involving others that activate unconscious memories of past experiences and which can thereby influence one's judgment in the present. On the positive side, if this aspect is handled with conscious awareness of the forces at play, one can resolve old hangups and negative situations and gain greater understanding and awareness through the process.

Transit Pluto Opposition Pluto

This transit only occurs in old age.

Breinigsville, PA USA
16 March 2010
234332BV00001BA/1/P